Signs and Wonders

Benedicta Ward S.L.G.

Benedicta Ward

Signs and Wonders

Saints, Miracles and Prayers from the 4th Century to the 14th

VARIORUM

Published by VARIORUM
Ashgate Publishing Limited
Gower House, Croft Road,
Hampshire GU11 3HR
Great Britain

Ashgate Publishing Company
Old Post Road
Brookfield, Vermont 05036
U S A

ISBN 0–86078–316–2

A CIP catalogue record for this book is available
from the British Library and the US Library of Congress.

Printed by Galliard (Printers) Ltd
Great Yarmouth, Norfolk
Great Britain

COLLECTED STUDIES SERIES CS361

CONTENTS

MIDDLE AGES: ELEVENTH TO FOURTEENTH CENTURIES

This volume contains xviii+ 300 pages

FOREWORD

The papers collected in this volume reflect my interest over the last twenty years in the concept of Christian holiness in the world of Late Antiquity, the Early Middle Ages, and the Central Middle Ages, which has also formed the subject of several more extended studies. They were prompted by requests for lectures or written papers and therefore owe much to the generous interest and challenging response of others. I have not arranged them in the chronological order in which they were presented but in three groups which correspond roughly with the three areas of my studies.

Papers I–VII concern aspects of early Christian monasticism and are related to my five books of translation and comment on the Desert Fathers, an interest first inspired by some remarks of Fr. David Knowles and further stimulated by the Metropolitan Antony of Sourohz. The encouragement of my own religious community, and especially of its late superior, Mother Mary Clare and its Warden, the Revd. A. M. Allchin, has given me the privilege of approaching this work as part of a continuing tradition of life and prayer.

Papers VIII, XVIII, XIX, and XXII, are connected with my doctoral thesis, later published as *Miracles and the Medieval Mind*, and were done in response to the interest of Fr Jean Leclercq as well as Benedictine and Cistercian communities in both Belgium and America.

Two great figures who lived and worked within the monastic tradition in England have dominated my studies, the first Anselm of Canterbury, the second the Venerable Bede. Papers XXV, XXVI, and XXVII followed from my translation of and commentary on the *Prayers and Meditations of St Anselm of Canterbury* while papers IX, X, XI, XII, and XIII are all related to my recent book *The Venerable Bede*. My enjoyment of the works of both Anselm and Bede began and continue under the inspiration and guidance of another 'doctor et magister Anglorum', Sir Richard Southern.

My aim in these papers has been to encourage others to look carefully at certain writings of the past and to stand back from modern questions, methods and preoccupations in order to discover what they meant to those who wrote and those who received them. By 'standing under' the texts in this way I hope both myself to 'understand' and perhaps to enable others to do the same.

I am grateful to Sister Christine SLG for the preparation of the Index and to *Variorum* for undertaking this volume. Bibliographical references for these papers are given in the Table of Contents, and I am very grateful to their editors and publishers for granting me permission to reprint them here.

BENEDICTA WARD SLG

Oxford, 1991

Hagiography and History: an Introduction

> *Christ is the morning star who when the night of this world is past will bring his saints to the promise of the light of life and everlasting day'*

What is meant by hagiography? The word means, literally, writings about the holy ones, the written accounts of saints. It has come to mean a story which is a pious invention, something not congruous with the known facts, a sort of supernatural flattery; 'mere hagiography' we call it. Now it seems to me that hagiography is denigrated in this way because it has been confused with a very different literary form, that of biography, 'mere biography', I might want to say. The father of modern biography, Dr Johnson, held that a biography should show man as he was, in the 'the domestic privacies and display of minute detail in daily life,' adding rather gloomily, 'whether to see life as it is will give us much consolation I do not know, but the consolation which is drawn from truth, if any, is solid and durable'. When asked by his own biographer, Boswell, if it was proper to include in a biography any account of peculiarities, Johnson replied, 'Sir, there is no doubt as to the peculiarities; the question is, whether a man's vices should be mentioned'. In his opinion they should and it has seemed that ever since biographers have included more and more vices until that is all that is there. Biography points backwards, to a man in his earthly relationships with other men, and that is so often an account of struggle and failure. 'Bios', after all is very different from 'hagios'.

A saint's life is not a biography; it is a highly stylized piece of writing in a different vein. A century ago, saints lives were thought unrewarding for the historian, primarily because they were not biographies. More recently attention has been given to hagiographical writing in all its aspects, with many serious attempts to use this seemingly unpromising material. Historians use the lives of the saints as a precious mine for information about the society they lived in, and they propose various methods for such study, but there seems to me to be a fundamental limitation in many such attempts. To look at a saint's life and discount more than three quarters of it and then use the other quarter to illuminate secular history is to miss the point of the material being handled. 'Social history' is not what the lives were written for and it is necessary both to see the limitations of the form clearly and take its real purpose into account before applying techniques of elucidation to the peripheral details. I do not think that this is to involve the historian in unsavory sentimentalities of religion nor does such a procedure necessarily imply personal committment; it is a rather to grasp the nettle firmly, and take into serious account the primary purpose of both the saints themselves and the written accounts of their lives. Whether the modern scholar likes the content or not is irrelevant. We do not treat other written material so selectively; what the writer meant by his text is always central, however else it is used.

It is perfectly true that saints' lives contain much material which is odd, non-factual, elusive; they have often been told and retold, altered and combined or reduced; they contain slippery sorts of material such as accounts of miracles, prayers, biblical allusions. But they were serious pieces of writing, on however humble a scale, with a purpose which was central to their writers and readers, however periferal it may appear to a secularized age. Some were written by simple and credulous men but many were composed by the finest minds of all time. For instance, in the hands of a great historian and a great theologian such as Bede, a master of both factual account and theological reality, the saint's life contains even more than the ordinary piece of writing for the historian.

The saint's *Life* contains two major elements. On the one hand, the historian who writes about a saint writes, as did the New Testament writers, first of all convinced of the plain existence of his subject. In nearly all saints' lives there are historical details of names and places and dates and they are important because Christianity is not a myth, a philosophy or a moral code; it is based on firm historical moments of living and dying in a time and place. The Gospels are historical documents first of all. Even in the instances where a name venerated as that of a saint is due to a misunderstanding of some kind, it is a sound instinct that causes people to invent detailed and practical accounts of saints about whom nothing whatever is known. To take an extreme instance, St Monday, St Tuesday and St Wednesday appear in saints' lists with short accounts of their lives, in spite of the basic fact that they are simply a misunderstanding of the names used for the days of the week before Easter, Holy Monday, Holy Tuesday and Holy Wednesday. Incarnation demands particularity; the saints are not mythical heroes but first of all flesh and blood entities in time and space, and where a saint is supposed, however erroneously, to have lived, details of his existence are supplied.

But secondly, on the other hand, Christianity is not simply about 'the historical Jesus' and hagiography is not just about historical figures. The

New Testament writers immediately saw in the person of Jesus Christ an ultimate significance, whose very existence in time changed all history:

> *'Then he said to them, O fools and slow of heart to believe all that the prophets have spoken. Ought not Christ to have suffered these things and to enter into his glory? And beginning at Moses and all the prophets, he expounded unto them in all the scriptures the things concerning himself'. (Luke 24:26,27)*

The writers of saints' lives look at their subjects in the same way. They are concerned to show the work of God within a human life as it relates to the person of Christ, and that will include both accounts of the breaking through of divinity in the form of prophetic signs at his birth, of miracles as well as virtues during his life, of the inner relationship he has through prayer with Christ. The miracles are not seen or presented as 'miracula', things to be wondered at, but under the Biblical word 'signa', as signs of a new reality. Prayer for a saint, as for Christ, is the very centre of his being, not a pious extra.

But the most crucial point in a saint's life for the hagiographer lies not in his virtues, his miracles, his prayers, but in his death. Just as the gospels are predominantly about the death and resurrection of Jesus, in quantity as well as in orientation, so the saints themselves approached death as the meeting place with the Saviour, the moment of passover into life. From the first days of the church the deaths of Christians were described in terms deliberately recalling the final and definitive death of Jesus; for example, when Stephen was stoned to death, the writer of Acts describes his last words in direct relation to those of Jesus on the Cross: 'Lord, lay not this sin to their charge' (Acts 7:60) at once echoes 'Father, forgive them for they know not what they do' (Luke 23; 34), while 'Lord Jesus, receive my spirit' (Acts 7; 59), deliberately recalls 'Father, into Thy hands I commend my spirit' (Luke 23:46). Moreover, the words and events of the death of Jesus are linked into accounts of the deaths of the saints by use of the images through which the evangelists described the resurrection of Christ: the moment of dawn, dazzling brightness, the sweet scents of a garden, white-robed figures. These are the consistent elements in accounts of the death of the saints in any century including our own, and their purpose is to place the death of the saint in the context which gives it ultimate meaning, the resurrection of Christ.

Hagiography is not tentative biography but a different literary form, a way of writing with its own means and ends and not an unformed and crude prelude to something better. There is in the accounts of the

Christian saints (and I am concerned exclusively with them) in any age a pattern integral to their subject. It was not imposed later by others to distort the facts; rather, the written account is there to highlight the pattern which made the subject a saint. This pattern has been from the first century until today the life, death and resurrection of Jesus Christ. Christians are saints not because they are brave or well-behaved, nice, intelligent, great or even good; they are saints insofar as they have 'put on the Lord Jesus' (Rom. 13:14) in whom dwelt 'all the fullness of the Godhead bodily' (Col. 2:9). The central the purpose of a hagiography is to present this Christ-likeness to others who run the same race, as encouragement, as assurance that they are surrounded by a great cloud of witnesses and that with God all things are possible. The question for the Christian is not how can I enjoy myself, do good, help others, get rich, happy, balanced or respected, but, how can I receive the gift of Christ most completely. The first question the hagiographer asks is not what school did this man go to, who were his friends and enemies, what were his hobbies, or what did he look like, but can we see in this human life and death the marks of the Lord Jesus. Moreover, one of the convictions of Christians is that the saints are not dead but more alive than those still on earth; there they can and will continue to aid their fellow-Christians by their prayers. They are simply on the other side of Christ, and there is a continuing relationship between them and us. Accounts of miracles therefore after the death of a saint are part of the pattern of hagiography; they are signs of the work of God in the world of men.

The primary pattern for a saint's life, therefore, is Christ and the primary pattern for the hagiographer is the Bible as understood in the life of the church. In reading a saint's life it is necessary to take seriously its form and purpose; and in this any Biblical references, together with their interpretation in early commentaries, will be illuminating. Unless the central purpose of hagiography is taken seriously and understood and explored it is valueless to mine such texts for periferal details which were important to neither saint, writer or hearers. Hagiography is closer, perhaps, to art than to science:

> *'Not everything has a name; some things lead us into a real beyond words. Art thaws even the frozen, darkened soul, opening it to lofty spiritual experiences. Through art we are sometimes sent indistinctly, briefly, revelations not to be achieved by rational thought'.*

PUBLISHER'S NOTE

The articles in this volume, as in all others in the Collected Studies Series, have not been given a new, continuous pagination. In order to avoid confusion, and to facilitate their use where these same studies have been referred to elsewhere, the original pagination has been maintained wherever possible.

Each article has been given a Roman number in order of appearance, as listed in the Contents. This number is repeated on each page and quoted in the index entries.

It has not been possible to reproduce all the illustrations originally included in these articles.

EARLY MONASTICISM

I

Apophthegmata Matrum

The position of women in the ancient world is still largely a matter for speculation rather than analysis. Thus any small contribution to the information available for what is significantly the 'patristic' period should be of interest. For this reason I have chosen to comment on a very small portion of the texts available for the beginnings of monasticism, that is, those Sayings in the *Apophthegmata Patrum* which are attributed to women or are about women. I have used the Greek text of the *Alphabetical Collection* printed in Migne[1] and many caveats must be entered about it, not least before attributing any saying definitively to any person. It is however clear that there were some women in the desert and that a few sayings were attributed to them rather than to the men. There are of course other sources which complement this one and which would have to be used if any adequate picture of the place of women in early monasticism were contemplated; there are for instance the lives of the women saints, especially of the great penitents, Mary of Egypt, Pelagia and Thais, and there is information available about the group of ladies who were the friends of St. Jerome. This does not however claim to be a complete picture but an attempt to illuminate some details in a neglected source.

The Sayings offer three kinds of information about women in the desert in the formative stages of monasticism; there are a few Sayings attributed to three women by name; there are occasional references to women ascetics; and there is the more nebulous theme of the place given to women in the symbolism used by the Fathers. These will be discussed in turn.

Two of the women whose sayings are recorded, Theodora and Syncletica, occupy the easily recognisable role of abbesses in charge of convents of nuns, of which there were a number in the desert. The sayings of Theodora reflect a background of the well-to-do and educated: the first is in the form of a question to Archbishop Theophilus[2], that ambiguous figure in the affairs of the desert; another saying mentions the difference between the teaching of Manicheans and Christians about the body[3]; another mentions a monk 'who

---

[1] *Apophthegmata Patrum* ed. J. P. Migne *Patrologia Cursus Completus Series Graeca* vol. 65, cols. 71–440. Paris 1868. (All references are to this unless stated otherwise).

[2] Theodora 1, col. 201.

[3] ibid 4, col. 201.

had been rich'[4] and a fourth refers to 'sitting at table where there are many courses'.[5] It seems that Theodora's convent was near Alexandria and her friends and advisors from that milieu. Her teaching in the sayings is concerned with patience and preserverance in asceticism. An instance of her particular combination of theological insight and entire simplicity is her saying about the resurrection of the dead: 'an old man asked Amma Theodora, "At the resurrection of the dead, how shall we rise?" She said, "as pledge, example and as proto-type we have him who died for us and is risen, Christ our God" '.[6]

Amma Syncletica was also in charge of a convent of nuns and the *Life of Saint Syncletica* is almost certainly of the same person in the Apophthegmata. Her sayings are recorded in the form of analysis of the ascetic life with shrewd comments upon it. She is speaking in the context of her own community and her words take the form of exhortations to her nuns. She uses the imagery of the laundry, the infirmary and the dinner table to express her ideas and there are also some striking images taken from sea-faring. Presumably she had lived near the sea and had observed the fishermen of the Mediterranean with as much astuteness as she later did her nuns. There is a wealth of experience behind such remarks as 'do not fill yourself with bread and you will not want wine'[7], 'when you have to fast, do not pretend you are ill'[8], and 'it is dangerous for anyone to teach who has not first been trained'[9], while her observation of hermits and cenobites is equally discerning: 'there are many who live in the mountains and behave as if they were in the town and they are wasting their time. It is possible to be a solitary in one's mind while living in a crowd and it is possible for one who is a solitary to live in the crowd of his own thoughts.'[10]

The convents of the desert are mentioned elsewhere in the Sayings. When, for instance, Abba Serapion converted a courtesan, he took her to a convent and left her in the charge of the amma. The spirit of such a place is illustrated by her treatment: she was allowed to do as she wished without rules or commandments and as her genuine desire for asceticism grew she was able to put it into practice and was eventually enclosed as an anchoress in the convent.[11] It is clear that women were able to follow a form of monastic life within the protection of a group. They were not to mingle with the men and it seems from another saying that the nuns were as conscious as the hermits

---

[4] J-C Guy, *Recherches sur la Tradition Grecque des Apophthegmata Patrum, Subsidia Hagiographica* no. 36, Brussels 1962, 23.

[5] Theodora 8, col. 204.

[6] J-C Guy, op. cit., p. 23.

[7] Syncletica 4, col. 421.

[8] ibid 9, col. 424.

[9] ibid 12, col. 425.

[10] J-C Guy, op. cit. p. 33.

[11] Serapion 1, col, 414.

of the need for this separation, though it is also apparent that they were more concerned about the temptation they might present to the men than vice versa: a monk wanted to visit his sister who was a nun and ill, but she would not see him, 'because' she said 'he would have to come into the midst of the women'.[12]

But there were also women in the desert who lived as solitaries. Some of these were not known to be women until their deaths. One of them was found by abba Besarion and his disciple[13] on their way to visit John of Lycopolis: 'we found the brother seated and engaged in plaiting a rope: he did not raise his eyes to us or greet us'. On their return they again passed the cave and entering they found he had died, 'when we took up the body to bury it we perceived that it was a women. Filled with astonishment, the old man said, "see how the women triumph over Satan while we still behave badly in the towns." ' The surprise expressed and the fact that the woman had lived entirely unknown point to the greater hazards involved in such a life for a woman; they had to be more rigorously alone than the men and their asceticism was greeted with more astonishment when it was known.

There appears in the Sayings however one woman who seems to have lived openly as an ascetic and to have been accepted as such. This was Amma Sarah. It can be deduced from her sayings that she was not an abbess of a convent; the tone of her remarks is not didactic and she speaks out of a different experience. It seems that she lived alone by the Nile for sixty years and for the first thirteen she had to fight against the demon of lust. It is significant that she dealt with this in exactly the same way as any of the hermits: 'she never prayed that the warfare should cease, but she said, "O Lord, give strength" '[14]. Sarah was accepted but it is clear that to achieve this she had in effect to become a man. When challenged by two visitors, she replied, 'according to nature I am a woman, but not according to my thoughts'.[15] To some other monks she said, 'It is I who am a man, you who are women'.[16] The way to find a place among the fathers was to transcend sex and, like them, return to the paradisal state of unfallen Adam. It was something hard enough for a man, for a woman it was deemed almost impossible; and if it were done, it was by first accepting the role of masculinity.

It was a man's world and women were almost excluded; almost but not quite. There was no concept of feminine spirituality as such and women who were able to compete with the men were rare. What then was the idea of woman in the minds of the desert fathers? First of all, they represented the

---

[12] Histoires des Solitaires Egyptiens, ed. F. Nau. Revue de l'Orient Chrétien 2nd Series vol III (XIII) 1908, Paris. cap. 153, p. 51.

[13] Besarion 4, col. 140–1.

[14] Sarah 1. col. 420.

[15] ibid 4. col. 420.

[16] J-C Guy, op. cit., p. 34.

temptation to lust. There are many Sayings in which women tempt monks to lust; even in one instance a monk admitted sadly that his temptations were not about real women at all but about 'old and new pictures of them'.[17] But an equal number of Sayings are about women as representing the temptation to return to the settled life of the village, where the mother and wife were central. These were both severe temptations and the fathers did not underestimate them. Women were harlots or hearth-keepers and as such a rigorous policy of exclusion seemed unavoidable; the only women permitted into the desert were the virgins and penitents, and they were kept as far away from the monks as possible either in a convent or hidden and unknown in a cell.

The desert fathers recognised that the desires roused in them by contact with women were among the most deep-seated in human nature and the most dominant. In their pursuit therefore of purity of heart they applied shock treatment to their relationships with women from the moment they undertook the ascetic life. But this was only a means and not an end; where the shock treatment worked, there was another stage in which a more positive approach was possible. In actual relationships with women, for instance, there was the abba Nilus who watched with appreciation while the harlot Pelagia rode naked through the streets, and the abba Abraham who disguised himself as a soldier and visited a brothel to find his niece Mary and bring her back to the desert. Even in that most dangerous realm of thoughts, images of women could eventually be used, even of harlots. John the Dwarf compared the soul to a courtesan with many lovers. Pambo wept over an actress in Alexandria and his phrase summarises the attitude of monks to harlots: 'Two things', he said, 'make me weep; one is the loss of this woman, the other is that I am not so concerned to please God as she is to please wicked men'.[18] For the desert monks, the soul was feminine towards God and in this sense the purified images of women had a place in their thoughts. They were acutely aware of women as temptation both in terms of sexuality and domestic security, and they told stories of children brought up in the desert who had never seen a women and yet who were tempted by them. Initially, they fled from every thought that could stir their imaginations about them. But there were fathers for whom the imagery was restored, and they could even use the language of that experience which is most central in sexuality to express their most intimate understanding of prayer: 'when the soul withdraws from bodily cares, the Holy Spirit comes upon her and since she is barren, she is able to conceive'.[19] There was also for them one woman who was a companion in the life of the desert and one to whom they could relate with confidence: 'Abba Joseph said, "My thoughts were with St. Mary the Mother of God as she wept by the cross of the Saviour. I wish that I could always weep like that"'.[20]

---

[17] Cyrus 1, col. 253. [18] Pambo 4, col. 369.
[19] Histoires des Solitaires, op cit., cap. 154, pp. 51–2. [20] Poemen 144, p. 357.

II

'Signs and Wonders'
Miracles in the Desert Tradition

THE understanding of miracles, whether biblical or contemporary, is at present limited and perhaps therefore distorted by the stress laid upon miracles as breaking the laws of nature. This is in line with the dictates of David Hume, for instance, who saw in a miracle-filled landscape 'the whole frame of nature disjointed'[1], or of Bishop Stubbs, who asked how seriously one could take 'the constant infraction by divine authority of the ordinary processes of the course of this world'.[2] This is however only one way of approaching the miraculous and one which would hardly have been understood before the twelfth century. If a man of the ancient or medieval world had said 'the world is full of miracles' he would not have meant 'the constant infraction...of the course of this world', principally because the concept of the 'laws of nature' in this sense was not yet devised. It seems therefore useful to consider at least one example of a different understanding of the miraculous and for this I have chosen to make a few remarks in connection with the text of the *Historia Monachorum in Aegypto*.[3] This is a text of the monastic world of fourth century Egypt and one which more than most can be seen to be full of miracles; perhaps this is why it had not been previously translated into English. I hope to indicate how these miracle stories were seen in their context, without our modern presuppositions imposed upon them, and to suggest that they provide an invaluable source not only for the social background to the period but also for the religious thought of that world.

First: what words are most commonly used in the ancient world to refer to what we call 'miracles' ? In the Vulgate, the term 'miraculum' is used only five times and in each case refers to something quite other than what is later meant by 'miracle'. The same is the case with the text of the *Historia Monachorum*. In the Greek text, the words used are ἰάσεις καὶ θαύματα καὶ δυνάμεις and elsewhere σημεῖα, ἰάσεις[4]; in the Latin text of Rufinus they are *signa*, *plurima et immensa signa*, or or *virtutes*.[5] They are not τέρατα nor ἄρεται, they are not *miracula* nor yet *mirabilia*. The terms which are used do not point to what is 'against nature' but describe 'miracles' in a more varied, subtle and discreet manner altogether. The stress in all the words used is not on any breaking of the laws of nature, but on the immense significance to be found in events that seem to men striking. They are not the breaking of a law but the special manifestation of the powers of heaven, which constitute the world at all times.

The events covered by these words in this text can be placed in four categories. First there are the cures, ἰάσεις, which are also called *signa* and *virtutes*. There are in fact singularly few of this kind of miraculous event. What they demonstrate is the conviction of the ordinary man in the desert that certain of the monks were holy men, in touch with the powers of heaven, and that they could be appealed to in all kinds of need including that of illness. The monks are not all held to be holy men, nor is it the head of a community who is automatically said to have this charism; it is the great ascetic, who is the *vir dei*, and who is seen by others (not by himself) as a focus of power. The stress in the stories of cures is not on the infraction of laws of nature; rather there is a long drawn out process of prayer and fasting and repentence, to provide a setting in which, once in a way, - and it is never assumed that all the sick are cured, - the sickness, a disorder of nature, will be set right: 'the wife of a senator who had lost her sight through developing cataracts on her eyes begged her husband that the saint should be told about her: he prayed for her and moreover sent her some oil that he had blessed. She bathed her eyes only three times and on the third day regained her sight and publically thanked God'.[6] But, as one of the old men said, cures were a very minor matter in the desert; could not even doctors, he said, do as much ?

Then secondly there are the works of power, the miracles which are seen as *signa*, as signs of the kingdom. They are events which illustrate the action of God in the world, in the new age, through these men. They affirm that God is acting now, that he has not been left behind with the apostles and prophets. These stories link the saints of the desert with the saints of the most authenticating text possible, the Bible, and parallels are drawn or implied: it was said that for Patermuthius, the sun stood still, as it did for Gideon, and Biblical texts are supplied to confirm the meaning of this. When abba Apollo is described, amazing for his his works of power, the writer tells us that Satan appeared to him, saying, 'are you not Elijah or one of the prophets and apostles ?' Apollo replied with the refreshing asperity of the desert, 'was God present then but is now away on a journey ? God can always do these things', and he added, never missing an opportunity, 'and if he is good why are you evil ?'[7] The saints of the desert are those through whom God acts now; it is not a question of authority or succession but of present charismata.

One of the most striking and appealing of this kind of miracle is in the stories that tell of the control of the holy men over animals. There are the snakes who guard the cave of an old man, the hyena who asks another saint to cure her blind cubs and bestows in return that sheepskin which was to end in the hands of Melania. Abba Apollo goes out secretly at night to give water to the gazelles; another old man uses a crocodile as a raft over the Nile. These are not sentimental animal stories in the English vein, but instances of the powers of heaven in the new Adam, of paradise restored, of man once more naming and controlling the animals, 'And Abba Bes commanded the hippopotamus in a gentle voice saying, "In the name of Jesus Christ I command you not to ravage the countryside any more". The hippopotamus went away as if driven by an angel... He also sent away a crocodile in the same gentle manner'.[8]

Thirdly, there are the more interior kinds of miracles: instances of foresight and insight so striking that they seemed to be miracles, wonders, θαύματα. These are also called prophecies: προφητείας χαρίσματα, *futura praedictiones*. These stories are meant to convey the fact that the desert saints were above all the ones who could discern reality; as the text says, 'through them the world is kept in being and through them human life is perserved and honoured by God'.[9] The fact that their discernment was almost always uncomfortable for the recipients is another part of their office of bringing judgement to bear on the affairs of men. When for instance a brother intent on getting a free set of new clothes came and told Abba Or his hard luck story, he 'reproved him in public and produced his clothes for all to see; no one as a result dared lie to him any longer'.[10] There is no suggestion in this story that the laws of nature were broken; it is a miracle because it is an instance of the powers of God at work in a man.

Fourthly, there are the dreams of the desert, a topic in themselves, about which I want to make only two points in the context of miracles. The dreams and visions were also called miracles, signs of power, wonders. First, they were not readily believed in. The dreams even of saints, it was held, were to be received with caution, since there were almost certainly the work of demons and a temptation to that last horror of the desert, loss of humility. Secondly, where a dream or vision is related and accepted as a wonder, it almost always gives focus to some dramatic turning point in the waking life of the dreamer. Abba Or, Abba Apollo and the Hermit John all passed many years in the solitude of the desert; and all eventually received instruction in dreams to return to society and teach their brethen; to this is added the authenticating reference to the promises of God to Abraham. Even more striking is the dream of Abba Patermuthius[11]: a robber for many years, he climbed onto the roof of the house of a lady hermit, and unfortunatley could not get down. In his uncomfortable sleep, he dreamt that Christ the Emperor came riding by and summoned him to a greater service in his army. When he awoke, Patermuthius went into the desert as a solitary for many years, and worked many wonders; perhaps from another point of view it is of interest to point out here that it was many years before he received Christian baptism. The dreams of the old men are part of the life of the ancient world; they are, for that world and in this literature, entirely acceptable and indeed commonplace; what would really have broken the laws of nature would have been *not* to dream, or not to act upon it.

In conclusion, I suggest that the theme of the signs, works of power, wonders in this text at least, are part of a world view of God as being sole lord of creation, manifesting his powers through his saints now as in other ages. The question asked of the events recorded is not 'how', what are the mechanics of this, but 'why', what is it saying to me now.

REFERENCES

1. David Hume, *An Inquiry Concerning Human Understanding*, Section X, Of Miracles, in *The Philosophical Works of David Hume* (Edinburgh, 1841), vol. iv, p. 138.

2. *Chronica Magistri Rogeri de Houdene*, ed. W. Stubbs (R.S. 1868-71), vol. iv, Preface, xiv.

3. The Greek version is edited by A.-J. Festugière, *Subsidia hagiographica* 34, (Brussels, 1961). Rufinus' version, *P.L.* 21, 387-462. A translation into English was published in 1981 (Mowbrays). Hereinafter referred to as *Historia*.

4. *Historia*, Prologue.

5. Rufinus, Prologue.

6. *Historia*, 1, John of Lykopolis.

7. *Ibid.*, 8, Apollo.

8. *Ibid.*, 4, Bes.

9. *Ibid.*, Prologue.

10. *Ibid.*, 2, Or.

11. *Ibid.*, 10, Copres.

III

The Desert of the Heart
Importance of the Desert Fathers Today

'In the deserts of the heart
Let the healing fountain start,
In the prison of his days
Teach the free man how to praise'.

My title is taken from the last verse of a poem by W. H Auden in memory of W B Yeats. It was written after Yeats' death in 1939, that year of the falling apart of Europe:

'In the nightmare of the dark
All the dogs of Europe bark,
And the living nations wait
Each sequestered in its hate'. [1]

It is not perhaps so far from our own situation over forty five years later. And it would have seemed just as appropriate more than a thousand years ago in the last days of the Roman Empire when, as Augustine said, 'The world grows old'. Auden looks for a 'healing fountain' and the place for that living water is 'the desert'. There is a link there for us with the desolations of the world of Augustine, when the deserts were again the place of healing and fruitfulness. In the year 386 the young Augustine was reading in a private garden in Milan among the ruins of the greatest empire known to man. He was visited by some friends who described how two of their collegues in the Imperial civil service had left the world in order to become monks after the example of St. Anthony of Egypt. Unspeakably moved, Augustine left them: 'I flung myself down' he wrote later, 'beneath a fig tree and gave way to tears... all at once I heard the singsong voice of a child, 'take it and read it, take it and read it' ... I opened the book of the Scriptures and read the first passage my eye fell on, for I had heard the story of Antony and I remembered how he happened to go into a church while the Gospel was being read and taken it as a counsel addressed to himself when he heard the words, 'Go home and sell all that belongs to you and give to the poor... and come and follow me'. [2]

The story of an uneducated peasant-farmer proved the turning point in the conversion of the formative theologian of medieval Europe. Such an experience may not be limited to that one situation, for when any man discovers the healing fountains they can fructify in any of the deserts of human experience. So perhaps it will not be a vain exercise in arid scholarship to look more closely at such texts, in case, who knows, another Augustine should 'take up and read' and exclaim 'what is the meaning of this story? These men have none of our education and yet they stand up and storm the gates of heaven. . .'

Who were these men? In the fourth century Egypt, Syria and Palestine were the scenes of intensive experiments in Christian living, of a kind new in the Christian world. Every form of monastic life was tried, every extreme, every experiment and in many ways it has never been surpassed. The great centre and the earliest was Egypt. By 400 A.D. Egypt could be described as a land of hermits, a source of exasperation to the civil authorities who wanted men to fight and pay taxes, not to pray; and a source of enthusiastic, if at times, uninformed, admiration to Christians in the east and gradually also in the west and to the north of the Mediterranean. The three main types of monastic experiment in Egypt correspond roughly to three geographical locations: first, Lower Egypt. Here Antony the Great settled in about 269 as a solitary, and gradually attractted many disciples who lived near him. These were the hermits, the ones who lived entirely alone, meeting only on rare occasions. In Upper Egypt at the same time, there evolved a different form for the radical break from society. These were men who lived together in communities, at first under the guidance of Pachomius, another Egyptian who, at the end of the third century, withdrew from society to serve God in the desert. A third kind of monastic life evolved in Nitria and Scetis, where the monks lived virtually solitary lives, but in groups of three or four, often as disciples of a master. It is with the first and third of these groups that I am concerned, though, of course, the second, the communities, was of vital importance for the development of religious community life.

First: How do we know about them? How accurate is our information? The experiment of ascetics in their withdrawal from society in Egypt in the fourth and fifth centuries produced some remarkable literary records. Chief among them was a new literary genre of the Sayings of the Fathers, akin to wisdom literature, but with a distinctive form and tone. Short stories and anecdotes and quotations were repeated and passed on around the desert, and were eventually written down. They took, on their literary form, either the shape of sayings related to a theme, such as silence, discretion, charity, etc; or they were grouped under the names of the monks best known in Egypt and attributed to them. Groups of monks would preserve the sayings of their founder or spiritual father and this nucleus would be enlarged and rearranged as time passed. These have preserved the unstructured, unsophisticated wisdom of the desert in simple language. They do not provide and should not be made to provide a full programme of monastic or of spiritual life, but they do give instances of the practical, down to earth affairs of early monastic life, and they were produced from the lives of experts. They are also a reminder of how slick and polished our spirituality has become. Just as the Gospels remind us of the crude and unstructured facts of the life of Jesus of Nazareth, so these records show us the real life of the desert, beyond our later idealisms and subtlties. Other records, for instance the lives of the desert fathers and the Conferences of Cassian, provide other insights into this world, but the Sayings are still the earliest, most basic source – the one to which I will be referring.

First, let us look at what they thought they were doing in withdrawing from the life of society and going off alone into the deserts of Egypt. It is just this fact of withdrawal, of going away, that has always been both the scandal and the justification of the ascetic life. I will read you first part of the account given by St. Athanasius of the beginning of monastic life for Antony the Great, the first hermit; it is worth looking at in itself, and also because it provided the pattern for later conversions, not only of Augustine, but also of St. Francis of Assisi:

> "Antony was an Egyptian by birth. His parents were of good stock and well to do and because they were Christians he himself had been brought up as a Christian. Upon his parents' death he was left alone with a sister who was very young. He was about 18 or 20 at the time... one day as he was walking along towards church he reflected how the apostles left everything and followed the saviour and also how the people in Acts sold everything and laid it at the feet of the apostles for distribution among the needy and what great hope is laid up in heaven for such as these. With these thoughts in his mind he entered the church. And it so happened that the Gospel was being read at that moment and he heard the passage in which the Lord says to the rich man 'if thou wilt be perfect, go, sell all that you have and give to the poor and come and follow me and you will have treasure in heaven' . . . Antony immediately left the church and gave to the townsfolk the property he had from his forebears, keeping only a little of the proceeds for his sister. But once again he entered the church and heard the Lord saying in the

> Gospel 'be not solicitous for the morrow'. He could not bear to wait any longer but went out and distributed everything to the poor. Then he devoted all his time to ascetic living near his own house. For there were not yet many monasteries in Egypt and no monk even knew of the faraway desert." [3]

So Antony lived for awhile near another older ascetic near his own village; later he withdrew into the desert and lived in one of the tombs for many years in total solitude. It is a story of continual withdrawal into greater solitude, and later he returned to the company of others only because they came to him and asked for his help and advice. Son of a Christian family, well to do farmers inthe Nile delta, he heard the Gospel read in church and took the words personally and literally; he sold everything and left the security and domesticity of his life in order to follow the command of the Lord which he saw in a practical and obvious sense.

Other stories of conversion fill out the picture. Let me give you the most extreme and dramatic. Apollo, a peasant and a shepherd, one of the roughest of the Coptic monks, committed an act of outrage: "he saw a pregnant woman in the field one day and said to himself, 'I should like to see how the child lies in her womb.' So he ripped her up and saw the foetus. Immediately his heart was troubled and filled with compunction he went to Scetis and told the fathers what he had done. Now he heard them chanting, 'the year of our age 3 score years and 10 and even by strength 4 score, yet their span is but toil and trouble' and he said to them, 'I am forty years old and I have not made one prayer; if I live another year I shall not cease to pray God that he may pardon my sins.' So he passed all his time in prayer saying, 'I as man have sinned, do thou as God forgive.' " [4] Again, the immediate departure from what is known and familiar; the literal interpretation of a passage from scripture heard in church, entire concentration on prayer and the need of a sinner for mercy. A rough man, a sinner in the most obvious sense, with an obvious and practical interpretation of the demands of the Lord.

Next, in contrast to these two Copts, let us look at some foreigners in Egypt. Macarius, one of the greatest of the fathers, used to tell visitors about two young Romans who came to see him one day and asked to be his disciples. He thought them too delicate, too well brought up for the rough life of the desert and refused to help them. But, like the Copts, they would not turn aside from their desire to live away from society, in silence and solitude, and they built themselves a cell; they lived there for three years without seeing anyone and finally Macarius decided, as much out of curiosity as anything else, to visit them. He prayed with them and shared their way of life for a day and a night, and finally concluded, "the first had become a perfect man while the enemy was still fighting the younger." Later when both had died, Macarius used to take visitors to their cell and say, "come and see the place of the martyrdom of the young strangers." [5] Martyrdom: this extreme of solitude and aloneness was seen as death, the death of the false self, a lifetime of ascetic endeavour.

There was also a very famous Roman in the desert, Arsenius, who was always cited as the extreme of cultivation among the monks. He had been at court with the young princes, Arcadius and Honorius, sons of the Emperor Theodosius I. In 394, he left the palace in Rome secretly and came to Egypt where he lived as a hermit for the rest of his life, known for his extreme asceticism and silence. "While living in the palace, Arsenius prayed to God in these words: 'Lord, lead me in the way of salvation' and a voice came to him saying, 'Arsenius, flee from men and you will be saved.' "[6] Having withdrawn into the solitary life he made the same prayer again and he heard a voice saying to him, 'Arsenius, flee, be silent, and pray always, for these are the sources of sinlessness.' The contrast between the luxuries the monks imagined he must have enjoyed in the palace and the simplicity of his later way of life delighted the other monks and again and again they told stories to point the contrast. Perhaps the most delightful, however, is one which contrasts the austere, educated, patrician Arsenius with a very simple monk, Moses the Black, an Ethiopian who had been a robber before he became a monk; a story which is more comprehensible perhaps when one remembers the background of Egypt and the boat of Horus on the river of the dead in which there were honey cakes:

> "It was told of a brother who came to see Abba Arsenius at Scetis that when he came to the church, he asked the clergy if he could visit Abba Arsenius. They said to him, 'Brother, have a little refreshment and then go and see him.' 'I shall not eat anything,' said he, 'till I have met him.' So, because Arsenius' cell was far away, they sent a brother with him. Having knocked on the door, they entered, greeted the old man and sat down without saying anything. Then the brother from the church said, 'I will leave you. Pray for me'. Now the visiting brother, not feeling at ease with the old man, said 'I will come with you,' and they went away together. Then the visitor asked, 'Take me to Abba Moses, who used to be a robber.' When they arrived the Abba welcomed them joyfully and then took leave of them with delight. The brother who had brought the other one said to his companion, 'See, I have taken you to the foreigner and to the Egyptian, which of the two do you prefer?' 'As for me,' he replied, 'I prefer the Egyptian.' Now a Father who heard this prayed to God saying, 'Lord, explain this matter to me: for Thy name's sake the one flees from men, and the other, for Thy name's sake, receives them with open arms.' Then two large boats were

> shown to him on a river and he saw Abba Arsenius and the Spirit of God sailing in the one, in perfect peace; and in the other was Abba Moses with the angels of God, and they were all eating honey cakes." [7]

So we have Antony, a middle class farmer's son, converted by the words of the Gospel, withdrawing into the utter solitude of the desert from his familiar way of life. Apollo, an ordinary, uneducated Egyptian, like the majority of the monks, committing a crime and turning from it to solitude and repentance. We have the educated, civilized young Romans and the great Arsenius, also choosing this flight from the world into the desert, to the ages without end of solitude. How are we to understand a desert full of monks who have gone outside the bond of society completely and for life ? What is there to be learnt from this way of life? First of all one must say this: they never claimed to be only nor even the ideal Christians. A later writer in the same tradition put it like this: 'God is for all those who chose him, life for all, salvation for all; faithful, unfaithful; just, unjust; religious, irreligious; passionate, passionless; monks, seculars; healthy, sick; young, advanced in age; even as the outpouring of the lights and the sight of the sun and the winds of heaven, so and not otherwise; for there is no respect of persons with God.' [8] Many stories are told of ascetics who have this brought home to them by discovering people living in the world who are counted as their superiors in virtute; perhaps the story I like best is that of the Emperor Theodosius: he was said to be the equal of the ascetics not for his almsgiving, nor for his simple way of life, but because 'during the races in the hippodrome he sat crowned and robed and copied manuscripts paying no attention to the cheers and praise of the crowd.' [9] Abba Mateos said, 'It is not through virtue that I live in solitude but through weakness; those who live among men are the strong ones.' [10]

I suggest that the sayings and lives of the monks of Egypt have a limited but quite definite value for us. It is possible, of course, to read these texts and be entirely untouched by them; they can jerk past like a series of old movie shots, of interest, but of little significance. But there is another way; it is like this. In the Coptic gallery of the British Museum there are some portraits which are startingly modern in appearance. Painted on wax, they show the faces of Egyptians of the Fayyum for the fourth century and earlier – the same time and place as the desert fathers. Here is a middle aged woman in all her best jewelry; there is a stern man, the head of a household; an old woman remarkable like a Bostonian aristocrat; and most moving of all, a young boy of fourteen or so. They look like the more decadent of the English gentry in the last century. Most striking of all are their eyes, great dark eyes widening suddenly in amazement and apprehension; because, you see, these faces are painted on mummy cases and those eyes look out upon death. The pagan dead stare into a frightening continuation of the old life: 'Homage to thee, lord of darkness, thou that art at the head of the great house, prince of the night and black darkness; I come to thee, a disembodied soul, guide me in this season where there is cloud and darkness.' On Mount Sinai there are some other wax portraits made at the same time and again the great dark eyes are the focus, but with a difference: these are the first icons, the wax portraits of Christ and St. Peter, the Christian dead. It is not so much that their eyes look through the gate and grave of death into life everlasting but that by looking into their eyes we can see how to come ourselves to the gateway of life; and so learn for ourselves how to go in and out and find pasture. I suggest that these sayings of the fathers are like that. Let me give you an example of how their literature can be entered into, and let me concentrate on that element of withdrawal which I have already illustrated. They go away suddenly, violently, breaking painfully with the life they have known, leaving not only what is bad but also what is good; it is a flight from sin; it is also a flight from domesticity, the hearth, the involvment with the bonds of society. There was always, it seems, the temptation to return: one brother who lived outside his village did not go there for many years and he said to the other monks, 'Look how many years I have been here and have not gone to my village and look how often you have been there;' they told Abba Poemen and he said, 'by night I used to go and walk round the fields of my village, lest I become proud of the fact that I had not been there.' [11] The pull of the village, but even within resisting that, a man might still trust in his own will power and become proud of going away. They go into the desert, where they are poor in actual fact. They have left all that completes the self, those extensions of the person into things, relationships and activities. This is not a search for silence, and the beauty of unspoiled countryside; the luxury of aloneness. They call it the 'harsh and rugged desert,' the 'terrible wilderness;' and pay the full price in hardship for leaving the rich valley of the Nile; There they learn to do one thing and one thing only: they stay there and they learn to know themselves; they come face to face with the false self, with negation, with what John of Lycopolis calls the serpent coiled about the heart, [12] that selfishness that burrows deeper always into oneself. They use the terminology of the demons, and through it they analyse with painful accuracy the limitation and destruction within themselves.

What do they mean by this life time of self-knowledge? They say that a monk must sit in his cell and his cell will teach him everything. [13] They learn that it is possible for a man to remain at the centre of the web of human suffering; or to use another metaphor, they learn how to remain with the raw edges of themselves pointing always upward to the healing that comes only from the heavens. They said, 'the cell of the monk is the furnace of Babylon, but it is also where the three children found the son of God; it is like the pillar of cloud, and it is where God spoke to Moses.'[14] To quote from a very different source,

> I tell you naught for your comfort, yea naught for your desire. But that the sky grows darker yet and the wind rises higher. [15]

God, they say, is here or he is nowhere, and all the limitations, the simplification, the external austerities are to enable the man concerned to come to that very quick of human existence and to find God there; at the centre, they tell us, is life and not death. Here they say is one point where God exists and loves mankind. It is the story of Jacob, perhaps, to take it another way: Jacob, alienated from his brother, wrestles with the traveller unknown in darkness; and crippled for life, he goes towards the brother whom he has betrayed and says,' I see your face as the face of God.' The monk is to experience an identification with the cross which is for life: 'I stood with St. Mary,' says one of them, 'as she wept by the cross of the saviour;' [16] 'the monk,' says another, 'is one with the crucified Lord who became obedient unto death; ' [17] the icon of the monastic life is of a monk crucified on a cross.

Of course, this is only one side of the story. Because the experience of these men is of God, who is, above all and beyond all, faithful. When all the other loves are broken, and these sayings show the extent of that breaking in their lives, there remains the unbroken everlasting love of God and underneath are the everlasting arms. There are as many stories of the true joy of these men as there are of their tears. As he was dying Benjamin said, 'be joyful at all times, pray without ceasing and give thanks for all things.' [18] Their faces shine with light, they are known for their courtesy, their joy, their welcome to visitors, their care for one another. [19] The life of Christ, the new Adam, flows so richly in them that they cast out demons, cure disease, and, most endearingly to an English public, play again with the animals. Bes talked gently to a hippopotamus and a crocodile and persuaded them not to lay waste the land anymore; Theon went out at night to give precious water to gazelles and antelopes; Macarius cured the blind cubs of an hyena and in return she gave him a sheepskin; Helle sailed over the Nile on a crocodile as a ferry. Perhaps the most telling thing of all, with one another they did not judge: Abba Macarius, they said, became like God towards Scetis, 'for just as God protects the world so Macarius would cover faults which he saw as if he did not see them and those he heard as if he did not see them.' [20] Moses the Black was once asked to join in condemnation of a brother who had sinned, and "took a leaking jug and filled it with water and carried it with him to the meeting place; they said to him, 'Father what is this, and he said to them: 'My sins run out behind me and I do not see them and today I am coming to judge the errors of another'. " [21]

This is not a comfortable literature but neither is it a fanciful one. There are stories in it of visions, dreams, miracles, wonders, and it would take at least another paper to explain what I think about them. They have significance only in the context of the life of death and resurrection, and they themselves are never central. When Pachomius was asked, 'tell us one of the visions you see, Father,' he replied, 'a sinner like me does not ask to see God that he may see visions for that is against his will and is error. Hear all the same a great vision; if you see a man pure and humble that is a great vision. For what is greater than such a vision, to see the invisible God in a visible man.' [22] That is one of the main lessons of this literature the vision of God in man, and the truth that is God who is faithful. I have found it worth pursuing through all the difficulties and strangeness of such texts and I find it abundantly worthwhile. There is a very simple and steady learning here, and it is both universal and particular at the same time. The exploration of these deserts of the heart lead to the healing fountains springing up into eternal life.

Follow, poet, follow right
To the bottom of the night;
With your unconstraining voice
Still persuade us to rejoice.

With the farming of a verse
Make a vineyard of the curse,
Sing of human unsuccess
In a rapture of distress.

In the deserts of the heart
Let the healing fountain start,
In the prison of his days
Teach the free man how to praise.
(Auden)

Abba Antony said, 'God requires nothing but the human heart;' he also said, 'I no longer fear God, I love Him.'

NOTES.

1. W H Auden, 'In Memory of W B Yeats,' in *Collected Shorter Poems 1927-57*, Faber and Faber, 1966, pp. 142-3.
2. St. Augustine's *Confessions* Bk VIII, cap. 6.
3. St. Athanasius' *Life of St. Antony* trans. R T Meyer (London, 1950) pp. 18-20.
4. *Saying of the Desert Fathers* trans. Benedicta Ward (Mowbrays, 1975) Apollo 1.
5. ibid. Macarius 33.
6. ibid. Arsenius 1 & 2.
7. ibid. Arsenius 38.
8. John Climacus, *The Ladder of Divine Ascent* trans. L. Moore (London 1959).
9. Quoted by Kallistos Ware, "The Monk and the Married Christian" in *Eastern Churches Review* VII; Spring 1974, pp. 75-6.
10. *Sayings* op. cit. Mateos 13.

11. ibid. Poemen 110.
12. *Lives of the Desert Fathers,* trans. and commentary, Benedicta Ward and Norman Russell (Mowbrays 1981) John of Lycopolis.
13. *Wisdom of the Desert Fathers* trans. Benedicta Ward (SLG Press 1975) 74, p. 24.
14. ibid. 63, p. 22.
15. G K Chesterton, 'The Ballad of the White Horse' in *Collected Poems,* (London 1930) p. 233.
16. *Sayings* op. cit. Poemen 144.
17. ibid. Hyperechios 8.
18. ibid. Benjamin 4.
19. *Lives of the Desert Fathers* op. cit. Nitria.
20. *Sayings* op. cit. Macarius 32.
21. ibid. Moses 2.
22. *Life of St. Pachomius,* caps. 47-8.

IV

THE IMAGE OF THE PROSTITUTE IN THE MIDDLE AGES

"Beauty consuming itself like incense burned before God in solitude far from the eyes of men became the most stirring image of penance conceivable . . . the generosity of expiation, the gift of tears, were to the Christian a perpetual subject of meditation."

Emile Male

The fourth century in Egypt produced some examples of outrageous sin turning to outrageous repentance, from the city to the desert. This centre of repentance is, in fact, the key to the lives of all the desert fathers, and its essence, as with repentance in any age, is not psychological but theological. What drew so many tears from the eyes of Arsenius that "he had a hollow in his chest channelled out by the tears that fell from his eyes all his life" (Arsenius 41) was not a gloomy reflection upon his own acts of sin in the past but the apprehension of the glory of Christ our God always before him: "It was said of him that on Saturday evenings preparing for the glory of Sunday, he would turn his back on the sun and stretch out his hands in prayer towards the heavens, till once again the sun shone on his face" (Arsenius 30).

Especially striking to the monks of the fourth century was the conversion of prostitutes, those involved in selling sexual love, and their turning to a life of receiving the gift of love. They even used the prostitute as an image for their own lives of prayer: John the Dwarf, for instance, in two of the Sayings attributed to him, compares the soul to a courtesan: "There was in the city a courtesan who had many lovers. One of the governors approached her saying, 'Promise me you will be good and I will marry you.' She promised this and he took her and brought her to his home. Her lovers, seeing her again, said one to another, 'Let us go to the back of the house and whistle for her' . . . But the woman stopped her ears and withdrew to the inner chamber and shut the door. The old man said that this courtesan is our soul, that her lovers are the passions, that the lord is Christ, that the inner chamber is the eternal dwelling; those who whistle are evil demons, but the soul always takes refuge in the Lord'' (John the Dwarf 16).

A second saying attributed to him is on the same theme, but more startling in its terseness: ''One of the old men said, 'John, you are like a courtesan who shows her beauty to increase the number of her lovers.' Abba John kissed him and said, 'You are quite right, father.' One of his disciples said to him, 'Do you not mind that in your heart?' But he said, 'No, I am the same inside as I am outside'' (John the Dwarf 46). The generosity of the prostitute is used as an image for the soul, as well as the need to flee from demons, who are compared to her lovers. Pambo wept over a sinful woman seen in Alexandria but not only because of her sins: ''Two things make me weep: one is the loss of this woman, the other is that I am not so concerned to please God as she is to please wicked men'' (Pambo 4). Nonnus, seeing the harlot Pelagia, was amazed at her beauty and turned to his companions saying ''How many hours has this woman spent in her chamber adorning herself . . . that she may be a joy to the eyes of men . . . and we with such a Bridegroom . . . we do not adorn ourselves nor take care to wash the filth from our miserable souls, but leave them in their squalor'' (PL 73, col. 665).

In his book *Monks and Marriage,* Fr. Jean Leclercq refers to the theme of the harlot as an image in the Bible of the unfaithfulness of Israel. ''Holy Scripture uses it [the image of the harlot] quite frequently as a symbol of certain periods of crisis between God and his chosen people'' (p. 87). This symbolic use of the image of the prostitute as the unfaithful people, or the unfaithful person, towards God is important and I will return to its use as a metaphor later. But in addition to the symbol there was and always had been the factual reality of historical persons who lived as prostitutes and were converted. These are not the adulterers, the ones involved in sex outside marriage: these are the ones who sell physical caresses for money, without personal commitment or prolonged relationship. In the Sayings attributed to John the Dwarf, for instance, there are not only instances of the uses of the prostitute as a metaphor; there is also the story, perhaps the earliest and simplest of its kind in this literature, of the conversion of Paesia:

> She prepared for him and lay down on the bed. Abba John entered and sat down beside her. Looking into her eyes, he said to her. 'What have you got against Jesus that you behave like this?' When she heard this she became completely rigid. Then Abba John bent his head and began to weep copiously. She asked him, 'Abba, why are you crying?' He raised his head, then lowered it again, weeping, and said to her, 'I see Satan playing in your face, how should I not weep?' Hearing this she said to him, 'Abba, is it possible to repent?' He replied, 'Yes.' She said, 'Take me wherever you wish.' 'Let us go' he said, and she got up and went with him (John the Dwarf 40).

Paesia is presented as an orphan who had given hospitality to the monks of Scetis and was therefore well known to them; she undertook a life of prostitution because she became poor and the implication is that she had beggared herself through charity towards them. She dies in the desert on the way there, and John comments, "One single hour of repentance has brought her more than the penitence of many who persevere without showing such fervour in repentance" (John the Dwarf 40). The Anonymous Series of Sayings likewise contains the use of the prostitute as an image of the spiritual life and also at least one story of the genuine conversion of a woman. This time it is the story of a brother whose natural sister became a prostitute in the city. He went to see her and was bringing her back, repenting, to the desert, but, like Paesia, she died before they reached it (Anon. 43).

Such stories were well known and much used as edifying tales for monks. Pre-eminent among them was a group of four longer stories, each written in Greek but translated into Latin and circulating as a group in the *Vitae Patrum,* that popular reading matter for monasteries and convents of the West throughout the Middle Ages. The story of St. Mary Magdalene was of course even more popular and better known, but the other four had a certain amount of popularity also. The first is the story of Mary of Egypt, the second the tale of Thaïs, the third that of Maria the niece of Abraham and the fourth the history of Pelagia.

Mary of Egypt was the heroine from the fifth century onwards of a story of dramatic repentance. Elaborated and extended, it still forms a central theme of the liturgy of the Eastern Orthodox Church for the fifth Sunday of Lent, the Sunday of St. Mary of Egypt, where the prostitute in need of redemption is seen as the sinful soul of everyman, unable to repent and asking only for the mercy of God: "Thee we have as a pattern of repentance, all-holy Mary, pray to Christ that in the season of the fast this gift may be conferred on us, to raise thee in our hymns with faith and love" (Exapostilarion for 5th Sunday of Lent).

Mary chose to live from childhood in Alexandria as a prostitute; it was said that she enjoyed her trade so much that she did not take money for it, but lived by spinning. Going to the harbour one day, she took ship for Jerusalem with a party of pilgrims, each of whom she seduced during the voyage. In Jerusalem she continued to find new lovers until one day she came with the crowd of pilgrims to the Holy Sepulchre where the relic of the Holy Cross was offered for veneration. Wishing to enter, she found herself held back by an invisible force until, turning to an icon of the Mother of God, she promised repentance and entire conversion if the Virgin would first allow her to venerate the Cross. This was allowed, and she then fled over the Jordan and lived in solitude for many years. Discovered one day by the good monk Zosimus, Mary tells him her story, receives from him communion and finally is buried by him, with the help of a lion from the desert.

Such a story is clearly packed with intricate symbols — the contrast of the good self-satisfied Zosimus with the penitent sinner is central to its message; the details of three loaves of bread which Mary takes with her into the desert, the action of passing over the waters of the Jordan, her appearance by moonlight, walking on the waters, the lion who comes out of the desert at her death — all are replete with Christian significance which would not be lost upon those who heard or read the story.

John Moschus records the story of Mary who lived as a hermit in Egypt and Cyril of Scythopolis who visited her tomb. Cyril, both in his *Life of St. Cyriacus* and *The Sayings of the Desert Fathers* (Bassarion 4), recounts the visit of two monks to an Egyptian hermit, who was recognised after death as a woman. It seems there may be here an historical foundation for the story, and certainly it is true that there were prostitutes in both Alexandria and Jerusalem, some of whom may well have retired to the desert as ascetics. Mary of Egypt was venerated in the West with a feast on April 2nd (sometimes the 9th or 10th) and her story in its more elaborate form became one of the miracles of the Virgin Mary. William of Malmesbury, for instance, lists it as no. 40

among his collection of *Miracles of the Blessed Virgin Mary.* He says her story is "venerable by long established tradition and the undoubted truth of the matter." William obtained the story from the cycle of Mary legends composed by Dominic of Evesham, who introduced it into the collections. Dominic used the Latin account of Paul the Deacon (PL 73, cols. 671-90) which is the text most usually found in the monastic Passionales. The miracles of St. William of Norwich contain a story clearly based on the story of Mary of Egypt, and which the author compares explicitly to that source. In 1168, Thomas of Monmouth claims that he was in a chapel recently consecrated to the boy William (April 27th) and that a party of pilgrims came there to pray. Among them was a woman who, like Mary, found she was unable to enter the shrine because of her sin, in this case, the sin of sorcery. After confession, she finds she can go in. The parallel is slight and depends only upon the similarity of a sinful woman who cannot enter a holy place, and is used by Thomas to emphasise the holiness of the new chapel of St. William; the real point of the story of Mary the great sinner, who turns only by the mercy of God towards great repentance, is entirely lost.

At times the story of Mary of Egypt was confused with the apocryphal legends about the later life of St. Mary Magdalene. Honorius of Autun, for instance, says of Mary Magdalene: "It is told that after she, with the other disciples, saw the Lord ascend into heaven, she received the Holy Spirit with the others. Afterwards, because of her love for Him, she did not wish to see any other man, but coming into the desert she lived for many years in a cave. When a certain wandering priest came to her and inquired who she was, she answered that she was Mary the Sinner and that he had been sent to bury her body. With these words she departed from this world which she had long despised, entering into glory and with angels singing a hymn she ascended to the Lord" (PL 172, col. 981). This somewhat garbled memory of the story of Mary of Egypt here attributed to St. Mary Magdalene is denounced by the tenth century author of the *Life of St. Mary Magdalene;* he includes some very lively information about the later career of his heroine and her brother and sister in southern France but he denies that this piece of legend belongs to her: "It is very false and borrowed by creators of fables from the deeds of the Egyptian penitent" (PL 122, col. 1486). The point of both stories is of course the same: the prostitute, the lover of many men, is turned by love of Christ to the solitude of the desert and undertakes there the ardours of prayer and penance.

When Humbert of Rome wrote a pattern sermon for preachers in the thirteenth century, he included one which could be preached to fallen women. Just how he expected his friars to meet these ladies is not clear and it may be that the sermon was included only for the sake of completeness. The penitent sinners whom he uses to illustrate the hope held out for prostitutes are St. Mary Magdalene, St. Mary of Egypt and St. Pelagia. All three, he says, found the sins of the flesh hard to relinquish; they enjoyed what they did, they were used to doing it and they were notorious for it. With many Biblical examples, Humbert goes on to show that they turned to three genuine ways of repentance: they wept much, they went away into solitude, and they suffered greatly in their penances. And at their deaths they were taken into very great glory. To expand that point, Humbert refers to another repentant whore, Thaïs, for whom Paul the Simple saw a marvellous bed prepared in heaven. Where sin abounded, concludes Humbert, grace did much more abound. (I am indebted to Fr. Simon Tugwell, OP, for a transcription of the Latin text of Humbert.)

Here two more of the *meretrices* of Egypt are introduced for the edification of the thirteenth century: Pelagia and Thaïs. Pelagia was an actress in Alexandria, and therefore presumed to belong to the class of immoral persons, such as jesters, mimics, jongleurs, clowns, etc. She passed along the road one day with her companions and was seen by a group of bishops, all of whom hid their faces in horror except for the Bishop Nonnus, a monk from the desert, who "did long and most intently regard her and after she had passed by still he gazed and his eyes went after her. Then turning his head he looked at the bishops sitting around him. 'Did not,' he said, 'her great beauty delight you?' " (PL 73, col. 665). Later, he baptised Pelagia and later still helped her to run away disguised as a man and become a hermit in Palestine. The deacon James who wrote the story visited the "hermit Pelagia," of whom so many wonders were told, and found her at the point of death. It is a story of great beauty told with a moving simplicity, in which the beauty of a woman revealed the glory of God to a monk and stood as judge to the whole of a timid and self-righteous episcopate. Perhaps writers did not re-tell it because it is already told superbly well; or perhaps the idea of the monk and bishop gazing in wonder at the naked actress on the road was felt to be too dangerous in a more prurient age; at any rate, there are few repetitions of the story of Pelagia in the Middle Ages, though the story formed part of the group in the *Vitae Patrum.*

More popular was the savage tale of Thaïs, the shortest and the least appealing of this groups of *'sanctae meretrices'*. Thaïs was a prostitute in Alexandria who attracted great trade and caused violence and even murder among her jealous lovers. Paphnutius, one of the more tough and unbending monks of the desert heard of this, disguised himself, and went to challenge her. At his stern words, she repented and followed him into the desert, first burning all her ill-gotten gains. Immured in a cell in a convent with no outlet, she passed three years alone in her own filth, praying only "O thou who didst create me, have mercy upon me" (PL 73, col.112). Paphnutius, urged on by St. Anthony and his disciple Paul, opened the cell to assure her that her repentance had been accepted in heaven; she died within a few days.

This story formed the basis for one of the plays of Hrotswitha, a canoness of the abbey of Gandersheim, in the tenth century. Hrotswitha admired the comedies of Terence and set herself to write plays which would praise the chastity of Christian women. In her play *Paphnutius* she uses the story with great skill and sensitivity. It belongs to a second groups of plays which she sent to the court of Otto II for admiration after her first plays had been welcomed there, and it may be that a certain desire to impress the *litterati* of the court induced her to place in the first act a long discussion of the liberal arts in the mouth of the unlikely figure of Paphnutius. In the rest of the play, however, Hrotswitha re-tells the story from the *Vitae Patrum,* making a vivid and dramatic scene out of the burning of Thaïs' goods, handling the dialogue before she is shut into her cell with great insight into her shrinking yet courageous words. At the end she concludes with a tender scene of the death of Thaïs, who dies in the company of Paphnutius. On her lips are the words of the only prayer he had ever allowed her to say, no longer experienced as a restriction but as a free choice.

Hrotswitha included among her plays another on the same theme; this is her play *Abraham,* a dramatic presentation of the story from the *Vitae Patrum* of Maria, the niece of Abraham. Here all her art as a dramatist reaches its height, inspired by the beauty of the text before her which was written by Ephraem, the friend and companion of Abraham and Maria. The story forms the end of the life of Abba

Abraham, a hermit, who received into his hermitage when he was old a small orphaned niece called Maria. He taught the seven year old heiress how to sing the psalms, how to fast and keep vigil, and disposed of her inheritance so that she might never be tempted by worldly goods. After many years of companionship in prayer, Maria is seduced by a visiting cleric and in despair runs away and becomes a prostitute in the city. Her uncle heard where she was and how she was employed and disguised himself as a soldier and went to find her. Entering the brothel, he approached Maria in her room as a lover and revealed himself to her, begging her to return and learn repentance in company with her uncle and Ephraem who loved her. She says: "Go before, and I will follow your goodness and kiss the traces of your footsteps; for you have so grieved for me that you would come and draw me out of this cesspit" (PL 73, col. 157). In the desert, Maria lived a life of true repentance and her tears and prayers became a source of healing to those who heard her.

In her play, Hrotswitha enlarges the character of Ephraem and gives him a series of conversations with Abraham, expanding the story with human detail. The scene with Abraham in the brothel with the brothel-keeper and Maria is excellently set out, and the dialogue between uncle and niece when they are alone catches the full agony and tenderness of the original perfectly. The play concludes as it began with a conversation between Abraham and Ephraem about Maria in her repentance and love. The point of the original story is that sexual sin is not unforgiveable but despair is; Maria, like so many young monks in the desert tradition, is shown as a young and self-assured person, relying on her own ability for virtue and therefore despairing when overthrown by lust. The restoration of love and humility leads her to the same practices of asceticism, but with her motive wholly changed. The story is given exactly the same point in the dactylic hexameters of Hrotswitha.

These stories of sin and repentance were popular especially in the monastic circles for which they were written. It is perhaps worth asking how they were read. In a world accustomed to reading the Scriptures with the inner eye of faith, no text, and especially no spiritual text, would be of interest simply for its surface meaning; that would be too thin by far. At times some of the parallels that were drawn with contemporary events missed the central point and used points which were peripheral and taken from the "literal" sense of the stories, as in the case of Thomas of Monmouth's use of the Mary of Egypt story. But this is rare; the main theme is the point. The key to the real appeal of these tales is the use made in them of Scripture. For example, in the story of Abraham and his niece Maria, Ephraem breaks off his narrative at a crucial point, indeed at the climax, to give what seems at first a rather obscure reference to Genesis. "Come now, beloved brethren, and let us marvel at this second Abraham. The first Abraham went forth to do battle with the kings and smote them and brought back his nephew Lot; but this second Abraham went forth to do battle with the Evil One and having vanquished him brought home again his niece in greater triumph" (PL 73, col. 655). The obvious parallels of the two Abrahams and the two nephew/nieces is not the whole nor the centre of this comparison. A glance at Commentaries on this passage from Genesis 14 shows how it was read habitually by the faithful: Abraham "the mystical figure of Christ, the seed of Abraham" goes to rescue Lot, who has been captured by "four kings with five," that is, "the four elements of the worlds are signified with the five senses by which man is taken captive"; "Abraham went forth to that battle with the Cross of Christ and in the name of Jesus, that strong sign, that banner of faith, and brought back the captive with triumph" (*Glossa Ordinaria,* Genesis 14). In other words, these stories of the *meretrices* of Egypt were presented and read as stories about the one theme of perennial interest in every age, the redemption of souls by Christ; His *kenosis* is paralled in the monks who go to save the women, who are themselves images of the captive human being, redeemed solely by the mercy of God. The drama of their great bondage is built up in order to stress the even greater wonder of their salvation and their consequent great love. The sinner becomes the contemplative, not out of merit or effort, but by the touch of God; all that is needed is to be at the point of need where such mercy can be received.

That the appeal of these stories is theological and not psychological is perhaps underlined by the kind of interest taken in them by later writers. In the Middle English collection of miracle stories known as the *Alphabet of Tales* among the first is the story of Thaïs; and when Anatole France published his deadly indictment of asceticism in 1890, he chose Thaïs as his base. Operas, stories, poems, even a strip cartoon in *Punch,* have chosen this most stark of the stories to illustrate the drama of the soul, the dilemma of redemption. When writers want to uncover the psychological dynamics of repentance, they chose other stories, as in Jonathan Heath-Stubbs' *Maria Aegyptica:*

Thrust back by hands from the sanctuary door
Mary of Egypt, that hot whore,
Fell on the threshold. Priests, candles, acolytes,
Shivered in flame upon her failing sight . . . .
And when at last she died,
With burning tender eyes, hair like dark flame,
The golden lion came;
And with his terrible claws scooped out a tomb,
Gently in the loose soil,
And gave that dry burnt corpse to the earth's womb.

To read these stories as they were meant to be read is to enter into that realm of monastic culture which Jean Leclercq has presented with such insight. "Medieval man took more interest in permanent and universal ideas than in specific events which are transitory by nature. To understand them, one must adopt their point of view. Once this is done, legend becomes, in a sense they themselves would have approved, truer than history (*The Love of Learning and the Desire for God,* Chapter 8, 'Literary Genres,' p. 206). Throughout the Middle Ages, this interest in "permanent and universal ideas" was fed by the stories in the *Vitae Patrum,* including the lives of the *meretrices.* They were re-written, quoted, used, included in artistic illustration. Above all they illustrated a central theme in the monastic life, in which the mercy of God towards the sinful, unfaithful, bound soul, was of primary concern. With a renewed interest in the actual state of harlots in the twelfth century, this theme again had an outside, physical relevance. But it should not be forgotten that in all ages readers of these stories saw in them the image of salvation totally received by sinners. The reflections of Ephriam the Deacon who had seen the lives of Abraham and his niece at first hand continued to be the response of the average to the lives of these stars: "Alas for me, for those two have fallen asleep and gone their way to the Lord in whom they believed; their minds were never occupied with worldly business, but only with the love of God. And I, unprepared and unfit, remain here, and lo winter has overtaken me and the winds of infinity find me naked and poor and without any covering of good deeds" (PL 73, col. 659). The application of the stories to oneself is to use the text as the text of the Scriptures was used, for the moral sense, the personal word of God to the soul of the reader. The colour and drama built around these stories at times has been more appealing than this personal and interior message, at times the details, pleasing to another age, have offended later readers. But the theme of the unfaithful soul turning at the point of unbearable need to the generosity of the mercy of Christ makes them in their first version, throughout the Middle Ages and now, an important part of the monastic and Christian tradition.

TEXTS

Translations from the *Sayings of the Desert Fathers* (Alphabetical Series) can be found in *Sayings of the Desert Fathers,* trans. B. Ward (Oxford 1975).

— of the *Anonymous Series,* in *Wisdom of the Desert Fathers,* trans. B. Ward (SLG Press, Oxford 1976). A new and enlarged edition is in preparation.

— of the *Lives of the Harlots,* see my forthcoming book for translations and commentary, *Harlots of the Desert: a study in repentance* (Mowbrays, Oxford).

An English translation of the plays of *Hrotswitha of Gandersheim,* by Christopher St. John, is available. (Latin text PL 137.) London 1973.

V

TRADITIONS OF SPIRITUAL GUIDANCE

Spiritual direction in the Desert Fathers

> Do not be afraid to hear about virtue and do not be a stranger to the term. For it is not distant from us nor does it stand external to us, but its realization lies within us and the task is easy if only we will it. Now the Greeks leave home and traverse the sea in order to gain an education but there is no need for us to go abroad on account of the Kingdom of Heaven nor to cross the sea for virtue. For the Lord has told us before, 'The Kingdom of God is within you'. The only thing goodness needs, then, is that which is within the human mind.[1]

'ITS REALIZATION lies within us': this conviction that the kingdom of God is to be discovered within the heart of man lies at the centre of the spiritual teaching of the desert. The fourth century in Egypt saw the invention of christian monasticism and it produced some of the finest texts ever written about conversion of the heart, that is to say, of the whole person, within the tradition of the gospel. The whole life of the monks was a training, not a search for 'illumination', but a training, an *ascesis*, both for and in the life of the kingdom of God. The perspective of things has subtly changed in the clear air of the desert, the 'huge quiet' of Nitria, Scetis and the Cells. They said:

> There is no labour greater than that of prayer to God. For every time a man wants to pray, his enemies the demons want to prevent him, for they know that it is only by turning him from prayer that they can hinder his journey. . . . Prayer is warfare to the last breath (Agathon 9 in *Sayings*).

And when Abba Sisoes was dying, even though his face 'shone like the sun', he said, 'I do not think I have even made a beginning yet' (Sisoes 14 in *Sayings*).

In this life-time of conversions, the monks found that they needed the assistance of others, not only in the practical matters of life in the desert, though that was of great importance to them, but in the inner ways of the heart. It would be an anachronism to talk about 'spiritual direction' among the desert fathers; they were very clear that the process of turning towards God was a matter of the spirit and the body together, and that this was given in direction only by Christ. Any help they asked or received from one another was with this in mind: 'we ought to live as having to give account to God for our way of life every day' (*Systematic Series* 4). They are like the dogs who hunt hares, the one who has seen the hare:

> pursues it until he catches it, without being concerned with anything else . . . so it is with him who seeks Christ as master: ever mindful of the cross, he cares for none of the scandals that occur, till he reaches the Crucified (*Systematic Series*, 71).

Their 'training' is a process of turning from the bonds and limitations of the self into the freedom of the sons of God, and any words spoken between them are for this end, the attainment of that stillness in which the Spirit of God alone guides the monk. For this reason they are very sparing with their words, and one should not be misled by the fact that the records of the desert come to us primarily in the form of conversations. They stand together on the page and we have the illusion that they were said one after another in a busy kind of dialogue, but in fact they are sentences remembered over many years and finally grouped together from several periods and areas. Some are so changed that their context and much of their meaning is lost. It is these fragmentary words which lead into the atmosphere of the desert more than the literary constructions created later by John Cassian in his *Institutes* and *Conferences*. More truly of the desert than those elegant reminiscences is, for instance, the story of Abba Macarius and the two young strangers who came to him for guidance: he showed them where to live and left them alone for three years before he inquired any further about them; or of Abba Sisoes who decided that his own part of the desert was becoming crowded and went to live on the mountain of Antony; there, he said to a brother, he lived peacefully for 'a little time', and when the brother asked how long this 'little time' of total silence and solitude was, he replied 'seventy-two years' (Sisoes 28 in *Sayings*).

Against this background of the 'ages of quiet without end', the timelessness and silence of the desert, is it possible to say anything about their assistance of each other in their lives of conversion? It would be wrong to look for a coherent programme of spiritual direction in such texts but it is possible to see something of their expectations and experiences through some of the *Sayings*. It is important to remember when looking at these texts, however, that they are in no sense a treatise on a theme, but fragments of stories glimpsed through many layers of transmission; sometimes they seem contradictory, sometimes inconclusive, and they should not be given a coherence they do not have. However, some practical ways of learning *metanoia* seem to emerge from the texts, and seem, moreover, to be virtually the same for both the hermits and the cenobites. I will therefore suggest certain 'sayings' as revealing the basic understanding of training in the monastic life in the desert. It is also perhaps worth recalling before I do so the conviction of the desert fathers that the life of salvation is for all, and is not the exclusive preserve of monks, a theme sometimes forgotten among themselves, but which was always there and is best expressed perhaps in the words of a later writer:

> God is for all those who chose him, life for all, salvation for all, faithful, unfaithful; just, unjust; religious, irreligious; passionate, passionless; monks, seculars; healthy, sick; young, advanced in age; even as the outpouring of the light and the sight of the sun, and the winds of heaven, so and not otherwise; for there is no respect of persons with God.[2]
>
> While still living in the palace, Abba Arsenius prayed to God in these words, 'Lord, lead me in the way of salvation', and a voice came saying to him, 'Arsenius, flee from men and you will be saved'. Having withdrawn to the solitary life he made the same prayer again and he heard a voice saying to him, 'Arsenius, flee, be silent, pray always, for these are the sources of sinlessness' (Arsenius 1 and 2 in *Sayings*).

These sayings, attributed to Arsenius, one of the most famous of the fathers of Scetis at the beginning of the fourth century, contain several things that are of the essence of the spirituality of the desert. There is the desire for one thing only, salvation; there is the immediate practical action of doing, not only thinking; there is the command to flee, to go away from what is familiar; then the idea of silence, solitude, aloneness, which is the desert; and the ideal of constant prayer for the whole of life. But there is also the 'voice', the direction which comes from God at the very beginning of this conversion and this is the first and perhaps the most vital of the ways of spiritual understanding in this tradition. There are many accounts of the way in which the monks decided to undertake their lives of asceticism, and always there is in some form this 'voice' this command from God. In the case of Arsenius, it is a direct answer to him when he prays. In the case of others, it is mediated through one or other of the many ways in which a Christian can expect to hear the will of God. For instance, Antony the Great, the father of hermits, heard the gospel read in church, 'if you will be perfect, go, sell all that you have and give to the poor and come and follow me and you will have treasure in heaven'. This time a word from the scriptures pierced his heart. It was followed by the same reaction as with Arsenius: 'Antony immediately left the church and gave to the townsfolk the property he had . . . then he devoted all his time to the ascetic living' and after a while, he went deeper and deeper into the desert (*Life of Antony*, 2,3 and 8). A practical action, and then flight, exile, a going away from the familiar world of the village, as Arsenius had fled from the palace of the Emperor. For Pachomius, the father of cenobites, it was the charity of

Christians that moved him, and caused him to leave his life as a soldier and go away into the solitude of the desert. For Apollo, a rough coptic peasant, it was horror at his own sin that caused him to flee, followed by a further piercing of his heart when he came near to Scetis and heard the monks repeating a psalm: 'So he passed all his time in prayer, saying "I as man have sinned, do thou as God forgive"' (Apollo 2 in *Sayings*).

This pattern of being moved by the action of God first, of leaving the familiar place, going away and giving oneself over to the action of God in silence and solitude is the gateway in the desert to prayer and conversion of heart. What follows until death is the hard work of becoming the new man in Christ: 'one of the Fathers asked Abba John the Dwarf, "What is a monk?" And he said, "He is toil. The monk toils at all he does. That is what a monk is"' (John the Dwarf 36 in *Sayings*). This 'toil', this 'hard work' lasted a lifetime. And the direction had to be constantly followed and kept clear. In this task, the monk had three assets: one was the cell; the second was the scriptures and the third was an old man, a father, as a point of reference in all he did.

The *Sayings* are full of references to the cell of the monk as the place which in itself directed the monk's life. The flight into the desert leads to a place of stability: 'Just as a tree cannot bring forth fruit if it is always being transplanted, so the monk who is always going from one place to another is not able to bring forth virtue' (*Systematic Series* 72). The first action of the newcomer to the desert was either to build a cell for himself, a simple one-roomed hut, or to join an established monk in his cell. The idea of staying in the cell is stressed again and again. 'Go, sit in your cell, and give your body in pledge to the walls of your cell, and do not come out of it' (*Systematic Series* 73). 'A brother came to Scetis to visit Abba Moses and asked him for a word. The old man said to him, "Go, sit in your cell and your cell will teach you everything"' (Moses 6 in *Sayings*). Why is it that they saw this stability in the cell as vital in their training? It was because they could learn there and there only that God exists, because if God is not here and now in this moment and in this place, he is nowhere. To remain in the cell was to stay at the centre of human suffering and discover that God is there, that at the centre there is life and not death, salvation not damnation, light and not darkness. They said, 'the cell of a monk is the furnace of Babylon, but it also is where the three children found the Son of God; it is like the pillar of cloud, and it is where God spoke to Moses' (*Systematic Series* 74). The cell was the place of hard work: Abba Sarapion once visited a celebrated recluse who lived always in one small room and he asked her, 'Why are you sitting here?' And she replied, 'I am not sitting. I am on a journey'.

The first teacher of the monk was God; the second was his cell. Within the cell, the monk had one sure guide and often it was the same guide that began his conversion — the scriptures. The language of the writings of the desert was so formed by the meditation of the scriptures that it is almost impossible to say where quotation ends and comments begin. The thought of the monks was shaped by constant reading and learning by heart of the text of the bible, and in particular by the constant repetition of the psalms in the cell. Later generations used also the constant prayer of the name of Jesus, and while this particular form of words ('Lord Jesus Christ Son of the Living God have mercy upon me a sinner') is not found in the *Apophthegmata*, the idea of continual prayer by using a set form of words in the psalms was central to it. The combination of attention to God, the stability of the cell and the meditation of the scriptures is found in a saying of Abba Antony:

> Always have God before your eyes; whatever you do, do it according to the testimony of the holy scriptures; in whatever place you live, do not easily leave it. Keep these three precepts and you will be saved (Antony 3 in *Sayings*).

Epiphanius of Cyprus urged the reading of the scriptures for the monk, 'Reading the scriptures is a great safeguard against sin. . . . Ignorance of the scriptures is a precipice and a deep abyss' (Epiphanius 9 and 11 in *Sayings*). But for the more simple coptic monks the scriptures were more than this. They were the bread of heaven on which they fed as often as they could and as literally as possible. The breaking of the bread of the scriptures was to them the bread of life, and there are stories of monks going for many days without food because they were fed by this bread of heaven. Abba Patermuthius, a robber, went after his conversion into the desert for three years, having learnt only the first psalm; he spent his time there 'praying and weeping, and wild plants were sufficient for his food'; when he returned to the church, he said that God had given him the power to recite all the scriptures by heart. The fathers were astonished at 'this high degree of ascesis' and baptized him as a Christian (*Lives*, ch X). The meditation of the scriptures, the main guide to the monk, is here presented as a sacrament; not as an intellectual study but as a free gift of God and, moreover, as the bread of life in the wilderness, even for one not yet baptized.

This consideration of the scriptures as sacrament leads to the next channel by which the monk learned the lessons of the desert, that is, the words of a father. The most frequent request of one monk to another was 'speak a word to me', and by this request the monk was not asking for either information or instruction. He was asking, as with the scriptures, for a sacrament. The 'word' was not to be discussed or analyzed or disputed in any way; at times, it was not even understood; but it was to be memorized and absorbed into life, as a sure way towards God. Pachomius even said that if someone asked for a 'word' and you could think of nothing to say, you should tell him a parable of some sort and God would still use it for his salvation. Again and again, there are stories of monks who would go to live with an old man, and find that he would never give them instructions or orders; they could imitate him if they wished; and if he spoke, the words were for them to use, not debate. A brother asked a monk what he should do because he always forgot whatever was said to him and the old man used the image of a jug which is frequently filled with oil and then emptied out: 'So it is with the soul; for even if it retains nothing of what it has been told, yet it is . . . purified' (*Systematic Series* 91). It was not the words of the father that mattered in themselves. Nor were his personality and treatment of the disciple central, a point made very clearly in a story of Abba Ammoes:

> At first Abba Ammoes said to Abba Isaiah (his disciple), 'What do you think of me?' And he said to him, 'You are an angel, father'. Later on he said to him, 'And now, what do you think of me?' He replied, 'You are like Satan. Even when you say a good word to me, it is like steel' (Ammoes 2 in *Sayings*).

The father of a monk in the desert was not a guru nor was he a master; he was a father and several things followed from this. The abba did not give 'spiritual direction'; if asked, he would give 'a word' which would become a sacrament to the hearer. The action of God was paramount and the only point of such 'words' was to free the disciple to be led by the Spirit of God, just as the abba himself would. In the desert there could only be one father to a disciple and even when he died, he was still the father of his sons. There was no need to change fathers, or to find a new one if one died. It was a lasting and permanent relationship. In such a relationship, tradition was passed on by life as well as by word; those who had already been a certain way into the experience of the monastic life must be able to become this channel of grace to others. But the aim was always for the abba to disappear. The real guide was the Holy Spirit, who would be given to those who learned to receive him. Moreover, in this relationship, it was almost always the disciple who asked for a word, not the abba who offered one. The lesson to be learnt, and the *Sayings* are full of stories of puzzled newcomers who found it incomprehensible not to be instructed, was that each one had to learn to receive the gift of God for himself; and it was precisely in learning this that the disciple began to pray. There was no set of instructions, no pattern, for the monk; just some simple external ways of living, the word of the scriptures and, if requested, the sacrament of the words of a fellow monk.

It was and remains a hard way, and in order to use it properly, the disciple needed to see it as a crucifixion with Christ, wound against wound, so that the life of the Spirit might be truly given.

> A brother asked an old man, 'How can I be saved?' The latter took off his habit, girded his loins, and raised his hands to heaven,

> saying, 'So should the monk be: denuded of all things in this world and crucified. In the contest, the athlete fights with his fists; in his thoughts, the monk stands, his arms stretched out in the form of a cross towards heaven, calling on God. The athlete stands naked when fighting in a contest; the monk stands naked and stripped of all things, anointed with oil and taught by his master how to fight. So God leads us to victory' (*Systematic Series* 11).

The necessary abdication of the selfish centre of a man, which John of Lycopolis saw as a serpent deeply coiled round the heart of men, so deeply embedded that it was impossible to remove it for oneself, demanded the full attention, daily and in minute detail, of the monk for his whole life. The literature of the desert is not about visions and spiritual experiences; it is about the long process of the breaking of hearts. The monks defined themselves as sinners, as penitents, as those who needed and would always need mercy.

There are, in this tradition, many things that resulted from this approach. One of them was that suppleness of the spirit which breaks through the stiff lines of determination and self-righteousness, and makes the soul supple and pliable to receive, as they would say, the impress of the Spirit as upon wax. One of the ways of discovering if this process was continuing lay in the acceptance of the abba by the disciple as the one who discerned reality, against the evidence of the senses; as the one who knew what should be done, against the limited understanding of family obligations; as one who knew what was possible, against the dictates of common sense. The well-known story of the disciple who was commanded to plant a dry stick and water it should be seen in this context; it is told in several versions, in some of which the story has gained picturesque imagery, with the dry stick flowering; but in its more primitive form it was simply an illustration of how supple and obedient the disciple had become to do such a thing. The words, the actions, the opinions, did not matter in themselves; what concerned the monk was his ability to listen and obey. So, when an old man said to his disciple, 'Look, there is a buffalo', the disciple looked and said, 'Yes, abba' even when his eyes told him that it was a wild boar (Mark 2 in *Sayings*).

This life of discovery of the power of the cross in a human life, lived practically and realistically, without notions and theories, produced three 'signs'. First, there was the sign of tears: it was said of Abba Arsenius that he wept so much that 'he had a hollow in his chest channelled out by the tears that fell from his eyes all his life' (Arsenius 41 in *Sayings*); and the young monk Theodore, the favourite disciple of Abba Pachomius, wept so much that his eyesight was endangered. Tears signified the baptism of repentance rather than superficial emotional disturbance in this tradition and were often associated with meditation on the passion of Christ. One old man asked another, 'Tell me where you were . . .' and he said, 'My thoughts were with St Mary the Mother of God as she wept by the cross of the Saviour. I would that I could always weep like that' (Poemen 144 in *Sayings*). These tears were valued, not ignored or explored; in this theme of weeping and allowing others to weep there is a vital element in the 'spiritual direction' in the desert. It is this: the monk undertook a life of ascetic prayer and it was held that this was what he most desired; so that when he wept or groaned or had to fight against temptations, in fact, whenever he suffered profoundly and continually, he was allowed to do so, indeed, he was encouraged by others, and especially by his abba, to stay at this point of pain in order to enter into the only true healing which is God. When Moses the Black, one of the most attractive of the monks of Scetis, was tempted to fornication, he came to Abba Isidore and told him he could not bear the temptation. Isidore urged him to return to his cell and continue the battle, but he said, 'Abba, I cannot'; Isidore then showed him the 'multitudes of angels shining with glory' who were fighting within the monks against the demons, and with this assurance, but with no alleviation of the suffering to be endured, he returned to his cell (Moses 1 in *Sayings*). The women of the desert seem to have been as clear about this as the men: 'It was said of Amma Sarah that for thirteen years she waged war against the demon of fornication. She never prayed that the warfare should cease but she said, "O God give me strength for the fight"' (Sarah 1 in *Sayings*).

This concentration upon the value of suffering in the light of the cross of Christ leads to the second sign which was seen as a mark of authenticity in the lives of the monks: charity. In so far as the monk truly found himself 'crucified with Christ', so far did he receive the Holy Spirit, and display in his life the gifts of the Spirit of God. The charity of the monks, their warmth, their unaffected welcome of each other and of strangers, their practical care of one another were as famous as their asceticism; the other side of their pain was their joy. This was not the kind of pleasure which is an alternative to and an escape from suffering nor is it an exploitation of others, but a realization of that 'Christ between us' that gives deep and true relationship. It is the life of the kingdom, of the Second Adam, of man restored to paradise, and though at no moment did they forget that this was only so through the cross at the centre of their lives, the result was not gloom but radiance. The most striking result of this spirituality is closely connected with the reserve of the elder fathers about giving orders or rebukes to the newcomers: they did not judge one another in any way. It was said of Abba Macarius that he 'became as it is written a god upon earth, because just as God protects the world, so Abba Macarius would cover the faults that he saw as if he did not see them, and those which he heard as though he did not hear them' (Macarius 32 in *Sayings*).

This freedom to live increasingly in the power of the Spirit points to the third sign of desert spirituality: there is a concern for unceasing prayer in this tradition, not as a support to works but as the life of the monk, and this is often expressed in terms of 'the prayer of fire'. The end and aim of the monk was to become so open to the action of God that his life would fill each moment of the day and night. Prayer was not a duty or obligation but a burning desire. The older monks never 'taught' prayer; they prayed and the newcomers could find in their prayer a way for them to follow. Abba Joseph said to Abba Lot, 'You cannot become a monk unless you become like a consuming fire', and when Abba Lot asked what more he could do beyond his moderate attention to prayer each day, 'the old man stood up and stretched his hands towards heaven his fingers became like ten lamps of fire and he said to him, "If you will, you can become all flame"' (Joseph Panephysis 6 and 7 in *Sayings*).

The search for God in the deserts of Egypt in the fourth century came to an end with the devastation of Egypt in 407, though there is at present a revival of this way of life in the monasteries of the Wadi al'Natrun, which is in some sense a continuation as well as a revival. What remains to us are the written records of their lives. Certain documents of the early generations, a few letters and some brief sayings of the fathers provide a clue to the lives they lived; the accounts of their actions and their conversations with visitors also survive, in the *Institutes* and *Conferences* of John Cassian, the *History of the monks of Egypt*, and the *Lausiac history*. The theology of the monastic life of Egypt was first analyzed by Evagrius Ponticus and John Cassian. In Palestine and in Syria, other men experimented with monastic life and left other records, most notable of which are the *Letters of Barsanulfus and John*. But it is in the sayings of the fathers, the collections of their words, that the spirit of the desert can best be found. They themselves began to commit their words to writing and many of them regretted that this had already become necessary even in Scetis and Nitria; the first fathers, they said, lived practical and realistic lives, the second generation seemed to them to rely upon that distorting mirror, the written word, more and more. Abba Poemen asked Abba Macarius, weeping, for a word, but he said, 'What you are looking for has disappeared among monks' (Macarius 25 in *Sayings*). Perhaps the essential message of the desert lies precisely there: it is not in reading or discussing or even in writing articles that the life of the soul is to be discovered; nor is it in the advice of anyone else however experienced; it lies in the simplicity of Antony the Great who, hearing the gospel read, went and did what he had heard said, and so came at the end of his life to such a point of discovery of the kingdom of God within himself that he could say, 'I no longer fear God; I love him' (Antony 32 in *Sayings*).

NOTES

[1] St Athanasius: *Life of Antony* translated by Robert C. Gregg (London, 1980), section 20. This will be referred to as *Life of Antony.* References in the text are to this and the following books:

Sayings of the Desert Fathers translated by Benedicta Ward (London, 1975) — to be referred to as *Sayings. Wisdom of the Desert Fathers* edited by Benedicta Ward (Systematic Series, SLG Press, Oxford, 1979) — to be quoted as *Systematic Series.*

Lives of the Desert Fathers translated by Norman Russell (Mowbrays, London, 1980), which is a translation of the *History of the monks of Egypt.* This will be referred to as *Lives.* The numbers refer to numbered sections in these works and not to pages.

[2] Climacus, John: *The ladder of divine ascent.*

VI

DISCERNMENT: A RARE BIRD

'Discretion is a very rare bird upon the earth' (Bernard of Clairvaux)

IN THE CHRISTIAN tradition, *diakresis*, discernment, has always been highly esteemed. It has been seen not as merely part of the natural virtue of prudence but as one of the direct gifts of the Holy Spirit, both the way into and the fruit of life in Christ. In the first thousand or more years of Christian living, discernment (also called discretion[1]) was discussed with complete unanimity, not because each writer repeated what his predecessors said without further thought but because the practice of Christian life continued to make abundantly clear the nature and purpose of discernment. It would be possible to summarize and examine what each writer has said in chronological order but because of the agreement between them perhaps a more fruitful approach would be to take the main points about discernment upon which there is notable agreement and illustrate this from selected sources over a span of 1,500 years. I use for illustration the experience of the first Christian monks in fourth-century Egypt, and the reflection upon that way of life by John Cassian and John Climacus, some texts from the central Middle Ages, and some material from the fourteenth century in the West, to cover as wide a span as possible.

First, what is 'discernment' in the Christian tradition? John Climacus calls it 'a solid understanding of the will of God',[2] while for Cassian it is 'the mother of virtues, as well as their guide and regulator'.[3] These are somewhat pedestrian descriptions, perhaps, and in them discretion is seen as a quality that orders and arranges the more vivid and dramatic virtues rather than doing anything in itself. Bernard of Clairvaux gives discernment the same quality when he comments on the passage in the *Song of Songs* 'Set love in order within me' (Cant 2, 5).[4] No-one could accuse Bernard of being lacking in zeal; he was enthusiastic, particularly with regard to asceticism, to such a point that he could be classed with the fools for Christ, those who follow with a single eye the wisdom of Christ so that it is vividly seen as 'folly to this world' (1 Cor 4, 10).[5] But he was as aware as the desert fathers of the need for this calm and sensible faculty as a point of control for zeal; he calls it 'the moderator of love' and adds 'discretion . . . is not so much a virtue as a moderator and a guide of the virtues, a director of the affections, a teacher of right living'.[6] Gregory the Great called discretion a nose, 'by which we discern good and evil odours' and he adds, 'he has a small nose who is not able to keep the measure of discernment.'[7] The image is of a wine-taster sniffing the bouquet of a wine or even of a dog raising its muzzle to sniff out the day before it goes beyond the doorstep. Such a faculty is not in itself the vision of God; it is that which finds the direction to it. So the author of the *Cloud of unknowing*, following Richard of St Victor, says it is Joseph, the beloved son of Jacob and Rachel, the forerunner of the Benjamin of contemplation: 'and he comes! Joseph is born late in time, but his father loves him most of all for without discretion goodness can neither be attained nor maintained.'[8]

Since discernment is valued so highly, how urgent is it for a Christian to have this faculty? Bernard of Clairvaux says it is 'utterly necessary', but this is an assertion within the context of a way of life very specifically directed to prayer: 'the more eager the zeal, the more vigorous the spirit, the more generous the love, so also the greater the need for more vigilant knowledge to restrain the zeal, to temper the spirit, to moderate the love'.[9] Elsewhere he calls discernment *rara avis*,[10] a rare and elusive quality of perception. John Climacus goes so far as to say that discernment, which he links with 'dispassion' is not essential to salvation: 'Not everyone can attain to dispassion but all can be saved and reconciled to God'.[11] Discernment is needed within the whole body of the Church, but is not a possession or a skill attained by individuals, a reminder that Christianity is not the property of an exclusive and sensitive elite but open to everyone, some of whom will be discerning, others not; it is not the equivalent of the enlightened state of the philosopher but a gift of God within the economy of salvation for all. The basic and essential question for each is 'how can I be saved?' and discernment is only to this end, a part of the way to the answer. Gregory the Great suggests that it is even possible to have too much discernment:

> there are some who . . . oftentimes exercise themselves more than is necessary in certain enquiries, and are mistaken through over much nicety, whence this is also added, 'or with a great and crooked nose'; for a great and crooked nose is an immoderate nicety of discernment when it has grown up beyond what is fitting and does itself confuse the righteousness of its actions![12]

Discernment is not to be confused either with curiosity or with a crippling insistence on getting it right in every way before acting.

It is clear from each instance quoted that this God-given light upon conduct has always been valued very highly in Christian life, though never out of context. But granted that discernment is desirable, the next question is how can this quality of life be attained and exercised? How do we know if we have it? It is often said that it is always possible to tell by negative results, when discernment turns out in its effects to lead away from the direct path of charity, that fundamental precept and promise that we 'shall love the Lord' and our 'neighbour as ourselves' (Matt. 22, 37–39). This is surely a rather defeatist way of learning, though in this looking-glass world of Christian life it is so often the only way; as the *Cloud*-author says, 'I have never yet known a sinner come to a perfect knowledge of himself and his basic temperament without having been taught it in the school of God by the exercise of many temptations and frequent stumblings and risings'.[13] Because humankind is fallen, it is impossible to become discerning easily and naturally by love and concern. Certainly the early writers connect discernment with love, and John Climacus admits that great love can give someone a particularly sensitive insight into another, but as everyone knows, love is not enough. There is a distorting lens in the eye of the soul which sends the most loving discernment awry. Have the early writers anything more to say about rectifying this squint than simply pointing to its dangerous effects? Discernment is above all about inner motive and begins with oneself and here they would say that the first step towards learning true self-knowledge is to be aware that it is lacking, and so the first virtue needed both in order and in priority is humility. John Climacus says, 'the sea is the source of the fountain, and humility is the source of discernment'[14] and in the desert tradition this is a constant theme. This is not a cringing and rather abstract idea in the desert literature but part of the way out from the illusions of a self-centred world towards an understanding of the reality of humankind before the Creator, of sinners before the Saviour. It is learned with consistency and great practical application, and the most important sign of the reality of this humility in all the desert literature is never for one moment to judge others.

> A brother in Scetis committed a fault and a council was called to which abba Moses was invited . . . He took a leaking jug filled with water and carried it with him . . . he said, 'My sins run out behind me and today I am coming to judge the errors of another'.[15]

This is a refusal to exercise the judgement which condemns others, that killing self-assertion that was the cause and result of the Fall and which continues to damage relationships with God and with others. This itch to condemn by our judgement can be transfigured into discernment which sees only the mercy and goodness of God in others. The way to allow this 'right judgement in all things' to be formed is through humility of heart which in practice involves a consistent refusal to exercise that self-assertion which forms hostile and negative judgements against the neighbour.

The true 'judgement' of others which is discernment is the God's eye view, which is always positive: as the *Cloud*-author puts it, 'Not what thou art, nor what thou hast been seeth God with his merciful eyes but what thou wouldst be'.[16] The difference between judgement and discernment is admirably illustrated in the life of Margery Kempe, a devout lady from Lynn in Norfolk. Margery's experience of the love of God was expressed in

> remarkable faces and gestures, with vehement sobbings and great abundance of tears, so that many people slandered her, not believing that it was the work of God, but that some evil spirit tormented her body or else that she had some bodily sickness.[17]

This negative criticism, based on externals only, made her unsure of herself and she began to ask advice from others, thus exercising the self-knowledge that is humility. She went to consult that sober and wise person, Julian of Norwich, and was met with true understanding and positive discernment of her inner motives instead of negative judgement of external phenomena. In spite of the obvious differences of temperament between them, Julian did not rebuke Margery as an irritating and embarassing hysteric. First she listened to her, and then thanked God for all his work in her; after that she reminded her very gently of the plain and basic virtues of obedience and charity in following Christ and added delicate support for Margery in dealing with her critics: 'Set all your trust in God and do not fear the talk of the world, for the more contempt, shame and reproof you have in this world, the more is your merit in the sight of God'.[18] True discernment is always life-giving and is concerned with motive: external actions vary and can be good or bad at different times and for different people; it is the motive behind them that needs discernment. It is an inner sensitivity that is needed and John Climacus compares it to the sense of smell; he says, 'Everyone with a healthy sense of smell can detect hidden perfumes and a pure soul can quickly recognize in others the sheer fragrance of goodness he himself has received from God'.[19] The results in one filled with this right spirit of discernment always issue in a positive but non-sentimental gentleness which is seen as God-like: 'Just as God protects the world, so abba Macarius would cover the faults that he saw as if he did not see them and those which he heard as though he did not hear them'.[20]

This way towards discernment in the Christian tradition is always very practical; no-one simply has discernment for its own sake, it is always known in its exercise in practical situations, whether it is used for oneself or for others. Nor is it an absolute, something that is always the same; on the contrary, it changes with the person learning it. John Climacus says that there are three kinds of discernment: that which is proper for beginners which he calls self-knowledge; another kind of discernment for 'those mid-way along the road' which is 'a spiritual capacity to distinguish unfalteringly between what is truly good and what in nature is opposed to the good'; and then there is for those he calls 'perfect' a discernment which is 'knowledge resulting from divine illumination which with its lamp can light up what is dark in others'. Moreover he says,

> for those of us who are untried recruits in the life of the spirit, growth in humility comes out of doing what the Lord wants, for those who have reached midway along the route the test is an end to inner conflict; and for the perfect there is increase and indeed a wealth of divine light.[21]

How does this practical course in discernment continue? The early writers are unanimous in saying that another aspect of humility and self-emptying is to ask advice, to place oneself in the hands of others and therefore to enter into the way of obedience. 'Ask advice humbly of the fathers and brothers', 'everything is to be declared before the elders'.[22] This is not necessarily consultation of someone more learned or even more spiritual than oneself and this is an important difference within the Christian tradition from other ways of attaining self-knowledge.

> One day abba Arsenius consulted an old Egyptian monk about his thoughts. Someone noticed this and said to him, 'Abba Arsenius, how is it that you, with such a good Latin and Greek education, ask this peasant about your thoughts?' He replied, 'I have indeed been taught Latin and Greek but I do not even know the alphabet of this peasant'.[23]

John Climacus says that maybe a guide we choose will be ignorant and stupid and will in fact be wrong about the details of what he suggests, but what God is waiting for is not a right conclusion about a matter but for our suppleness in falling into his hands for him to work in us.[24] This attitude of attention to inner disposition rather than external facts is admirably illustrated by a story from the desert: one day, an old man was walking with a disciple and he saw a small wild boar. He said to him, 'Boy, do you see that buffalo?' He said to the disciple 'Yes, abba'.[25] The disciple was not interested in wild animals but in his own reliance on his abba as the one who truly discerned reality, even in such a trivial matter. The point is that the Christian is not looking for wisdom from a master but is seeking to become open to the only teacher of the Christian who is Christ.

The paradox is that in order to learn from him and him only, the blinding pride of self-confidence has to be eliminated and this can only be done by placing oneself in the hands of others. This can apply to long-term issues, such as of the way of life by which to follow Christ or to details of that way. For instance, when Anselm of Canterbury wanted to choose in what way he would best serve the Lord, he placed himself entirely in the hands of Lanfranc: 'He came to him and told him that he was undecided between three courses of action but he would hold to the one that Lanfranc judged the best'. Lanfranc hesitated to give an opinion but took Anselm with him to consult Maurillius, the bishop of Rouen, asking him to discern the right way, thus both testing Anselm's flexibility and trust and also adding another strand, that of the opinion of a bishop, to the situation. In fact Maurillius said that Anselm should become a monk at Bec, something Anselm had already considered and rejected from motives which were particularly self-orientated but, because he chose to receive the decision from the hands of another and not by self-choice, it became for him his own chosen way to God.[26] Anselm was not of course choosing by magic, by a kind of sortilege, from a refusal of responsibility; he exercised his mind to its limit to hear what God was asking of him in all the normal ways open to the Christian, i.e. scripture, tradition, doctrine, sacraments, natural order, actual circumstances, conscience, etc. but knowing himself to be blinded by self-will he found it prudent to place himself in the hands of another human being, and to experience in this choice a freedom from self which could then whole-heartedly welcome the choice made. Discernment through others, not for their skill or intelligence but in order to be free to hear the will of God truly, is not confined to individuals. The *Rule of St Benedict* was described by Gregory the Great as 'conspicuous for its discretion'[27] and contains directions for consultation between the abbot of the monastery and the brothers; everyone is to be consulted because 'God often reveals what is better to the younger'.[28] Nor is it only with regard to major decisions but also in the details of serving

God in daily life that discernment has to be sought; it would be possible to describe the *Rule of St Benedict* in its entirety as a guide to discernment through daily life.

The early writers are also unanimous in saying that 'spiritual' matters need as much discernment as 'material' matters. Man is fallen and his sight is wrong about both equally. To be intent on a spiritual way is not necessarily any better than to be absorbed in earthly affairs. The *Cloud*-author has some scathing pages devoted to the false mystics with their exaggerated external signs of devotion[29] and makes it clear that what looks like eager self-denial can come simply from a desire to show off, a longing to feel one is doing something, or from even more basic natural urges. Such things, he says, are in fact very dangerous because they nourish pride of heart in an especially subtle way. The early monastic tradition is filled with examples of those good men who failed because they were intent on their own exercise of austerity rather than letting such things remain linked to humility, charity and flexibility. There is a steady refusal among the desert fathers to trust in anything merely because it is 'spiritual': again and again they told stories of monks to whom the devil appeared as an angel or as Christ, and their instant recourse to humility, saying, 'See if it is not someone else to whom you have been sent; as for me, I am not worthy of it'.[30] Cassian has instances of monks renowned for their goodness; their knowledge of spiritual matters was extensive but this also made them open to a world of spirits, not all of them good, and by lack of discernment among them some were led to suicide, murder or despair.[31] Discernment is more necessary in spiritual matters as in material ones, because the danger is greater and more hidden. Just as telling, and in the same tradition, are the pithy remarks made by the *Cloud*-author in his short treatise *On the discerning of spirits*. For him, the real teacher of Christian virtue which is love is 'a still, loving contemplation' of God: it is by the experience of this 'blind movement of love towards God that a contemplative soul comes more quickly to the grace of discernment which knows how to speak and when to be quiet, when to eat and when to fast, when to mix and when to be alone'.[32] Until that point is reached, however, there are signs which will enable a distinction to be made between the motives of the heart in whatever is done or proposed: what is basically necessary, the writer says, is genuine belief that God is faithful and will perform what he has promised: 'really believe you are forgiven'; then, if what you want to do is really because of love of personal comfort and ease, or out of a desire, however secret, for praise and the good opinion of others, it comes from self-love; and if what we want to do proceeds out of bitterness and desire to belittle others, then it comes from the devil and must be firmly rejected.[33] It is the same teaching as the desert and the early Middle Ages, but here expressed with great directness and vividness.

Discernment in the early Christian tradition, then, was concerned with the examination of motives for each individual in his following of Christ. They would say that when the light of discernment is turned towards oneself, it must be ruthless in its refusal of illusion, however comforting, but when turned towards others it must be truly the light of God which is always positive. It was not perceived as a special or rare ability but a part of Christian life for all, whether in oneself or by consultation with others. It is in fact connected with two aspects of *kenosis*: the cross of Christ and humility. It depends upon faith that when I say I do not know, there is One who always does, which is a real and active knowledge of Christ crucified as risen and victor. God does not impose goodness on anyone, but what he waits for is the humility that can trust what is outside the limiting circle of the self. He waits to be asked and trusted and has given us one another as an immediate way towards this trust. Discernment is not a technique nor is it something high-class in a special spiritual world but it is part of the way of the cross, where each follows in company with 'a great cloud of witnesses': 'Without form or comeliness and nailed to a cross, thus is truth known'.[32]

NOTES

[1] Since the eighteenth century, 'discretion' has been increasingly used in connection with good behaviour, especially in speech, but earlier it was synonymous with 'discernment', both coming from '*discretio*' the Latin form of '*diakresis*'. Hence 'discretion' will be used here in quotations with this meaning, as in 'a discretion of spirits'.

[2] John Climacus, *The ladder of divine ascent* trans. C. Luibhied and N. Russell, (Classics of Western Spirituality, SPCK/Paulist Press, 1982), Step 26 'On discernment', p 229. (Hereafter referred to as 'John Climacus').

[3] John Cassian, *Conferences*, trans. E. G. S. Gibson, (Nicene and Post-Nicene Fathers of the Christian Church, vol. XI, reprinted Michigan, 1973), 2nd Conference of Abba Moses, cap. IV, p 310. (Hereafter referred to as 'Cassian').

[4] Bernard of Clairvaux, *On the Song of Songs* trans. K. Walsh and I. M. Edmonds, (Cistercian Fathers Series 31, Kalamazoo, Michigan, 1962), vol 3, p 25.

[5] I Cor 4, 10. Cf John Saward, *Perfect fools: folly for Christ's sake in Catholic and Orthodox spirituality* (Oxford, 1980), pp 58–79.

[6] Bernard, *op cit.*, p 25.

[7] Gregory the Great, *The pastoral charge*, trans. H. R. Bramley (Oxford, 1874), Bk.1, pp 40–42. (Hereafter referred to as *Pastoral charge*).

[8] 'Benjamin', by the author of the *Cloud of unknowing,* trans. by Clifton Walters in *A study of wisdom* (Oxford, 1980), pp 18–21. Cf. Richard of St Victor, 'The Twelve Patriarchs',

cap. lxvii in *Richard of St Victor* trans. by Grover A. Zinn, (Classics of Western Spirituality, SPCK/Paulist Press, 1979), pp 124–5.
[9] Bernard, *On the Song of Songs*, *op. cit.*, p 25.
[10] Bernard, 'Sermon 3 on The Circumcision'.
[11] John Climacus, p 240.
[12] *Pastoral charge*, Bk I, p 141.
[13] *A discernment of stirrings*, trans C. Wolters in *A study of wisdom* (SLG Press, 1980), p 28.
[14] John Climacus, p 228.
[15] *Sayings of the Desert Fathers*, trans. B. Ward (Oxford, 1975/88), Moses 2.
[16] *The cloud of unknowing*, trans. C. Wolters, (Penguin Classics, 1961–82), p 152.
[17] *The Book of Margery Kempe*, trans. Windeatt (Penguin Books, 1985), p 77.
[18] *Ibid.*, pp 78–80.
[19] John Climacus, p 240.
[20] *Sayings of the Desert Fathers*, Macarius, 32.
[21] John Climacus, p 229.
[22] Cassian, p 310.
[23] *Sayings of the Desert Fathers*, Arsenius, 6.
[24] John Climacus, p 244.
[25] *Sayings of the Desert Fathers*, Mark the disciple of abba Sylvanus, 2.
[26] Eadmer, *Vita S. Anselmi*, ed and trans. R. W. Southern (Oxford, 1962), pp 10–11.
[27] Gregory the Great, *Dialogues*, 11, 36.
[28] *The Rule of St. Benedict*, trans J. McCann, (London, 1952), cap. 3, p 24.
[29] *The cloud of unknowing*, caps. 53 and 54, pp 122–126.
[30] *The wisdom of the Desert Fathers*, trans. B. Ward (SLG Press, 1981/8), p 50.
[31] Cassian, caps 5, 6, 7, 8; pp 310–311.
[32] *A discernment of stirrings*, p 43.
[33] *Ibid.*
[34] Guigo of the Chartreuse, *Méditations*, traduction et rédaction par un Chartreux (Sources Chrétiennes, 308, Paris, 1983), Meditation 5, p 104.

VII

A Tractarian Inheritance: the religious life in a patristic perspective

> Let us now praise famous men and our fathers in their generation; their bodies are buried in peace and their name lives to all generations; people will declare their wisdom and the congregation proclaim their praise. (Eccles. 44:1, 14, 15)

Those 'famous men' Newman, Pusey and Keble are in a special sense 'our fathers' in the generation of the religious communities of the Anglican Church. 'Their name lives' most especially through those communities and above all in the city where they lived and became friends in that bond of *amicitia* which many have seen as the kindly face of God.[1] Their bodies are 'buried in peace' all, except Pusey, in other places, but Oxford remains especially the centre and heart of their shared vision, the 'Oxford Movement', as we call it. I would like to make some remarks about three aspects of this Oxford Movement which perhaps sound rather tangential and disparate but are in fact three parts of a single theme: first the link formed by Newman, Pusey and Keble with the monastic past of Christendom through their editions and translations of the Fathers of the Church; secondly their understanding and implementation of this monastic theme that they discovered there in re-establishing religious life in England; and thirdly their popularisation of this theme in their lighter works, poems, hymns, and that quintessential Victorian form of literature, the novel.

First; the Library of the Fathers. It is a commonplace to say that the Oxford Movement was based upon the theology of the undivided Church and its understanding of the Scriptures. This is a tradition within the Church of England which goes back to the sixteenth century, and in emphasising and exploring it the founders of the Oxford Movement were not innovators; they were re-discovering something at the heart of Anglicanism. There is inevitably an attraction for Anglicans to the Church of the first centuries and with it often goes an appreciation of the churches which still hold the Fathers as contemporaries, those 'ancient orients kirks' the eastern Orthodox churches. This was recognised among the Tractarians and bore especially rich fruit in the lively genius of J. M. Neale in his translations of eastern liturgical texts and in his amazing knowledge of eastern Orthodoxy. This deep and rich tradition of the theology of the undivided Church was however out of fashion in the rationalist atmosphere of nineteenth-century England. When Dean Gaisford conducted a visitor round the library at Christ Church, he dismissed the sombre volumes of the Fathers of the Church with a wave of the hand and the two words: 'sad rubbish'.[2] But from an early age Pusey had felt their attraction; as a present for attaining his degree he asked his father for a folio set (presumably the Mabillon edition) of the Fathers of the Church. Keble and Newman were equally aware of the Church Fathers, Newman in particular reading them at Oriel and using them as the basis for those writings which were to give him a permanent place among the theologians of Europe. These men were all scholars and classicists; they read Greek and Latin as easily as English, and wrote it too: Pusey's preface to his edition of Augustine's *Confessions* is in a Latin as clear and fine as Augustine's own. They were men who approached religion through reading – not only Pusey at Eton, Christ Church and as Hebrew Professor and editor of that amazing work, the list of Arabic manuscripts in Bodley; but Newman, student at Trinity and fellow of Oriel; and Keble, brilliant student at Corpus, also a fellow of Oriel, elected when he was only nineteen, and later Professor of Poetry at Oxford. It seems inevitable that so bookish a crew should turn to publication.

The Library of the Fathers, conceived by Newman, Pusey and Keble, was their most useful contribution to the spread of patristic studies in England. But it was not their only kind of publication. Before they turned to translations they put their hands to editions. The production of critical editions of ancient texts was in the air in the nineteenth century and it is necessary first to see the Tractarians in the wider world of academic scholarship before noticing how they went beyond this. The nineteenth century invented the scientific study of history as we know it, most of all by the careful collation of manuscripts in critical editions. This is the century which saw the flowering of the work of the Bollandists in Belgium with the *Acta Sanctorum* series in the able hands of Albert Poncelet, François van Ortroy and above all Hippolyte Delehaye. In Germany Georg Pertz and his most able pupil Jaffé continued the *Monumenta Germanica Historica*, that series of texts indispensable to medievalists still. In France, the Maurists had reached the end of their editions of patristic and medieval texts connected most of all with the names of Mabillon and d'Archery, which were to have a further popularity in their use, and even at times their misuse, by J. P. Migne in the massive series of *Patrologia Latina, Graeca et Orientalis*. The Alcuin Club, the Early English Text Society, the Camden Society and innumerable local antiquarian societies undertook in England the publication of records; above all, this was the moment when English public records were collected and published in the work of the Rolls Series, begun in

1822 when the House of Commons successfully petitioned George IV for the publication of the sources of English history. (Incidentally it is interesting to observe that while the government-sponsored project of the Rolls Series kept several historians in comfort for years, the editors of the Tractarian projects always needed to beg for money and were partly subsidised by the founders, partly by public subscription.) These vast and scholarly concerns certainly influenced Pusey, Newman and Keble in their presentation of Latin and Greek texts in critical editions. They were acquainted with the editions made by the Maurists, and there were personal connections with the Rolls Series in at least two ways: Henry Bickersteth, first Lord Langdale, was largely responsible for establishing the Public Records Office and was also notorious among Tractarians for his judgment in the celebrated case of *Gorham v. the Bishop of Exeter*. Joseph Stevenson, known for his work at the Records Office and for his catalogue of English historical writers, shared the doubts of Newman about the Anglican Church and in 1863 was received into the Catholic Church, a move which cost him his job; he retired to Birmingham to work for the Historical Manuscripts Commission and later became a Jesuit, completing his historical studies in the Vatican and at Farm Street.

The Tractarians edited the texts of Augustine, Chrysostom, Theodoret, and Cyril of Alexandria, the latter being the monumental work of Philip, the son of Dr Pusey, a task which took him to the libraries of Europe including those of Mount Athos. They are editions now largely superseded, but for their time they belong to the mainstream of European critical scholarship. In this, the Tractarians were no mere pedants. They wanted to present the works of the past as accurately as possible; to stand back from the texts and let them speak for themselves. Just as in prayer they learned the asceticism of standing back to allow God to speak without their interpretations and ideas, so in their scholarship they stood back, so that the writers of the past could be clearly heard. They might have remained only editors of texts; but they went further than their contemporaries. They presented also translations into English, in a great series of forty-eight volumes in the Library of the Fathers. It says a great deal for their insight and their energy that they conceived and carried out such a series, when they themselves were perfectly content for the texts to remain in the original languages and were even urging the retention of such languages in their university at the same time. It has been said that the central tradition of English scholarship lies not in the exploration of the past for its own sake but in 'the recurrent need to understand and stabilize the present by reviving the experience of the past;[3] it is to this stream of English scholarship that the Tractarians belong. They were realists, practical men, wanting to be in touch with the theology of the first centuries in order to 'understand and stabilize the present'. Realising that the revival of the Church ought not to be in the hands of a few dons but in the hands of the people of God, and realising moreover that few of those would have a first-rate reading knowledge of Latin and Greek much less Syriac, they decided to make translations into English of the texts of the early Fathers. They wanted to expand minds by contact with the sources: 'It is a vulgar and commonplace prejudice' wrote Pusey, 'which would censure everything by its own habit of mind and condemn as fanciful that to which it is unaccustomed.'[4] There was a practical need to have translations; the editors were equally aware of the need for the translations to be in no way beneath the new and exacting standards of the day. The friends had severe critics; not only the formidable Jowett at Balliol; but an earlier fellow of Oriel, to whom they referred as 'poor Arnold', at Rugby; poor because he did not believe as they did, but a fine Latinist and with an interest in the Fathers of the Church. Through a friend, Arnold asked Pusey for guidance about reading the Fathers and Pusey gave it hesitantly, as one afraid to cast pearls before swine; Arnold must have put him to shame with his generous comment on Pusey when he wrote, 'from Pusey you will learn, I am sure, nothing virulent or proud or false, but self-denial in its true form imbued with humility and loyalty'.[5]

Translation – one of the most difficult arts of mankind. Newman and Pusey were aware of the pitfalls, indeed in one exchange they present the continual problem of translation precisely: Newman, only too well acquainted with the crabbed and pedantic style of Pusey's English, feared for the style of his rendering of Latin; Pusey feared rather more the freedom Newman might take with the text; he wrote,, 'the object of all translation must be to present the ideas of the author as clearly as may be with as little sacrifice as may be of what is peculiar to them – the greatest clearness with the greatest faithfulness.[6] So the translations were commissioned and eventually produced. Augustine, Cyril, Chrysostom, Athanasius, Gregory Nazianzen, Ephraim the Syrian, all began to speak precise and rather pedantic English. Each volume was produced with a most valuable preface, many by Pusey himself. The idea of a translation series was very much a part of the mood of the times, but ahead of its time in being a translation series. Many translations have followed those early volumes, they have been superseded and are out of print; but they were the way in which the Tractarians sought to present the theology of the undivided Church to Englishmen for their use, not just for their pleasure.

What did the Tractarians themselves find in these texts which they spent the greater part of their lives and incomes in presenting? First they found the spiritual sense of the Scriptures, for the majority of the texts they used were commentaries on the sacred page. Pusey contrasted the commentaries of the Fathers on the Bible as 'ancient and catholic truth' compared with 'modern private opinion.[7] 'The Word', he wrote, 'is greater than the words and the Spirit greater than the letter', echoing the phrase of Claudius of Turin's preface to his Commentary on Leviticus: 'Blessed are the eyes which see divine spirit through the letter's veil.'[8] The mystical sense of the Scriptures absorbed the Tractarians; for them the Bible was indeed the sword of the Spirit, piercing the heart, and no mere collection of historical documents. Secondly they found in these texts, of course, the doctrine of the undivided Church. Thirdly they found there an essential concern for the poor, a concern which took root and flourished in the early Tractarian parishes such as St Saviour's, Leeds; and fourthly they found there that reverence for God expressed in forms of worship which sees the liturgy as the corporate prayer of the people of God with the hosts of heaven, a vision so magnificently expounded by J. M. Neale and so disastrously deformed by later ritualists.

But these were not the heart of the matter. What had aroused the Tractarians originally and continued to enrage them was not so much the apathy of Christians but their 'liberalism'. By this they meant that attitude to the Christianity which absorbs and is absorbed by the ideals and trends of the age instead of transfiguring those trends by the gospel of Christ; that attitude in which culture becomes an excuse for not obeying the commands of the gospel. The ideal of a Christianity which is a challenge to the world, which is in the margin of culture, a scandal and an offence, they found in the early Church, in the lives of the martyrs but also and perhaps especially in the accounts of the monks. What lies at the heart of the Oxford Movement as a direct inheritance from the early Church is the religion of the heart, the ideal of a life lived in conformity with the cross of Christ and this ideal is that which was central to early monasticism. Pusey, Newman and Keble were not unaware that almost every writer they admired, both in the early Church and in the Middle Ages, was a monk. All the Christian writings they proposed to their fellow Christians came from the milieu of monasticism. This central theme of monasticism remains still largely undiscovered, a secret to be explored and unpacked still further. There is more here than even the establishment of monastic communities for women, for men and the possibilities of hermit-life which have already appeared among us. But what in the context of the Tractarian Movement and the nineteenth century did this theme of monasticism mean?

First of all it meant opposition, criticism, incomprehension. The Tractarians were aware that the idea of vows, of celibacy, of a life apart from the well-known Christian ways, was not going to be well received in Victorian England. An instance of this peculiarly Protestant spirit is to be found in some sentences from an American publication. As Pusey had hoped, the Library of the Fathers translations were well received in America and soon the Americans were producing their own translations in the series of Ante Nicene, Nicene and Post Nicene Fathers. The volume of translations of Augustine's doctrinal treatises contains his *Praise of Virginity* and the sentence 'therefore go on saints of God, boys and girls, men and women, unmarried men and women . . . ye shall bring unto the marriage of the Lamb a new song which ye shall sing on your harps' is quoted but with the following austere reminder:

> We must admire [the fathers for] their power of self-denial . . . though we may dissent from their theory . . . The Reformation has abolished the system of monasticism and clerical celibacy, and substituted for it . . . the purity, chastity and beauty of family life, instituted by God in Paradise and sanctioned by our Saviour's presence at the wedding at Cana.[9]

The Tractarians were at pains to subdue any rumours that they wished to revive monastic life in England; the idea could only have brought the movement into disrepute; moreover it would have been distinctly contrary to their principle of reserve and restraint. So at the inception of Anglican monastic life, the idea proceeded against criticism, both inside and outside the Church. In this, the communities are most clearly seen as a protest, a comment from the outside, a challenge, to the Establishment. And in this also they are at one with the religious of the fourth century and in sharp contrast to the great churches of East and West in the Middle Ages and today, where monastic life is so integrated into the fabric of the church structures that its protest can rarely be heard. Rutilius Claudius Namatianus called the early monks 'squalid fugitives from the light' and referred to a friend who became one as a 'poor fool';[10] words that found an echo in many English minds when they encountered the first attempts in the Anglican Church at such a way of life.

The monastic life was, then, seen by the Tractarians first of all as a protest against the established liberalism of the age; but secondly, for the Tractarians themselves, monasticism was at the centre of their own lives. Keble might write:

> We need not bid, for cloistered cell,
> Our neighbour and our work farewell

but the same hymn embodies not only the 'little way' of St Thérèse of Lisieux, but the whole point of monasticism:

> The trivial round the common task,
> Will furnish all we ought to ask,
> Room to deny ourselves, a road
> To bring us daily nearer God'.[11]

Newman, a celibate priest, intent at first on founding a community at Littlemore, then involved in the Oratory at Birmingham, quite clearly found in primitive monasticism echoes of his own asceticism, as did the founder of the Oratory, St Philip Neri. Pusey saw the consecrated life of the priest as a total and monastic dedication and after the death of his wife undertook it as such. Moreover again and again these men proposed religious consecration for women quite specifically as a parallel to their own consecration through their ordination to the priesthood: for the women, they felt, there should be a similar possibility, and they presented it as the religious life.

Thirdly there were those within the Church of England who heard and understood the call of monasticism and those the Tractarians protected and encouraged. They found a way to present the total dedication of the sisters to an uncomprehending and hostile public through the grievous social needs of the day. To serve the sick and destitute without fear or care for self was comprehensible and within the understanding of Protestant England; indeed it went well with the philanthropy of the day. The idea, first proposed by Froude, was that religious life could be established under cover of certain pressing social needs.[12] The Park Village sisterhood, for instance, had for its works 'visiting the sick and poor in their own homes; visiting hospitals; workhouses and prisons; feeding, clothing and instructing destitute children, and (evocation of another age) giving shelter to distressed gentlewomen of good character, as well as assisting at the burial of the dead.'[13] Miss Sellon and her sisters made themselves acceptable through their work in a cholera epidemic; the sisters at Wantage, East Grinstead and Clewer, earned the same recognition for similar works.[14]

But it should be remembered that, as with the early monks, the works of mercy were not of the essence of the Anglican religious life. In all the Anglican communities, whether involved in active works or not, the priority was, and is, quite other. From the *outside*, in the deserts of fourth-century Egypt, it seemed that the withdrawal of the monks was justified because they offered the service of prayer for the world, 'These are they by whom the world is kept in being';[15] or by the care they had for the poor in the towns by their work and gifts of food; or by their support of those suffering for the faith. But the reality of both early monasticism and the Anglican communities, seen on the *inside* by their members, is quite other. The hard word of the desert was a call to repentance and the beginnings of monastic life in the Christian Church was in the discovery of the brokenness and hopeless scarring of human lives, which find their healing only and always in the life that comes from the cross of Christ. Abba Antony said, 'the greatest thing a man can do is to throw his faults before the Lord and expect temptation to his last breath'[16] 'if a man does not think in his heart that he is a sinner, God will not hear him';[17] and Abba Apollo prayed only: 'I as man have sinned, do thou as God forgive'.[18] Abba Pinufius said:

> our cross is the fear of the Lord. He who is crucified can no longer move his limbs and so should we become, attached, nailed to the cross, so that we can no longer follow our own will or desires . . . this fear creates in us compunction and leads us towards poverty and nakedness . . . it is a death which destroys our sin and gives

> in return that purity of heart which is Christ; and that is perfect love.[19]

Another writer presented even more specifically the monk as crucified, standing with his arms held out and saying, 'so should the monk be, denuded of all the things of this world and crucified . . . in his thoughts the monk stands, his arms stretched out in the form of a cross to heaven calling upon God'.[20]

It is this discovery of compunction as the gateway to life that colours the sermons and letters of Pusey and it is there that the essential nature of Anglican religious life should be sought. In a well-known letter to Keble Pusey describes his own vivid apprehension of his sinfulness and he uses terms familiar to the monastic tradition from the beginning: 'I am seared all over and scarred with sin so that I am a monster to myself.'[21] Let me say, in parenthesis, that the phrases of this letter are so close as to be a paraphrase of another monastic writer in this tradition, Anselm of Canterbury, a translation of whose prayers and meditations (or rather whose supposed prayers and meditations) was published with an introduction by Pusey himself.[22] A later sermon suggests in calmer terms the way of the ascetic as a result of this conviction of sin:

> to empty ourselves of our self conceit, our notions of station, our costliness of dress, our jewellery, our luxuries, our self-love, even as He emptied himself of the glory He had with the Father, the brightness of his majesty, the worshipping hosts of heaven and made himself poor to make us rich[23] . . . He would give us all that He is; He asks in return the nothingness that we are.[24]

And elsewhere:

> it were a dream to think we could love the Passion of Christ and not engrave it on our lives . . . that we could be melted by his sorrows and not sorrow or suffer with him . . .[25]
>
> Our life from baptism to death should be a practice of the cross, a learning to be crucified, a crucifixion of our passions, appetite, desires, will, until one by one they be all nailed and we have no will but the will of our Father who is in heaven.[26]

The idea of a whole life of asceticism in union with the cross of Christ is the ideal of the desert; it is vividly there in the founder and inspirer of the first Anglican communities. Moreover Pusey, like the first monks, was quite practical about it: 'we are not formed to seek conviction', he wrote, 'but to have it'; and when consulted about the possibility of unceasing prayer, another great theme of the desert, he said merely, 'the one plain rule is to set about doing it'.[27] Did Pusey in fact know the writings of the Desert Fathers or is it only a case of parallelism, the same desert air which blows through later texts? There is indication that he had some acquaintance with the primary sources of early monasticism, probably in Roswede's version of the *Vitae Patrum*. There he would have found the story which he quotes of a monk who was asked by the devil, 'Who are the sheep and who are the goats?' and who replied, 'I am one of the goats, as for who the sheep are, God alone knows.' Another story, told also in the *Life of St Martin*, which he refers to, is familiar in this tradition of the desert and occurs in many versions: the monk to whom the devil appears dressed in majesty and claiming to be Christ, and who is dispelled by the monk who refuses to see Christ glorified while on earth.[28] A quotation from Athanasius, *Life of St Antony*, 'All who saw him took delight in him', reveals his familiarity with this basic monastic source, a familiarity confirmed by his reference to the *Life of Antony the Great* in his edition of Augustine's *Confessions*.[29]

But what is most striking, beyond quotations, is the sense one has in reading Pusey's works of the 'huge silence and great quiet'[30] of Nitria, Scetis and the Cells, within the nineteenth-century pages. The lifelong programme of conversion of life according to the gospel, the identification with Christ crucified, lies at the centre of fourth-century Egypt and the Anglican religious revival. Nor was Pusey, like the monks, without a deep apprehension of the life of the Spirit which is given to those who so embrace the cross, without which the language of crucifixion and sorrow of heart can be simply self-pity and destruction. The proof that it is indeed the cross of Christ that is embraced lies in the life of the monk with Christ in his resurrection: 'they who so pray', he wrote, 'will find that their last prayer upon earth in the name of Jesus will melt itself into the first halleluia of heaven'.[31] Most movingly, both in his preface to the translation he made of the forbidding Surin and in his own fierce sermon, 'Christianity without the cross a corruption of the Gospel of Christ', he makes use of a translation of the most tender of medieval monastic hymns, St Bernard on the Name of Jesus: 'No tongue of man hath power to tell/ No written words can prove/ But he who loveth knoweth well/ what Jesus is to love.'[32]

The Oxford apostles, like the desert monks, strike a sombre note when they write of the inner life of repentance; but, like the monks, they were not always grave. It was said of Abba Antony that one day he was relaxing with some of the brothers and a hunter came by and was shocked at such levity. So Antony told him to bend his bow and shoot an arrow; and another; and another; until the hunter protested that if he kept his bow always strung tight it would snap; even so, said Antony, even so is the life of the monk.[33] So we find the good Keble unable to accept the proposal of his new penitent Pusey that he should not smile (an asceticism as familiar in the desert as in the Rule of St Benedict), protesting that he should remember the care he had for others, especially children.[34] Newman also could relax, and coming one day to visit Mr Pusey for solemn conversation instead took the young Puseys on his knees and told them about an old woman who had a magic broomstick that went to the well to fetch water for her; until she became tired of it and broke it in two; and what did she have but two little broomsticks going to the well to fetch water for her.[35] Pusey himself could relax with children and not only with his own Lucy and Philip who shared so closely his ideals. It is no surprise then to notice that these grave divines adopted one of the popular literary styles of the day in order to popularise the religious life, and wrote novels. Keble of course was the overwhelmingly popular poet of the group; Newman, like Wiseman, produced his novel of the early Church, *Callista*, to Wiseman's *Fabiola*. Others followed them – Shorthouse had popularised Little Gidding in his novel *John Inglesant*; John Mason Neale was to write and publish many short stories and novels, popularising the early Church and monasticism. Apart from the most famous, *Ayton Priory*, there is for instance *The Quai of the Discori*, a novel about Arius, who looks remarkably like a nineteenth-century heretic, with his daughter Helladia, dying of that interesting scourge of the nineteenth century, tuberculosis. To her bedside Neale brings, in fact, Antony the Great and his words echo the tradition of the desert: 'My child,' he says, 'I am a sinner who dwells in the desert.'[36] In another novel, *The Lazar House of Leros*, an amazing book, centred around that strange figure the seventeenth-century Patriach of Constantinople, Cyril Lucaris is who had Calvinist sympathies. Sophia, the heroine, becomes a nun and undertakes work which would have appealed to many an Anglican sister of mercy – nursing those with leprosy. Significantly she does not die of this, but as a martyr, that other kind of witness to total consecration to God, which has always given to monasticism its chief image.[37] From Dr Pusey we have, alas, no novel. But once on holiday on Hayling Island with Philip and Lucy he became the centre of a group of children: 'We were very merry at times,' wrote one of the adults later, 'little children were more at home with him than the rest of the world'. To them he told at least one story and his choice is perhaps typical of his life and prayer:

> one day one of the boys asked him to tell them a story. He agreed, and taking down a beautiful print of the Good Shepherd, gathered us all around him and drew out the story of the lost sheep and the Good Shepherd in such language as the little ones could well understand and with many a word of help for the elder children around whose little troubles he knew a good deal about.[38]

The lives and writings of Pusey, Newman and Keble became a new spring of life within the Church of England. Today the external expressions of their work have largely disappeared or changed radically; but the secret of love, prayer and sacrifice hidden in the heart of the movement survives and still carries with it their conviction of the power of God in the lives of men. Perhaps, if we called for rebels like the Tractarians, they would place the sign of the cross again over the secularisation of the world. There is already within the Church of England a silent rebellion of the heart, which follows and deepens the teaching of the first Oxford rebels and makes its own a prayer from the Evangelical tradition of the Church of England: 'O Lord, revive Thy Church; and begin with me'.

1. e.g. Aelred of Rievaulx, *On Spiritual Friendship*, ed. A. Hoste and C. H. Talbot (Corpus Christianorum 1981), Bk 1.69, p. 301, '*Deus amicitia est*'.
2. H. P. Liddon, *Life of E. B. Pusey*, 4 vols (London 1894), I, ch. 18, p. 434 (hereinafter 'Liddon').
3. R. W. Southern, Presidential Address, *RHS*, *Aspects of the European Tradition of Historical Writing*, IV, 'The Sense of the Past', iv.p.263, in *TRHS*, 5th ser., 23 (1973).
4. Liddon I, p. 419.
5. ibid. p. 410.
6. ibid. p. 423.
7. Quoted by G. Rowell, in *The Vision Glorious* (Oxford 1983), p. 78 (hereinafter 'Rowell').
8. Claudius of Turin, *P.L.*, civ. Col. 617.
9. Philip Schaff, in Preface to *Nicene and Post-Nicene Fathers*, III (New York 1887), p. iv.
10. Claudius Rutilius Namatianus, *De Reditu Suo* ed. J. Vessereau (1933), Book 1, 439–452, p. 23.
11. J. Keble, *The Christian Year* (London 1827).
12. R. H. Froude, *Remains* (London 1838), I, p. 322.
13. Quoted by A. M. Allchin: *The Silent Rebellion: Anglican religious communities 1845–1900* (London 1958), p. 62. This invaluable book remains the key to an understanding of religious life in the Church of England.
14. ibid. esp. ch. 3–8.
15. *Lives of the Desert Fathers*, ed. N. Russell and B. Ward (Oxford 1979), Introduction, p. 50.
16. *Sayings of the Desert Fathers* tr. B. Ward (Oxford 1974), Antony, 4, p. 2.
17. ibid. Moses, 3, p. 141.
18. ibid. Apollo, 2, p. 31.
19. Cassian, *Institutes*, Book IV, xxxiii.
20. B. Ward, tr., *The Wisdom of the Desert Fathers* (The Apophthegmata Patrum, Anonymous Series) (Oxford 1975), p. 3, No. 11.
21. Liddon, III, p. 96.
22. *Prayers and Meditations to the Holy Trinity and our Lord Jesus Christ, by St Anselm of Canterbury* (London 1856). Preface by E. B. Pusey.
23. E. B. Pusey, *Sermons during the Season from Advent to Whitsuntide* (London 1848²), p. 59, quoted, Rowell, p. 82.
24. ibid. p. 355, quoted, Rowell, p. 83.
25. id., Leeds Sermons (London 1847²) p. 176, quoted, Rowell, p. 85.
26. id., *Parochial Sermons* (London 1878, rev. edn), III, p. 50, quoted, Rowell, p. 84.
27. ibid. p. 211, quoted, Rowell, p. 86.
28. Quoted by E. B. Pusey in his preface to *Foundations of the Spiritual Life* by Jean Joseph Surin (London 1844).

29. E. B. Pusey, ed., St Augustine, *Confessions*, Bibliotheca Patrum (Oxford 1838), I, pp. 134–5.
30. *Lives of the Desert Fathers*, p. 149.
31. E. B. Pusey, *The Miracles of Prayer* (London 1866), pp. 28–30, quoted, Rowell, p. 87.
32. id., preface to Surin.
33. *Sayings of the Desert Fathers*, Antony 13, p. 3.
34. Liddon, III, p. 108.
35. ibid. I, pp. 407–8.
36. J. M. Neale, *The Quai of the Discori* (London 1847), p. 83.
37. id., *The Lazar House of Leros* (London 1849), p. 95.
38. Liddon, III, p. 187.

MIDDLE AGES: SEVENTH AND EIGHTH CENTURIES

VIII

THE MIRACLES OF SAINT BENEDICT

'One day when the brethren of this monastery were quarreling, one of them met St Benedict outside the door and the saint immediately gave him this command: "Go and tell the brethren that they give me no rest. I am leaving this house and let them know that I shall not return until I bring from Aquitaine a man who shall be after my own heart."'[1] The place is the abbey of St Benoît-sur-Loire at Fleury; the man from Aquitaine Odo of Cluny, the reforming abbot called in to deal with that turbulent house; and when the monk met St Benedict in the cloister, the father of monasticism had been dead for about four hundred years. It is a story with many layers of interest, and one which provides an entrance into the later tradition about St Benedict of Nursia. Here there is a monastery being refounded in France after the Norse invasions, a rough, undisciplined group who, as the writer says, 'had been scattered far and wide through fear of the enemy,' and were 'now united in body but divided in heart. The turbulence of society is reflected in the cloister and the level of comprehension of the monks is further illustrated by the fact that when they were told that St Benedict had left them, 'they did not have recourse to prayers and tears...but getting on their horses they rode hither and thither to find him and bring him back by force.' John of Salerno, the writer of this life of Odo of Cluny, scorns such a literal reaction; he is a monk of the spiritualizing tradition of Gregory the Great himself, and he tells the story as a vivid image of the place of St Benedict as the peace-maker within the community of monks, 'those who choose the narrow way...so that not living by their own will and obeying their own desires and passions, but walking by anothers judgement and orders, they dwell in monasteries and desire to have an abbot over them.'[2] But the reaction of the monks was not by any means unusual in tenth century Europe; the location of the saints was taken very literally indeed, and the relationship men made with them differed little if at all from their human relationships. If a great lord withdrew his patronage, it was only reasonable to go and force him to return to his duties if you could.

But what was St Benedict, the father of monks, the *advocatus monachorum* to do with Fleury anyway? What has Odo of Cluny to say in the matter? Why start so far away from St Benedict's own monastery in Italy, when he himself seems to have left it so rarely? Cluny, Fleury, Monte Cassino: one of the links between them is undoubtedly the miracles of St Benedict, that tradition of signs and wonders which is there in the first account by Saint Gregory the Great and continues for many centuries elsewhere. I propose to examine briefly some miracles connected with the name of St Benedict in order to see what insight can be gained from such material.

First of all there are the miracles of St Benedict which are related by St Gregory in the second book of the *Dialogues*. These claim to be miracles connected with the life of St Benedict; they are presented as his *res gesta*, what St Benedict did when he was alive. Now there are two aspects for comment here about such an account. The first is the purpose of the account; it was specifically written for the edification and encouragement of the reader; the second is that it is not a biography but a hagiography. These are stories which above all link the saint with the scriptural tradition of sanctity; the miracles validate St Benedict, they place him in the main stream of christian witness: 'I will tell you about the miracles of the venerable man Benedict, *in praise of the Redeemer*.'[3] So we find that St Benedict brings water from the rock, like Moses; he makes iron float like Elisha; he causes Marus to walk on the water like St Peter; ravens who feed him recall the feeding of Elijah in the wilderness; like David, he grieves at the death of an enemy. He possesses, comments Peter, the interlocutor in the *Dialogues*, 'the spirit of all the just'; but St Gregory as the narrator corrects him, 'Benedict' he says 'possessed the spirit of one man only, the Saviour, who fills the hearts of the faithful.'[4] Such miracles are related for a specific purpose; they are not the accidental deeds of a good man, they are the miracles of a saint. They link him with the wonders God showed through his predecessors, as an authentic saint of God, and above all, as St Gregory says, they give to his life the only test of christian sanctity, the likeness to Christ.

The miracles of St Benedict in the *Dialogues* of St Gregory can be discussed in many ways, but this hagiographical dimension is fundamental to them. They are not primarily intended as an account of the actions of the man Benedict (though that is not to say that they weren't). They are about holiness of life in a christian context. They are, for instance, about man restored to his right relationship in control of the natural world--a broken dish mended, a man walking on water, a thunderstorm obedient to a woman's prayers. They are about insight so profound that it pierces the clouds that divide men from one another, so that they are known for what they are, and a servant cannot be mistaken for a king, nor can Exhilaratus take even a sip of wine undetected. It is about that understanding of the vision of God that sees the whole of creation in a ray of the sun. And it is about the battle with the demons, a fight so central to the monastic life that it becomes visible in images and sounds: the demons shout and rage, they even sit on a stone to prevent it from forming part of the house of God; like a dragon coiled round the monastery, the devil lay outside the walls, and the sight of him was shock treatment enough for any monk who turned away in discouragement.

I do not wish to be misunderstood here. I am not saying that these stories are literary fictions of no consequence. I mean that the truth they embody and are designed to convey are more subtle and important than a simplistic reading of the narrative suggests. The images used to denote Christian sanctity are loaded with resonance and meaning and they are equally at the disposal of writer, of observers, and of the saints themselves. This is not an easy point to make clear but it has something to do with the fact that one apprehends realities through the images at ones disposal and not otherwise. We need a way of perceiving in order to see, and especially we need a way of writing in order to convey our understanding. To say that an image is a type, that it is there in similar stories, that it is found in previous accounts, does not mean that it can be dismissed, as if we had found out the writer in the act of copying from his neighbour in class; the resonances, the previous meaning, the allusion, is precisely what the writer wishes us to discover. The images are a lens, a telescope through which we view reality in its long perspective. For instance when the death of St Benedict is described in terms of light, brightness, and a road towards the east, this echoes not only his own vision of 'the whole world gathered in a single ray of light,'[5] it also contains all the echoes of heaven in the Scriptures, and most of all the stories of the resurrection of Christ, as it is meant to do. This man, they tell us, is dead and alive unto God in Christ: 'the tomb of Christ who is risen, the glory of Jesus' resurrection' still exists as the gate and entrance into heaven and the images tell us far more than any amount of argument can.

St Gregory presents St Benedict as the *vir dei*, the man of God before all else. It is an ideal of holiness set in a scriptural pattern and it is presented for edification: imitation of virtues, not amazement at wonders is Gregory's purpose. The miracles of St Benedict are the climax of St Gregory's description of the true christian man, whose virtues have made him so like Christ that the wonders and signs of the life of the new Adam flow again in the world through his life and actions.

Later, the second book of the *Dialogues* became in itself one of the great patterns for accounts of sanctity. Again and again in the Middle Ages saints' lives are modelled on either the *Life of St Benedict*, or the *Life of St Antony*, or the *Life of St Martin*. They become authenticating patterns, just as they themselves found authentication in the scriptures. For instance, when St Anselm strikes water from the rock at Liberi, his biographer has in mind not only Moses but also St Benedict;[6] when iron floats at Monte Cassino, the reference is to both Elijah and to St Benedict.[7] Odo of Cluny delivered from an accident at sea, recalls to his biographer 'what Peter and Paul and then our father Benedict had previously merited.'[8] The curious habit of receiving food from birds afflicted not only Elijah and Benedict but their successors, such as Cuthbert of Lindisfarne. The first account of St Benedict then is no simple record of events, but a highly sophisticated piece of theological writing.

But what became of this image of St Benedict in later accounts of him, above all in stories told after his death? For the Middle Ages had no doubt that a saint continues his work after his death; he is in fact more alive unto God and therefore more powerful and more accessible to men. The long tradition of northern Europe centres on the graves of the dead, on their relics, their dead bodies. Devotion in the early Middle Ages north of the Mediterranean could be called almost exclusively a thaumaturgy of the dead. Now the dead have one advantage over the living which gives them at once a popularity which is unique: they are dead, and they cannot answer back. If you consult a Simon Stylites, or an Antony, or a Macarius, you encounter a living person, whose replies are his own and not shaped by your predilections. You say, 'Father, speak a word to me' and you may be disconcerned, to say the least, by a reply listing your most private and secret faults and suggesting some practical remedies: 'Poemen said to Isaac, "Let go of a small part of your righteousness and in a few days you will be at peace."[9] 'Blessed Symeon said to Batacos, "for what reasons have you come here?" Batacos said, "I hope to transact business and bow before the feet of your holiness." "Wretched man," replied Symeon, "you don't mention that you are really here to act against Gelasios the man of God; go and ask to pardon at once."'[10]

St Benedict himself had not always in his lifetime been a comfort to his petitioners: 'he warned them to curb their sharp tongues and added that he would have them excommunicated if they did not.'[11] But go to the tomb of a dead saint and you have a quite different kind of freedom. You shape your requests, and by and large you hear the reply that your mind and imagination suggests to you. The stories of the posthumous miracles of the saints may reflect some aspects of the original tradition created around the living man, but ninety-nine percent of the time they reflect nothing of the kind. They are the reflection of an age, the record of the needs, sorrows, ambitions and ideals of each generation, each person, who experiences the contact with the dead. As such these collected stories of the miracles of the saints provide historical material of an unparalleled value. It is not the part of a historian, of course, to assess the supernatural value or content of such tales; but what he has to accept is the value given to them by medieval men and the vital role they actually played in their world. Once that is said, there are in these records glimpses of that person who is so rarely heard of as to be virtually unknown and inaudible, the medieval man in the street, or rather, the medieval monk in his cloister, since it was the monks who were the guardians of the relics and the recorders of the miracles. One does not expect to find out anything at all about St Benedict from such records; but one can see in a bewildering kaleidoscope of material what generation after generation made of him.

Let us look at two such records. First there are the *Miracles of St Benedict*, written under that title by Desiderius, abbot of Monte Cassino, in the second half of the eleventh century in Italy at St Benedict's own monastery. The account is in three books, and in form it follows the pattern of the *Dialogues* of St Gregory; there is an interlocutor, Theophilus in place of Peter, who encourages the discourse with his questions and comments. The intention of the writer is similar to that of St Gregory: to show the action of God among contemporaries for the encouragement of faith.[12] As well as the similarity in form and intention between the two accounts, there are close parallels between the content and even the phrases. The second book of the *Dialogues* provided an exemplar for the work by Desiderius, thus creating a continuity between the early tradition and the later one. But the content is very different when taken as a whole. Few of the stories turn out to be about St Benedict at all: there are far more instances of supernatural rewards and punishments meted out to monks and their neighbours. The monastic practices of fasting, obedience, humility, simplicity, stability, are rewarded; demons are rebuked; and enemies of the monastery receive severe and dramatic punishments for their crimes. In two cases only are there accounts of men cured of illness at the tomb of St Benedict: a boy visiting the abbey with his father is cured of insanity by lying all night before the altar of St Benedict;[13] the nephew of a monk of the house, Theoderic, was paralyzed and cured after praying before the altar of St Benedict and also having had the relics of St Maur placed on his chest.[14] The stories recorded in the last book by Desiderius hardly concern either St Benedict or the monastery, but are set in Rome and are connected with the reforms of Pope Gregory VII. What can be discovered from this account, then, is first, the interest in the tradition of St Benedict by an eleventh century abbot and his desire to show that St Benedict's protection and power are still at work in his monastery; secondly, a shift in interest from St Benedict as the father of monks to St Benedict as the protector of his own monastery at Monte Cassino; thirdly, a curious lack of miracles actually performed by St Benedict in connection with the tomb where St Gregory says he was buried. This is not a collection of posthumous shrine miracles in any ordinary sense of the term, and perhaps this was because the claim of Monte Cassino to exclusive rights in the body of St Benedict had been challenged.

This brings us at once to a very difficult question indeed: where is the body of St Benedict? Monte Cassino assumed that St Benedict was buried there, as St Gregory says, and that he either never went away or if he did at least some of him returned. But the abbey of Fleury claimed, and still claims with startling perseverance, that they once stole the body of the saint and took it to France and kept it there. It is still a debatable question. For the purpose of this paper, it is what each side said and claimed that matters--not, note, what each side really believed, because it would be a mistake to think medieval men, least of all monks, were deceived by their own reasoning. To summarize the rival claims: the body of St Benedict was said to have been stolen from its sepulchre at Monte Cassino by the monk Aigulf sent by Mummoldus, second abbot of Fleury, at the end of the eighth century. Desiderius does not allude to this, either to deny or admit it, nor does he use a quotation from the *Dialogues* of St Gregory which would have fitted the case: 'the holy martyrs can perform outstanding miracles where their bodies rest; but...in places where their bodies do not actually lie buried,...they must perform still greater miracles.'[15] The theft is, however, mentioned in Paul the Deacon's *History of the Lombards;* and it forms the basis of the *History of the Translation* by Adrevald of Fleury. It was necessary at Fleury to emphasize the point that these were really the relics of St Benedict, and throughout the Fleury collection this recurrs: in the story of the translation, the first book by Adrevald, there is a story about *quidam* "someone", who warned the pope in a dream that the relics were being stolen from Italy.[16] The legal question of the ownership of the relics is mentioned in two chapters of Adrevald's first book of miracles, where he describes a request from the pope for their return; Fleury is represented as having no counter-claim, and therefore being ready to surrender the body. Adrevald says it was St Benedict himself who refused to go back--he came to Fleury *propria sponte* and will not leave it unless he chooses to do so.[17] Another vision recorded by Andrew of Fleury at the end of the eleventh century continues the theme of the favour of St Benedict towards Fleury, but here it is also said that St Benedict shares his favours equally with Fleury and Monte Cassino: Richard, abbot of Monte Cassino, is said to have had a vision of St Benedict assuring him that this was so.[18]

The account written by Adrevald is an instance of a theme familiar in the ninth and tenth centuries of *pius furtus*. Adrevald had to show that the relics taken to Fleury where genuine; this meant that he had to show equally clearly that they were stolen. Phrases like 'by divine revelation' or 'St Benedict wills it' are the only justification for keeping what was taken; there is no attempt to show that the relics were in any way the legal property of Fleury. To have the body was all important, and the next most important thing was to show that it worked. It was genuine because it was really taken from its original shrine, and Monte Cassino was shown to admit this even in its counter-claims. It was also genuine because it worked miracles. The remainder of the books of miracles of St Benedict at Fleury are the assertion of just this claim; where the miracle collection is, there is the body--at Fleury and not at Monte Cassino.

At Fleury the tradition of the miracles of St Benedict underwent a further change. The book of miracles of St Benedict at

Fleury covers two and a half centuries and comes from the hands of five different writers, each with his own style, interests, and background. They reflect changes in culture, secular as well as monastic, to an amazing degree and, not surprisingly, they say virtually nothing about St Benedict.

The possible qualification to this is that there was an indirect concern at Fleury to present a continuation with the tradition of the miracles of St Benedict as recorded in the *Dialogues* of St Gregory. In the abbey church at Fleury there are carvings on some of the pillars from the twelfth century and earlier. They show scenes from the miracles of St Benedict as recorded by St Gregory: St Benedict fed by a raven, tempted by a devil, holding his Rule, and finally shown giving his blessing to the family of the carver, the monk Hugh de St Marie, who was also the writer of the last book of miracles. It is an amazing piece of propaganda by which the standard, authentic miracles of St Benedict are transferred visually to Fleury. Over the lintel of a door a scene is carved of the translation of the relics and the first cures at the shrine, a suggestion of continuity which is permanent and vivid and beyond argument.

Another visual aid at the abbey shows another side of the change in location perhaps even more radically. The carvings say, St Benedict is here; there is an unbroken tradition from his life until this moment and this place. In the excavations under the high altar the first place where the shrine of the supposed relics was placed has been uncovered. Around it, facing towards it, are stone sarcophagi of the ninth century containing the bodies of local magnates, determined to be as close as possible to this great friend of God at the resurrection, when they were certain to need all the help they could get. This practical concern with *Dies illa, dies ira* led these men, who, if the miracle-books are to be believed, were no great friends of the abbey during their lives, to take this final step to secure the saint's intercession in the next world:

> 'what shall I, frail man, be pleading,
> who for me be interceeding
> when the just are mercy needing?'

The coffins provide a very firm statement about the position St Benedict had come to hold in the countryside of the Loire.

St Benedict is seen, therefore, as the intercessor for Fleury and its dependants. The carvings and the coffins tell the same story and the miracles fill in the details. Each writer presents St Benedict in different situations but in each story the image has a remarkable consistancy: he is now no longer the father of monks, the abbot of a monastery, but the lord of his domains, the patron of a house and its inmates, responsible for them, as they are also responsible to him. The stories contain a wealth of detail therefore about monks and lay people living near the abbey, and their relationship to it. In the first book of miracles, for instance, written by Adrevald about 878/9, soon after the translation of the relics, the overwhelming impression is of a violent society, of small knights at war with one another, to whom the possessions of the abbey are fair game in a continual struggle for land and loot. In seven instances, the stories show the anger of St Benedict falling upon those who attacked the monastery, in four instances his protection is extended towards its inmates. What is interesting for the historian is to trace the dynamics of power, the aggression and defence pattern in this small part of tenth-century Europe. What is the significance of this anger of a saint? Who sees him as active and what does this mean in society? When Rohan, count of Orleons, for instance, attacks the lands of Fleury in a small piece of ground ajoining his own property, he is acting according to obvious methods for obvious ends; what defense does a monastery have? It needs to protect and consolidate lands just as much as the count, and it has at its disposal a force more potent than any army of knights: when the count falls ill, the abbey, through the writer Adrevald who records the sequence of events, sees the attack and the illness as cause and effect: St Benedict, he says, has acted mysteriously to defend his own and punish aggressors.[19] The relics of the saint are recognized as possessing mysterious but incalculable powers and in each incident where this supernatural sanction is asserted to have acted, the abbey is that much more secure. Imagination can be a more forceful shield than swords. The most notable characteristic of St Benedict at Fleury is that he proves his presence there by miracles; and the social situation in which the abbey exists determines that those miracles shall be above all acts of power and ferocity. Adrevald explicitly compares the relationship between St Benedict and Fleury with the covenant between Jehovah and Israel in which devotion is repayed by protection and the destruction of enemies. It was a covenant of mutual help and dependance, in which the monks were by no means always submissive. The monk Christian, the sacristan, guarded the shrine of the saint with energy, and when some treasures were stolen from it he confronted St Benedict with displeasure: 'Believe me, father Benedict,' he said, 'if you do not see to it that those bracelets are returned to me, I will never light another candle to you.'[20] A strange transformation for Saint Benedict, 'beloved of the Lord.'

After a long gap occasioned by the disturbances of the tenth century and the Norse invasions, Aimon of Fleury wrote two more books of the miracles of St Benedict. Odo of Cluny had taken control of the abbey and under his successor, Abbo, Fleury knew sufficient security for monastic life and learning to emerge. Aimon was a child-oblate, coming from a noble family in the Périgord, and he proved to be an able writer. Beginning in 1000, he records instances of miracles connected with the body of St Benedict at Fleury; again there is the firm assertion that the saint is really there by the proof of his miracles in that place. And what, beyond that central fact, emerges in these stories? In nine instances punishment falls upon the enemies of the abbey; the local knights have by no means learned their lesson, nor have conditions become much more peaceable than when Adrevald wrote; Fleury and its lands are still a focus for hostility and attack, and the assertion of the power of St Benedict must still be made. Rainald, Gerard of Limoges, Herbert of Sully, Romuald of Chartres, pass through these pages, with their attempts to acquire monastic property and the penalty this brings upon them. The point the writer is making is that St Benedict is *tutor loci*, the protector of that place, a violent saint with unlimited power who will repay attacks on what is his by supernatural retribution. Once the ills that happen to these men have been linked with their inroads on the abbey lands, a powerful piece of propaganda is in existance and it is at least meant as a deterrent. It needed only a few instances of misfortunes to befall those who trespassed against the abbey and its patron for the power of St Benedict to become an established feature of social life in the valley of the Loire. Romuald, a citizen from Chartres, let his pigs root in the part of a forest belonging to Fleury; he resisted the orders of the monks, even appealed to the bishop of Orleans: it was not his fault that the pigs had strayed. But he fell ill with a fever and was dead by daybreak. The monks were not slow to point to this as condemnation by their saint: 'Lo,' they said, 'the decree of the most just Judge has fallen upon him.'[21] So we find the name of St Benedict taken up as a war-cry in local fights: when, for instance, Adhemar of Chabannais fought with a friend of the abbey, Boso of Poitou, Boso's men were quick to use the name of the saint: 'they shouted the name of St Benedict to the heavens; the whole valley echoed with it and the woods threw back the name Benedict.'[22] A woman who lived near the abbey entertained a travelling knight who was ignorant of the powers at her disposal, and when he stole one of her geese she could rest assured in the protection of 'the most holy Benedict who has jurisdiction over this whole countryside.' Needless to say, the knight fell from his horse and sustained lasting injuries, which in turn increased respect for the saint.[23] The monks themselves were particularly alert to the responsibility St Benedict had for them, and when one of them was insulted and called a fool he felt justly aggrieved with his saint: 'Most holy Benedict, my lord, are you then sound asleep that you let one of your sons be insulted thus?'[24]

St Benedict has become in the imagination of local society a power to be reckoned with; a terror to the enemies of the abbey, a strong protector of its monks. It is a further stage in the projection of local needs and values onto the saint. It is a development from the original image of St Benedict at Fleury. There is, however, another element in these stories of Aimon. As well as marauding knights and cunning monks, there are pilgrims--men, women, and children--who come to the shrine to pray to St Benedict and offer gifts, rich gifts very often and eventually enough to rebuild the church. The pilgrims are also presented in the stories as the people of St Benedict; his protective power extends from his own monks to them, and at times his power is displayed in curing their diseases. Moreover, another element in these stories is significant: St Benedict is not the only saint who works miracles now at Fleury; at his side stands St Mary, the lady of Fleury, lending him her assistance in at least half the miracles recorded by Aimon. It is a common phenomenon of the times: St Mary moves into the centre of medieval devotion from this time onwards, and eventually miracles which were once attributed to the prayers of saints such as St Benedict were not only shared with her but transferred totally to her. But here it is of particular interest for Fleury, since it is in contrast to the early exclusive claim that St Benedict alone worked wonders there. Perhaps the suggestion is that his place at Fleury is now well-established and no longer needs quite such exclusive emphasis.

Aimon wished to continue this record but was deflected to writing the *Lives of the Abbots of Fleury*. The work of recording the miracles of St Benedict was taken up by another monk of Fleury, Andrew. He began in 1043 and was still writing in 1056. He was the son of a local noble family and entered Fleury under the abbot Gauzelin. The four books of miracles which he wrote are in a style notably more ornate than that of his predecessors, a symptom of the times as well as a reflection of his own interests. Again, the preponderance of miracles are those of vengeance: knights die suddenly after pillaging the lands of the abbey; serfs become paralyzed when they work on festivals; the serf Stabilis who ran away from the abbey and lived as free man in the town for several years is summoned in a dream by his lord, St Benedict, and returns to his former serfdom.[25] Litigation over monastic property results in punishments by the saint not only of the ones who bring the cases but for the lawyers involved in opposition to the monks. St Benedict is still shown as having a care for his own people, and for the pilgrims: in time of plague, his relics are taken in procession over the countryside as a pledge of his power to deliver his own. Several of the sick are reported as receiving healing by prayer at his shrine. And the stories are no longer confined to Fleury: St Benedict is now venerated in Spain and Aquitaine, and pilgrims come from there to give thanks to him at Fleury, thus continuing to focus veneration for St Benedict there.

The next writer to take up the tale of violence in high places is the monk-poet Ralph of Tortaire, who was born in 1063 and became a monk at Fleury. He recorded eighteen miracles of vengeance, thirteen instances of protection and favour, and three cures at the shrine.

Ralph is a lively and enterprising writer, and in his stories there are instances of the power of the saint exercised against animals--dogs, pigs, and peacocks. The increasing interest in miracles connected with the sacraments is illustrated here, too: a dying man is miraculously enabled to recover sufficiently to make his confession, by prayer to St Benedict. Ralph feels compelled, as none of his predecessors did, to explain the miracles of vengeance in theological terms: for our profit, for the chastisement of our souls, for our eternal benefit, he says; not at all how the earlier writers thought about it. For them punishment had a more practical and immediate value. But the old theme of St Benedict as a stern patron is still prominent: in his first chapter, Ralph ascribes the death of Eudes, the brother of King Henry, to his contempt for the possessions of the abbey.[26] The sick were still cured by the relics of the saint, but equally those who attacked his lands or worked on his feast day or molested his people were punished. Warinus, for instance, a peasant on the lands of the abbey, was attacked by a knight, Hugh Bidulf, and had his arm broken; he complained to St Benedict before his shrine: 'My lord, St Benedict, I am your slave; you are my lord. This arm which is broken then belongs to you. I would not complain if you had broken it yourself, but why should Hugh Bidulf be allowed to do it?'[27] Belinus, another servant of the abbey, turned to the saint in illness saying, 'if foreigners can secure my lord's favour, how much more should he care for me, since he is my lord according to law and they only come here from a far country?'[28] The powers of St Benedict continue, then, into the eleventhe century; what has changed is the increase in foreigners, pilgrims, who now seem to have first claim on the saint, so that one of the saint's own people has to remind himself that he also can appeal to him.

The last miracles in the collection were recorded by the monk of Hugh of St Mary, who added eleven miracles in 1118. The collection ends there, either from a break in the manuscript or in reality. There is a marked difference in these stories from their predecessors: apart from the first miracle, which is an account of the deliverance of a captive, they are all cures of pilgrims. They happened at the shrine, and are recorded in detail, with names, dates, diseases, and the manner of the cure. One instance from Hugh's record will show how similar these were to cures at other healing shrines and how different from the usual miracles of St Benedict which were best described thus: 'This punishment was deserved, since he had opposed the friend of Christ with all the pride of his heart, and was laid low because of his sin.'[29]

> A woman from the town, who was called Hosanna, on that same night [the feast of the Annunciation, 25 March 1114] lay prostrate before the altar,

> holding out her arm and hand which were in need of healing. For a grievous sickness had taken all the strength from both and she could not even flex her fingers. When she had prayed earnestly, she found that she was cured and felt no pain at all.[30]

By 1118 the miracles of St Benedict had achieved their primary purpose of focusing devotion to St Benedict on the place where his body was buried at Fleury. How strong this centralization was can be further illustrated by reference to the veneration of the monks of Cluny for St Benedict. This was primarily focused on his shrine at Fleury. Relations between Cluny and Monte Cassino were, in the eleventh century, cordial: Hugh of Cluny visited Monte Cassino in 1083 and established a confraternity between the two abbeys,[31] Peter Damian visited and admired the life at both monasteries.[32] But nevertheless, the veneration of the Cluniacs for St Benedict's relics was focused on Fleury. The feast of the translation of the body of St Benedict to Fleury was celebrated at Cluny in the eleventh century[33] and Peter the Venerable supplied a new hymn for it in the twelfth, acclaiming the wonders surrounding the body of the Italian saint in his new shrine in Gaul:

> Claris coniubila Gallia cantibus
> Laetaris Benedicti patris ossibus
> Felix quae gremio condita proprio
> Servas membra celebria.
>
> Miris Italiae fulserat actibus
> Gallos irradiat corpore mortuus
> Signis ad tumuim crebrius emicat
> Illustrans patriam novam.[34]

The vital contact between the two monasteries had been made long before, when Odo of Cluny became abbot of Fleury. John of Salerno says, as we have seen, that Odo was called, elected, and pre-ordained to be abbot of Fleury by St Benedict himself. During Odo's abbacy, St Benedict appeared in visions, supporting his reforms, and he appeared also to Odo himself while he was keeping vigil at Fleury 'before the body of the saint.'[35] It also seems from this account of St Odo that the body of St Benedict had been removed from Fleury during the Norse invasions and was restored, amid miracles, at this time. This complete acceptance of Fleury as the miracle-working shrine of St Benedict containing his body by the monks of Cluny is a strong indication of the triumph of the propanganda of Fleury through the records of miracles there.

While these miracles do not add directly to our knowledge of St Benedict, they hold up a mirror to an age with exceptional clarity.

They point perhaps towards another fact about the place of the saints in history. We have for some years been demythologizers of the saints; if their legends are found to be unrelated to the facts of an edifying life, we dismiss them from the kalendar and from consideration, even when they are such major figures as St George and St Christopher. But the tradition about St Benedict indicates something further for consideration: the stories told about a saint after his death can have a more creative role in the lives of others than any plain historical facts about his life. Of course, with St Benedict there is always the fact to be borne in mind that his major contribution to civilization is that unique document of the human spirit, *The Rule*. But in addition, the legends, miracles, and stories provide not a dead weight of fanciful but outdated tradition, but a record of a living current of human experience, continually alive and infinitely varied. The texture of life is as varied as we care to make it, and for the monk especially one strand in it can still be the deeds of St Benedict.

NOTES

1. John of Salerno, *Life of St Odo of Cluny, Bibliotheca Cluniacensis*, 51E-2A; ed. Marrier and Duchesne (Paris, 1618).
2. *Rule of St Benedict*, ch. 5; ed. Justin McCann (London, 1952).
3. St Gregory the Great, *Dialogues* Bk. 1, p. 70; ed. U. Moricca (Rome, 1934).
4. Ibid., Bk. 11, p. 93.
5. Ibid., Bk. 11, p. 129.
6. Eadmer, *Life of St Anselm* Bk. 11, cap. xxxi; ed. R. W. Southern (Oxford, 1962).
7. Desiderius, *Dialogi di Miraculis Sancti Benedicti*, Bk. II, cap. 6; ed. G. Schwartz and A. Hofmeister (*MGH* XXXII, 1934).
8. *Life of St Odo*, 48A.
9. *Sayings of the Desert Fathers*, trans. Benedicta Ward (Kalamazoo-Oxford, 1975) 157.
10. Ibid., p. 39.
11. *Dialogues*, Bk. 11, p. 109.
12. Desiderius' *Dialogi*, Prologue, p. 1117.
13. Ibid., p. 1134.
14. Ibid., p. 1135.
15. Gregory, *Dialogues*, Bk. II, p. 134.
16. *Les Miracles de S Benoit écrits par Adrewald, Aimon, André, Raoul Tortaire et Hugues de Sainte Marie*, Cap. 1, Histoire de la Translation de Saint Benoit, viii, pp. 28-9; ed. E de Certain (Paris, 1858).
17. Ibid., Bk. 1, cap. xvii, pp. 40-46.
18. Ibid., Bk. VII, cap. xv, pp. 273-4.
19. Ibid., Bk. 1, cap. xix, p. 46.
20. Ibid., Bk. 1, cap. xxv, pp. 56-60.
21. Ibid., Bk. 11, cap. viii, pp. 109-10.
22. Ibid., Bk. 111, cap. v, pp. 135-42.
23. Ibid., Bk. 11, cap. xiv, pp. 116-17.
24. Ibid., Bk. III, cap viii, pp. 148-50.
25. Ibid., bk. VI, cap ii, pp. 218-20.
26. Ibid., Bk. VIII, cap. i, pp. 277-78.
27. Ibid., Bk. VIII, cap. xlvi, pp. 353-54.
28. Ibid., Bk. VIII, cap. xxxix, pp. 342-44.
29. Ibid., Bk. IV, cap. iv, pp. 179.
30. Ibid., Bk. IX, cap. xi, pp. 370-71.
31. *Chronica Monasterii Casinensis*, *MGH SS* VII, p. 741.
32. Peter Damian, 'Sermon for the Vigil of St Benedict,' *PL*. 144.
33. Udalric, *Consuetudines Cluniacensis*, i, 34; *PL*. 149:637.
34. Peter the Venerable, *Letters*; ed. G. Constable, (Harvard, 1967), vol. i, p. 320.
35. *Life of St Odo*, p. 53 D and E.

IX

Miracles and History
A Reconsideration of the Miracle Stories used by Bede

There is still a question mark against that part of the material in Bede's writings that concerns miracles. This has caused them to be either ignored by historians or treated to a cautious defusing so that they become safe to handle; at best they are considered as primitive survivals of white magic[1] or as a different kind of truth.[2] In Mr Colgrave's introduction to his edition of the *Ecclesiastical History*[3] he expresses the doubts felt about miracles in the query, 'How is it that one who is supposed to be our greatest medieval historian can spend so much time telling wonder-tales?'[4]

It seems to me that the answer to this question is not to be found only in seeing miracle stories in the light of anthropology and folk-lore, or even in terms of theological definition, but by looking also at the miracles recorded by Bede in relation to miracle material used by other medieval writers, particularly historians. Miracle stories are not the perquisite of the simple-minded and uneducated; they are there in the writings of some of the most sophisticated men of the Middle Ages: even Abailard has them.[5] Miracle stories were told and retold in the circle that included Anselm of Canterbury, Hugh of Cluny, Hugh of Lyons; John of Salisbury was as concerned with miracles as the more credulous Herbert of Bosham; there is hardly a medieval chronicler who does not have miracles to record. Accounts of miracles were part of the material available to all writers in the Middle Ages. It is useful for theologians to see how this was understood and integrated into the Christian scheme of things; it is useful for others with different concerns to discover the sources, conscious or unconscious, of this way of understanding reality. But for the historians there are two more important questions: first, how far is a miracle story an account of events and facts? and second, what use did medieval writers make of this material when it became articulate in their writings?

It is clear, first of all, that Bede and other writers who record miracles believed they were recording facts about events. People believed they had witnessed these events, and they told Bede what they believed had happened; there is no question of deliberate fraud or falsehood. But to believe that what you write about actually happened is not in itself a guarantee that it did, and with miracle material it is peculiarly difficult to find any valid way of checking the personal affirmation. The essence of a miracle is in itself unverifiable, especially after a lapse of time; all that can be said is: here was an event that caused wonder, that was said by sincere and truthful men to be the direct intervention of God in human affairs. Certainly, something was thought to have happened; the rest is interpretation.

In considering this interpretation of the material the first thing to take into account is a world-view very different from our own. In a pre-scientific world which did not depend on the modern notion of causation, what distinguished a miracle from other events? For us, the interesting question about a miracle is 'how?': how was this effect caused, how did it work, what were the mechanics of this event? In the sixth century exegetes had asked that question, too:[6] how did Peter walk on the water? did the water solidify or did Peter become light? It was not asked again until Robert of Melun and Robert Pullen took it up. For Bede and his contemporaries, the important question was not 'how?' but 'what?' and 'why?' It was not the mechanics of the miracle that mattered, but its significance. For Bede the world was shot through with divinity, and a miracle was not just any inexplicable event but an event that was also a sign of God's relationship with man. Bede himself records the extreme of this view when he sets down what Trumbert, 'one of those who taught me the Scriptures', had told him. Chad had said: 'The Lord moves the air, raises the wind, hurls the lightnings and thunders forth from heaven so as to arouse the inhabitants of the world to fear him.'[7] Here the external world is seen as an extension of man, inextricably bound up with his relationship to God. It was not until the twelfth century that miracles were seen in a different context with nature as an entity in itself; and significantly it is only then that miracles can properly be described as 'wonder-tales'.

Bede certainly believed that miracles happened; it was an integral part of his understanding of reality; but what is remarkable is the way in which he controls and uses this material. He was not primarily interested in the external marvellousness of miracles. His most usual word for miracles is not *miracula* but *signa*. It was what was signified that mattered; the wonder itself was secondary. Like St Gregory the Great he saw that 'it is a greater miracle . . . to convert a sinner than to raise up a dead man'.[8] In his account of the only instance of this, the supreme miracle, in the *Ecclesiastical History*, Bede follows just that presumption: Drythelm returned from the dead, but upon that fact Bede spends no time at all. This happened, he says, *namque ad excitationem viventium de morte animae*,[9] and the other importance that it has for Bede is that it happened in Britain, *in Brittania factum est*. There are few if any instances in Bede's works where he tells a story simply for the sake of causing wonder: the wonder is always subservient to the main issue, which is salvation. This is a use of miracles which comes from inside; they are events made integral to his main theme, a part of his deepest convictions about the dealings of God with man. This integral use of miracles has an appearance of simplicity but, to quote Mr Mayr-Harting, 'the appearance of naïveté here is very deceptive indeed'.[10] Bede understood the material he was using from the inside and was not concerned to assert or emphasize the marvellous elements in the traditions he received. As with his other material, Bede verified very carefully just what the best traditions were about a holy man or miraculous event. With St Cuthbert, he submitted his account to the brethren at Lindisfarne, for instance, and they could find no fault in it. He had recorded the consensus of opinion about the meaning of the life and miracles of St Cuthbert as it was seen by those who still lived in that tradition. They agreed that he was right about what happened and why: the significance of Cuthbert's life was to be seen through the details of events rather than in isolated facts devoid of significance.

Bede was careful also to name the people who were witnesses to miracles, as well as giving his written sources, which he does not do when relating political or military events. This is because the miracle is for Bede part of a living tradition, and its interpretation is vital. The witnesses are 'true and religious men', those in fact who can be relied upon to judge events rightly and see what is significant about them, rather than the most accurate observers of facts. This oral tradition of good men, *ex traditione maiorum*, is a source no longer available for historians; it belongs to the close-knit society of another age, where what is agreed to have happened is held to be a stronger guide than the observations of individuals. The fact that this source is not available now does not invalidate Bede in his use of it.

Bede is concerned primarily with the moral truth and inner

meaning of miracle stories, and secondarily with their significance within the story he is writing, whether it is the life of Cuthbert or the missionary saga of the conversion of the English people. He does not leave the miracles as marvellous anecdotes, though, incidentally, he uses the dramatic implications of the material to the full simply as a story-teller. But beyond this moral and missionary bias, Bede uses miracle material from within in yet a third way. I would like to look briefly at a few of Bede's miracle stories and show how an unprejudiced attention to the points Bede is making leads right away from an obsession with wonder-details and gives at least three dimensions to the material used.

First, there is one of Bede's most famous stories: Cædmon's gift of song.[11] Bede is certainly saying what a wonderful thing it is that this unlettered man learnt to sing; he is also saying what a splendid instance this is of God's goodness towards the English nation; and he is also concerned with the moral edification of Cædmon's death. But the story is far more than that; it is also a piece of literary criticism. Bede introduces the story by contrasting Caedmon's poetry with that of other writers; none of them equal him, he says, *nullus eum aequiperare potuit*,[12] and he asks what makes Cædmon a better poet than the rest. The answer is given in vivid and dramatic form based on the traditions at Whitby about the poet and used by Bede in a subtle and sophisticated way. First, he makes it clear that Cædmon had always been a frustrated poet, not someone who had never wanted to sing; and it was with this unresolved tension uppermost in his mind that Bede pictures Cædmon going to sleep one night. Then, in the long tradition of poets and prophets, Cædmon dreams. He does not dream of a saint or an angel, as in a miracle story, but of *quidam*, 'someone', who stands beside him. And what does he tell Cædmon to sing? *Canta*, he says, *principium creaturarum*,[13] the basic subject of all poetry. Cædmon wakes with the tension of his life resolved; he adds more verses, turning the *principium creaturarum* theme into its Christian dimension, 'praising God in fitting style'. Next day he is examined about his experience, not by the 'reverend and holy men' who would judge a miracle, but by *multis doctoribus viris*, men of skill and technical ability. From then on, Cædmon was subject to the ordinary disciplines of a poet—metrical form, style, melodious verse—his gift was not simply a wonder, unconnected with abilities and skills. Significantly, too, the subjects he wrote about were history and moral instruction; the subjects proper to a Christian poet are those Bede himself wrote about. Bede is of course writing about a divine gift of language, and his main point is that God has acted towards the poor and simple; but Bede is also talking about literature and the essence of poetry. Cædmon, he says, was inspired by God and therefore in the mainstream of inspiration that runs through great poetry; he chose subjects within the Christian economy which improved his verse, and he developed a technique to express his inspiration. But Bede asserts that it is the divine gift of poetry that made Cædmon supreme; the others just did not have what it takes.

There is here no dwelling on a wonder for its own sake, and it is revealing to contrast this with other miracle stories about the gift of language. For instance, Roger of Hoveden tells how at the funeral of St Hugh of Lincoln a thief tried to ply his trade; he was rooted to the spot, 'impelled to compose rather inferior Latin verses whether he would or no'.[14] Walter, a lay-brother at Clairvaux, was visited in his sleep by a saint who taught him the mass of the Holy Spirit; when he woke up, he remembered it, but had the ability neither to learn more nor to use what he had learnt.[15] Or there is the story of the dumb lay-brother, William of Ford, who had his speech restored at the prayers of a saint, only to find to his disgust that he spoke low-class English rather than aristocratic French.[16] These are indeed ornamental 'wonder-tales', and the contrast with Bede need not be stressed further.

Another instance of this subtle use of the miracle story is in Bede's account of the dream of Bishop Laurence.[17] Laurence, faced with a crisis in the affairs of the English Church, spent the night in the church of St Peter and St Paul. He dreamed of St Peter, who chided and whipped him; next day he could show the king his wounds. A story of primitive incubation, no doubt; also a story about God's concern for the English people; but for Bede it is far more than this. It is the chief of the apostles who chides Laurence, asserting his own responsibility for the Church in Britain and the responsibility of Laurence as his representative in the line of the Apostles. Bede's theme here is authority in the Christian Church; through the story he says that authority derives from Christ through the Apostles to the bishops, that it centres on the see of St Peter, that it is a matter not of domination but of a responsibility that cannot be evaded or abandoned, and that it is exercised in service and suffering after the pattern of Christ crucified. This is a serious and indeed vital theme, presented under dramatic images; it resolved an otherwise insoluble conflict. Mellitus and Justus returned to England and the king received baptism; he was 'greatly alarmed' (*extimuit multum*) by the dream of Bishop Laurence—and well he might be.

A third instance of this contrast between Bede's use of miracles and that of other writers is to be found in the matter of cures. To take only one example: Roger of Hoveden describes the cure of a woman of Wye[18] by that dubious person Abbot Eustace of Flay, as follows: 'She drank the water from the fountain he had blessed and at once vomited two large black toads, which at once turned into two huge black dogs and then into asses.' The keeper of the fountain sprinkled her with water, and 'at once the creatures ascended into the sky, leaving behind a bad smell'. It is perhaps unfair to take such an extreme example, which is only a wonder-tale—unless perhaps it is used in a study of delusions—but it is the wonder-tale in its extreme form. In Bede there is no such thing. Take, for instance, the story of the cure of Herebald by Bishop John of Beverley.[19] It is an immensely interesting story, with its interaction of spiritual healing by the bishop and physical cure by the infirmarian. And it was Herebald himself who decided it was a miracle, not the onlookers: it was a miracle for him not because it was unusual but because it was significant. He was, he said, cured in order to make good deficiencies in his baptism; and this cure of the soul was to him and to Bede the true miracle.

It is clear that we are misled if we class Bede's accounts of miracles as 'mere wonder-tales'; it is to place an emphasis on the wonder that is not there in Bede himself. There is a use of miracle material that can be called merely decorative, external, concerned chiefly with the element of the unusual, even if for a moral purpose. In Florence of Worcester, for instance, miracles are prodigies, like the movements of the stars or an eclipse of the sun; in Ordericus Vitalis, miracle material is recorded in lumps, taken whole from the shrine of a saint or a saint's life; in William of Malmesbury, who is in some ways closer to Bede, miracles are often mere wonders. In the *Gesta Regum*, for instance, in one section the miracles at the death of Pope Gregory are put alongside the story of the witch of Berkely *non superno miraculo sed inferno praestigio*,[20] a story of a magical statue of Venus in Rome, a *portenta* of Siamese twins, and the miracle of the uncorrupt bodies of the royal English saints, in such a way that what they have in common is simply their sensational value.

Bede is not, then, concerned with facts for themselves in the miracles; and indeed as his use of the anonymous *Life of Cuthbert* shows, he could alter facts to suit his theme if necessary. Do we then err if we look for factual information in the miracles recorded by Bede? I think there is historical information there, and that it is as great as in the rest of his work, but it is subject to more layers of use and interpretation than the other material. It is essential, therefore, to be aware of the use Bede makes of this material, his preconceptions about it as well as the aims and purposes he has in using it, and to realize that the events reach us essentially through interpretations. Bede is using his miracle material from the inside, and he shapes it according to his purposes. If we try to see the miracles as a simple record of facts we show ourselves more credulous and naive than Bede himself; perhaps it is not only in Bede's miracle material but in all his material that we should exercise some degree of this gift of discernment.

NOTES

1 Cf. Loomis, 'The Miracle Traditions of the Venerable Bede', *Speculum* xxi (1946), pp. 404ff.

2 Cf. C. W. Jones, *Saints' Lives and Chronicles in Early England.* Ithaca, N.Y. 1947.

3 Bede, *Ecclesiastical History*, ed. B. Colgrave and R. A. B. Mynors. Oxford 1969. (All quotations here from the *Ecclesiastical History* are from that edition.)

4 *HE* p. xxxv.

5 E.g. Abailard *Sic et Non. PL* clxxviii, 1525–6.

6 Cf. *De Mirabilibus, PL* xxxv, 2147ff.

7 *HE* iv.3 (p. 343).

8 Gregory the Great, *Dialogus* (*PL* lxxvii, 264–5).

9 *HE* v.12 (p. 489).

10 H. Mayr-Harting, *The Coming of Christianity to Anglo-Saxon England* (London 1972), p. 50.

11 *HE* iv.24 (pp. 414–21).

12 Ibid., p. 414.

13 Ibid., p. 416.

14 Roger of Hoveden, ed. W. Stubbs. Vol. IV (*RS* 51d, 1871), p. 143.

15 *Exordium Magnum Cisterciense*, ed. B. Griesser (Rome 1961), p. 240.

16 *Wulfric of Haselmere* by John, Abbot of Ford, Book I, c.14, ed. Dom Maurice Bell (Somerset Record Society, vol. XLVII, 1933), pp. 28–9.

17 *HE* ii.6 (pp. 154–5).

18 Roger of Hoveden, vol. IV, p. 123.

19 *HE* v.6, pp. 464–9.

20 William of Malmesbury, *Gesta Regum* (*PL* clxxix, 1187–93).

X

The Spirituality of St Cuthbert

Forty-seven years ago, Bertram Colgrave wrote in his preface to the *Two Lives of St Cuthbert*, 'These Lives of St Cuthbert throw considerable light on the secular history of the golden age of Northumbria. They also illustrate one of the most important periods of the English Church'.[1] Rarely has an historian been so prophetic. Since then, scholarship has continued to illustrate the truth of that comment, showing each year how the *Lives* of St Cuthbert, combined with the study of art, archaeology, and artifacts as well as charters and laws, do indeed throw light upon many facets of life in Northumbria in the seventh century. Moreover, it has been equally clear that the cult of St Cuthbert, like so many saints' cults, throws even more light upon many and varied facets of later medieval life, whether in the times of the Danish invasions, the monastic revival, or the Norman conquest. There is much profit in exploring the *Lives* in this way; but how it would have surprised Bede, let alone Cuthbert. For Bede did not write his *Life of St Cuthbert* to provide later historians with interesting information about 'the secular history of the golden age of Northumbria', nor was he intending to give later readers a biography in the style of Boswell, of 'Cuthbert in His Times'. It is right to look carefully at the form of the work and examine its sources and antecedents, to see it as a reflection of its cultural setting, to look at the audience for which such work was intended; but it seems only fair to try also to see what Bede himself wanted to convey in his picture of Cuthbert.

The 'horizontal' approach to Cuthbert as a man related to other men needs to be complemented by the 'vertical' approach to Cuthbert as he related to God, for in the *Life of St Cuthbert*, both in verse and in prose, Bede, like the anonymous writer before him, was writing the life of a saint; the form of their texts and the content of them were both part of the tradition of Christian hagiography. Their aim was to show that Cuthbert was holy, that is, that he showed in his life the marks of Christ crucified and that God had shown his love for that life of discipleship by signs and wonders, before and after death, just as he had done in the case of other holy ones in earlier times and other places. Moreover, their aim was to write in such a way that Cuthbert's

[1] *Two Lives*, p. vii.

holiness should continue to have meaning in the lives of others. A hagiography is above all pragmatic, practical: it shows one of that great cloud of witnesses in the detail of his life on earth as he walked in the footsteps of the Man of Galilee; and it poses the invitation of the angels at the tomb: 'Come and see; he is not here, he is risen.' The accounts of Cuthbert are not only a window onto the dead past; they are a stream of living water where he who is alive in Christ shows the race that is set before those who come after. They are not rather poor biographies; they are first-rate hagiographies.

I intend therefore to speak about the 'spirituality' of Cuthbert, as about something alive and immediate. But at once there are problems in even getting beyond the first word. What is 'spirituality'? It is not a word Cuthbert would have recognized, nor indeed a medieval word at all. Its earlier use was in the plural, 'spiritualities', referring to spiritual jurisdiction as opposed to temporal jurisdiction, the 'lords spiritual' as opposed (and how often literally opposed) to the 'lords temporal'. 'Spiritualité' has of course undergone a later transformation and in its French form there is a very good chance that 'un spirituel' will be someone who is witty, lively, or even mad. These are not the uses of the word Dr Stancliffe had in mind, I think, when she asked me to talk about the 'spirituality of St Cuthbert'. There is another use of the word 'spirituality' nowadays, which I regard with caution, since it seems vaguely gnostic, in which it means the non-material aspect of things, as in 'the spirituality of the motor bike', 'the spirituality of progress', 'the spirituality of electronics': a passive use of the phrase, referring, I hope, to human reaction to these objects. A more active use of the phrase is current in 'the spirituality of Islamic culture', and this is closer to the use I want to make of the term. To see the desires and religious aspirations of men within their cultural context can be extremely illuminating, especially in connection with non-literate societies, and is perhaps partly what has been done in many discussions this week. But as far as Cuthbert is concerned it has its limits, partly because much of the information about his society comes in fact from the *Life* itself, but also because this is still an approach which differs from that of the writers of the earliest *Lives*. I prefer, therefore, to take a middle way, and combine this modern use of the word 'spirituality' (which is perhaps closer to 'mentality') with another meaning given to it in the nineteenth century when it was coined. It was used then to describe a field of study earlier called ascetic theology, and/or mystical prayer. By 'spirituality', then, I mean what Cuthbert himself thought and said and did and prayed in the light of the Gospel of Christ. It seems to me that both Bede and Cuthbert would recognize this approach.

But this at once poses another problem, for what can be known about this inner kingdom? The way to know the heart of a man of the past is usually through his writings, and nothing survives directly from Cuthbert himself. He is seen only through the lens of observers, and moreover neither of his earliest biographers ever met him. That is surely a perilous way to see anyone, especially when I am proposing to look at what Thomas Merton described as

> a point of pure truth [at the centre of our being], a point or spark which belongs entirely to God, which is never at our disposal, from which God disposes of our lives, which is inaccessible to the fantasies of our mind or the brutalities of our own will.[2]

It is rare to reach any awareness of that kind of 'spirituality' in oneself — how much less in others — ; but it is such a centre that illuminates and governs thought, word, and action, and by looking wisely at the external moments, some apprehension of the centre can be touched. I want to suggest that the early *Lives* of St Cuthbert give us that wise view; but before examining them in order to come near the inner life of Cuthbert as he faced towards Christ, there is one obvious method of narrowing the scope of the inquiry. That is by saying at once what his life of prayer was not: it was not, for instance, the rosary, it was not the Stations of the Cross, it was not matins and evensong, it was not the piety of fourth-century Egypt or eleventh-century Canterbury, or sixteenth-century Spain. Cuthbert was not a monk of Jarrow in the days of Bede, nor was he a monk of Durham either in the time of Symeon, or in the time of Reginald, nor was he a Benedictine in any sense whatever; and he was not a Sister of the Love of God, either.

That is rather a negative comment; but perhaps it has at least been a warning signal not to shape Cuthbert in our own image. He was a man of his own time and place, and much about him ought to be alien, strange, perhaps at times entirely opaque. But while bearing that essential element of otherness in mind, I want to suggest that there is a more positive approach possible to Cuthbert. After all, there is a minimum of fact about Cuthbert which is agreed upon even by the severest historians: he actually lived. No one has ever suggested, as they have with both St Antony of Egypt and St Benedict of Nursia, that he was made up; and he lived in Northumbria in the mid seventh century. He chose to be a monk and hermit and he was also a bishop. I suggest that it can safely be inferred also that Cuthbert, noble or poor, was a man for whom his Christian life was a serious matter; and that his friends and colleagues were also men of integrity and not hypocrites. Cuthbert was known to them as a man of prayer, like them concerned primarily with what Jeremy Taylor called 'Following after the most holy Jesus, which is truest religion and most solemn adoration'.[3] It was two such men, Cuthbert's near contemporaries, following a way of life very like his own, who wrote about him fairly soon after his death, while there were still people alive who had known him well. They also were neither fools not liars but men of excellent intelligence and literary competence, one of them the first in the great tradition of English historians. The question these men asked about Cuthbert may not be ours, but it is a valid one; they were not interested in his noble connections, his love of gold, beer, or small animals, not even in whether he was clever, brave, or

[2] Thomas Merton, *Conjectures of a Guilty Bystander* (London, 1965), p. 142.

[3] Jeremy Taylor, *The Life of our Blessed Lord and Saviour, Jesus Christ, the Great Exemplar of Sanctity and Holy Life*, in *Complete Works*, ed. R. Heber, revised J. Eden (6 vols; London, 1847), II, 47 – 8.

great; they only wanted to know how this frail human being had put on the Lord Jesus Christ through life and into death. There are always those who do and those who write and the life of Cuthbert was made articulate by those who wrote about him. They chose small pictures from his life, and presented them with a wealth of interpretation directed to elucidating this central theme.

With this agreed minimum of fact in mind and accepting the innate honesty of the writers in terms of their own concerns, I suggest that there is one way in which these, and indeed other, hagiographies, can shed light upon their subject. Recently in the cathedral church of Durham, the manuscript of the Lindisfarne Gospels was placed on the grave of Cuthbert; I suggest that this is what both the anonymous monk of Lindisfarne and Bede did in their *Lives* of St Cuthbert: they placed over Cuthbert's life the Bible. With that overwhelmingly beautiful book, the Lindisfarne Gospels, the most beautiful thing about it is not its decoration but its content, the Gospel, the Good News, of Jesus Christ; just so the most important part of the *Lives* of St Cuthbert are not in the beauty of detail but those parts that link Cuthbert with the biblical tradition of sanctity, which is done most of all by the quotations the writers give from the Scriptures. In a first glance through a hagiography or any ancient text, the modern eye tends to skip the biblical quotations as mere pious trimming. I believe this to be an error of method. The illuminations of the Lindisfarne Gospel take on a world of new meaning if seen in connection with the text; the inner meaning of the *Lives* of St Cuthbert is made clearer, not more obscure, by examining the parts of the Scriptures that are placed over that life.

The best text for this examination is the prose *Life* by Bede, pre-eminently a man of the Bible, whom Boniface called 'that keen investigator of the Holy Scriptures;[4] and for Bede, the text of the Bible was not read alone. The fathers of the church had read the sacred page and commented on its various layers of meaning, in the conviction that the Holy Spirit was continually revealing the full truth of the written word, and it is just these interpretations that Bede collected and extended in his commentaries on the Bible. It seems to me useful therefore to examine the biblical quotations used by Bede, and to some extent by the anonymous writer, in connection with the standard patristic interpretations of those passages, which were familiar to those reading the *Lives* as they no longer are to most of us. Such study is particularly illuminating in this case since very often Bede himself gave the common interpretation of the texts is his commentaries on the Scriptures. The texts can be used as a lens held over the life of Cuthbert to show more distinctly the intimacies of a life lived in the light of the sacred page. It is possible that what will emerge most of all will be the spirituality of Bede, but I think this is not altogether the case. Bede looked deeply into the *Life* already written at Lindisfarne, and in his metrical *Life* he had already pointed out the interior

[4] *Letters of St Boniface*, trans. E. Emerton (Columbia, 1940), Letter to Ecgberht, no. 75, p. 168 (= ep. no. 91 in Tangl edition, cit. Lapidge, below p. 78, n. 7).

meaning of many episodes, using the *Life* as he used the Scriptures.[5] With the information about Cuthbert before him, supplemented by other sources, he set about presenting the inner significance of the text. This was the common approach to a text in the ancient world, where the surface meaning was seen as a thin layer, beyond which lay riches for the taking, and this was pre-eminently true of the text of the Bible as both Bede and Cuthbert used it. Such meditation of the text was to them common ground, not a different way of looking at things. While Cuthbert had never seen the Lindisfarne Gospels, he knew the Scriptures so well that he staked his life on the message they contain. In writing his account of Cuthbert, Bede is using the Scriptures as a lens, but it need not be a distorting lens. It is necessary to be alert in case what is revealed is the spirituality of the observers, for one sees what one is able to see, what one expects to be there; and, indeed, there is no objective observer of saints. Some of what the anonymous monk and Bede wrote is coloured by their own prejudice and more is coloured by a standard tradition of hagiography; yet the early lives are the nearest documents to Cuthbert in time, they come from men with similar preoccupations, they are directly concerned with Cuthbert's 'spirituality', and they are especially sensitive to the words of the Scriptures which formed the basis of his life. It seems to me therefore at least instructive not to try to sift factual detail from hagiographical *topos* in the *Lives* but rather to examine certain biblical texts that Bede (and to some extent the anonymous writer also) used to convey their understanding of the inner life of Cuthbert. Since it would be a very lengthy task to look at all the quotations from the Bible in the *Lives*, I want to look at the use of three biblical quotations which are used at key points in the *Life of St Cuthbert* and see what they convey about the inner truth of the stories they illustrate.

The first text I want to examine is the account which only Bede gives of the monastic education of Cuthbert at Melrose, which he says he heard from Herefrith of Lindisfarne, who knew it from Cuthbert himself. Cuthbert was received at Melrose by Boisil, and after his sojourn at Ripon returned there, where 'most diligently he paid heed both to the words and the deeds of the blessed Boisil as he had been accustomed to do before.'[6] Boisil died of a plague which had affected Cuthbert also. Herefrith, a priest of Lindisfarne and later abbot there, who was in the monastery at the time, told Bede how, in the last week of his life, Boisil proposed to spend his time teaching his disciple:

> Cuthbert . . . answered, 'And what, I ask you, is it best for me to read, which I can yet finish in one week?' He replied: 'The evangelist John. I have a book consisting of seven gatherings of which we can get through one every day, with the Lord's help, reading it and discussing it between ourselves so far as it is necessary.'[7]

[5] Cf. Michael Lapidge, below pp. 86 – 93.
[6] *VCP* 8, pp. 180 – 1.
[7] Ibid. pp. 182 – 3.

Fifty years later, perhaps these words were remembered at another deathbed and with another Cuthbert: ' "There is still one sentence not completed, dear master." "Then write it quickly." "Now it is done." '[8] Bede's last anxious gift to the Anglo-Saxon Christians was a translation of St John; perhaps it was the story told him by Herefrith that so moved Bede that he chose to communicate St John to others at his own death. There are three points I want to make about this passage. First, why did two teachers offer St John to their Anglo-Saxon converts? How did they understand him? St John's is called 'the eagle gospel' by St Jerome, in his Preface which was as well known as the text, because it is 'about the divinity of Christ . . . the rest of contemplation . . . the mysteries of God.'[9] It is this fact of the divinity of Christ that Boisil conveys to his disciple in those last days as the fundamental basis of faith. Secondly, not only the content but the fact that they spent seven days in reading were significant for Bede. In his commentary on Genesis,[10] Bede devotes some time to the mystical meaning of six and eight, relating such measurements of time to the whole work of creation and recreation, in which the eighth day is the everlasting day of the great Easter of heaven. So it was not lightly said that they read the Gospel together for seven days, for the eighth was the entry of Boisil into heaven, into the rest of the day that is forever. Thirdly, and for Bede this was the most important aspect of the story, he saw significance in the way in which they read the Scriptures: 'They dealt', he says, 'with the simple things of "the faith that works by love" ' (Gal. 5:6).[11] A later commentary expressed exactly Bede's understanding of this verse from Galatians as being about faith which finds its expression in love:

> Without love faith is useless; faith with love is Christian. Otherwise it is demonic. The devils also believe and tremble (James 2:19). Those who do not believe are lower and worse than the demons. But there is a great difference whether one believes Him to be Christ or believes in Christ. Even the devils believe Him to be Christ; he who believes in Christ, however, is he who hopes in Christ and loves him.[12]

In this seven days of reading, Boisil 'declared all Cuthbert's future to him,'[13] but this was no special and secret revelation or prophecy; Boisil's insight into Cuthbert's future came *because* they were reading the Scriptures, not apart from it. This reading became in itself the fundamental basis for the whole of Cuthbert's life as a servant of God. This light from the sacred page was to lead Cuthbert to Farne; but even more, as Boisil saw, it was to bring

8 *De Obitu Baedae*, ed. Plummer, *Op. hist.* I, pp. clxiii – clxiv.

9 Jerome, 'Preface to the Gospels': *Biblia Sacra juxta Vulgatem Versionem*, ed. B. Fisher *et al.* (2 vols.; Stuttgart, 1983) II, p. 1516.

10 Bede, *Libri quattuor in principium Genesis usque ad nativitatem Isaac et eiectionam Ismahelis adnotationum*, ed. C. W. Jones, CCSL 118A, p. 103.

11 *VCP* 8, p. 182.

12 Walafrid Strabo, *Glossa Ordinaria*, 'Epistola ad Galatas', PL 114, cols. 582 – 3.

13 *VCP* 8, p. 182.

him back to the service of 'the faith that works by love' as bishop. On the island, Cuthbert was alone, sealed into prayer, grounded more and more into faith; as monk and especially as bishop he did not stay in a cell or even in a monastery; he was always away, preaching, weeping with the penitent, in the faith that finds its issue in love. The biblical context of the quotation underlines the training Boisil gave through St John's Gospel: 'for in Christ Jesus there is neither circumcision nor uncircumcision but the faith that works by love' (Gal. 5:6). As bishop, Cuthbert was not a monk's monk, nor did he confine himself to a select group; his teaching was for the poor and needy, and his companions were lay men and even women. The close walk with God that he knew on Farne came from the light of the Scriptures as he read them with Boisil, and that love of God issued in the service of love for all. He was not a divided man torn by two vocations, the one to solitude, the other to service, but someone who from the basis of faith did the works of love whatever the circumstances. In his *Ecclesiastical History of the English Nation*, Bede's final summary of Cuthbert's life is that he 'received from [Boisil] a knowledge of the Scriptures and the example of a life of good works.'[14] *Verbo et exemplo docere*: his was a faith exercised both in solitude and in preaching to the poor.

My second example is perhaps the most familar section of the *Life of Cuthbert*. Cuthbert, as a monk of Melrose, was invited to visit Aebbe, the abbess of Coldingham, and sister of King Oswiu. Coldingham was a monastery which, it seems from Bede's *Ecclesiastical History*, may have needed all the instruction, both in word and example, that its royal abbess could get for it. When the Irish ascetic, Adomnan, saw the abbey some years later, he wept and told the abbess that the behaviour of her community was a scandal:

> All of them, men and women alike, are sunk in slothful slumbers or else they remain awake for the purposes of sin. And the cells that were built for praying and reading have become haunts of feasting, drinking, gossip, and other delights; even the virgins who are dedicated to God put aside all respect for their profession and, whenever they have leisure, spend their time weaving elaborate garments with which to adorn themselves as if they were brides, so imperilling their virginity, or else to make friends with strange men.[15]

The frivolity of the gay young nuns of Coldingham raises a smile now, but no one smiled at the time; to assume the life of a monk or nun was a serious matter even for royalty and decadence was not accepted as either normal or nice. Such a relaxed state of affairs was dangerous and it could hardly be the work of a few years. Perhaps when Cuthbert went there, it was this atmosphere of scarcely subdued eroticism which troubled him when he followed his custom of praying at night and which sent him to the beach to stand praying in the icy waters of the sea, that old monastic remedy for lust. What followed when he returned to the sand is another theme altogether:

[14] *HE* IV, 27 (25) (C and M, pp. 432–3).
[15] Ibid. IV, 25, pp. 424–7.

> There followed in his footsteps two little sea animals, humbly prostrating themselves on the earth; and, licking his feet, they rolled upon them, wiping them with their skins and warming them with their breath.[16]

A walk on the beach at night, so often fruitful for the English. A man alone by the sea, singing to himself and taking a dip, with small furry animals rubbing round his ankles. How attractive; is this perhaps, and how consoling it would be, the spirituality of Cuthbert? But this most private, intimate moment of the prayer of Cuthbert is not so superficial for either the anonymous writer or Bede when they place over it the lens of the Scriptures. For the anonymous, Cuthbert is Daniel, thrown into danger of lust, as Daniel was thrown into the den of lions; and Cuthbert, like Daniel, is ministered to by the animals.[17] For the fathers of the church, Daniel was never just the eunuch of King Nebuchadnezzar; he was Christ, who 'thought it not robbery to be equal with God but emptied himself' (Philippians 2:7) and came down, a new Daniel, into this animal den of the world. For Bede the emphasis is different though equally scriptural; he uses the words of the Gospel spoken by Jesus to his disciples after the Transfiguration, 'Tell the vision to no man until the Son of Man be risen again from the dead.' (Matth. 17:19) In his commentary on the Transfiguration Bede restated the patristic understanding of this moment of vision as the second epiphany of Christ, parallel to the baptism of Christ in the Jordan, the two revelations of the Christ as the Son of God.[18] The 'vision' seen on the shore of the North Sea centuries later was for Bede the same epiphany of God, by water and by light. It was a moment of such awe and terror that the observer, like the disciples, 'was stricken with . . . deadly fear'.[19] He had not been watching a man on a beach with his pets; he had seen the face of Christ in a man so transfigured in prayer that the right order of creation was in him restored. For Bede, Cuthbert with the animals was an even more awesome sight than for the anonymous writer: he was the new Adam, once more at peace with all creation, naming the animals, who were the first servant and the first friend. And as in the story of Cuthbert and Boisil, this is also a scene which leads towards entry into the kingdom through the gateway that is called death. There are two other points Bede is making here: one is that Cuthbert, renewed and purged by prayer, goes back to '[sing] the canonical hymns with the brethren':[20] the common life of charity and praise, however lax, is still the place for the exercise of the faith that works by love. And secondly there is a third otter. Bede describes the two otters as 'prostrate before him on the sand';[21] and when he describes the cleric of Coldingham, lying trembling before the feet of Cuthbert, he describes him in the same attitude: 'he

[16] *VCA* II, 3, pp. 80 – 1; cf. *VCP* 10.
[17] *VCA* II, 3, pp. 82 – 3.
[18] Bede, *In Lucae evangelium expositio*; ed. D. Hurst, CCSL 120, p. 205.
[19] *VCP* 10, pp. 190 – 1.
[20] *VCP* 10.
[21] *VCP* 10, pp. 190 – 1.

approached Cuthbert and, stretching himself on the ground, tearfully entreated his pardon'.[22] The relationship of man with the animals is transfigured easily and naturally in the love and worship of the first two otters, and while the third otter is also taken into that same transfiguration, it is by tears of repentance and through the gate and grave of death.

For my third passage I have chosen the moment when that death was fulfilled, and again Bede's source was Herefrith. When the anonymous author describes the death of Cuthbert, he presents a picture of peace and order:

> Being attracted by the love of his former solitary life he returned to the island . . . He remained alone, satisfied with the converse and ministry of angels, full of hope and putting his trust wholly in God.[23]

It is a bland enough description; but there is a discreet hint of something more harsh in his choice of a phrase from Mark 1:13, where angels ministered to Christ, but after the forty days of temptation in the wilderness. Bede dares to go closer to the last days of Cuthbert through what he heard from Herefrith who was with him, and he makes of it a revelation of the ultimate truth of the life of the saint. Herefrith had described how Cuthbert was left alone on Farne before his death, suffering in the darkness of a storm for five days.[24] Bad weather had prevented Herefrith's return to the sick man, and Cuthbert had also been subject to a tempest both external and interior. He had dragged himself to the hut on the shore, out of a great courtesy towards the brothers who would come back, and Herefrith found him there, without food or drink, his face marked by disease and pain. It was not a quiet and interesting illness that he was suffering but a disgusting sore that suppurated. And he had endured also that ultimate terror, about which Herefrith says he did not dare to inquire. It was surely the dereliction which is at the heart of the Gospel, when God was forsaken by God. This last darkness of the saints in their union with Christ is the most fundamental part of Christian sanctity and perhaps the most difficult to approach. It is not, I think, something interesting to endure nor a particularly spiritual condition. Often it consists in disgusting disease, long pain, loneliness, sometimes the anguish of doubt and despair, helplessness mental as well as physical. And it is not confined to those officially called saints. Perhaps it is not inappropriate to draw a parallel with the last years of a very great medieval historian and contemporary, Helen Waddell:

> Helen Waddell's life seemingly ceased in the 1950s with the total eclipse of her dazzling gifts of intellect, winning charm, balance and humour, her ripe scholarship and deep spirituality. Mute, unheeding, unfeeling, blind to all beauty, a stranger to the family she had so loved, she sat day after day before a picture of Christ crucified . . .[25]

[22] Loc. cit.
[23] *VCA* IV, 11, pp. 128 – 9.
[24] *VCP* 37.
[25] Felicitas Corrigan, *Helen Waddell: a Biography* (London, 1986), pp. 355 – 6.

For Helen, the darkness lasted for fifteen years, for Cuthbert, for five days; but time, I think, is not here measured by the clock. It had never been the beauty of scenery that had drawn Cuthbert to Farne — indeed he seems to have taken great pains not to see it at all. For him it was the desert, the place of the cross. There was nothing there for Cuthbert but the stars and water among the rocks; and no one had really understood. Whenever the brothers came they got it wrong, right up to their demands for his body after his death. Even Herefrith could not speak clearly about the real significance of the island and the anonymous writer made no attempt. It was Bede, with his intuitive sympathy for the hermit and the ascetic, who perceived the truth, and it was Bede who provided a clear lens to see both those last mysterious days and the whole meaning of Cuthbert's life on the island. He does so not at the end but at the very beginning of the *Life of St Cuthbert*:

> The prophet Jeremiah consecrates for us the beginning of our account of the life and miracles of the blessed father, Cuthbert, when, praising the hermit's state of perfection, he says: 'It is good for a man to have borne the yoke in his youth; he sitteth alone and keepeth silence because he hath borne it upon him.'[26]

This is no random phrase from the Old Testament, nor a pious cliché about solitude. The commentary which gives this passage from Lamentations its solemnity is from the liturgy rather than the patristic texts and it is from the readings at night office for the last days of Holy Week in the Office of Tenebrae. The reading of Lamentations at Tenebrae belongs to one of the oldest layers of Christian liturgy,[27] and it seems certain that Bede knew the lessons in this form. When John the Chanter revised the liturgy at Wearmouth/Jarrow,[28] it is more than possible that he introduced there the readings for the last days of Holy Week that were already common in Rome.[29] These included the reading of the Lamentations of Jeremiah at Tenebrae, where they are set among responses about the passion and death of Christ. In one of the most beautiful pieces of liturgy ever written, these verses from Lamentations become the cry of the crucified: 'He sitteth alone and keepeth silence because he hath borne it upon him', with the respond, 'He was led as a lamb to the slaughter and while he was evil entreated he opened not his mouth; he was delivered unto death that he might give life unto his people.'[30] It may well have been with this interpretation in mind that Bede used this phrase of Cuthbert, seeing him in his life, and especially in that mysterious

[26] *VCP* 1, p. 154, and using the Authorised Version of Lam. 3:28, quoted there.
[27] *Dictionnaire d'archéologie chrétienne et de liturgie*, ed. F. Cabrol and H. Leclercq (15 vols.; Paris, 1903 – 53), XV, i, under 'Semaine sainte', cols. 1165 – 9.
[28] Bede, *Lives of the Abbots* 6; ed. Plummer, *Op. hist.* I, 369; trans. D. H. Farmer, in *The Age of Bede*, ed. Farmer (London, 1965/1985), p. 190.
[29] Cf. Cabrol and Leclercq, *DACL* XV, i, col. 1166, and XII, ii, cols. 2436 – 7 (under '*Ordines romani*').
[30] Office of Tenebrae, Holy Saturday, 1st Nocturn.

darkness before his death, identified with Christ on the cross through the faith that worked continually by love.

Surely this is the real point about the early lives of Cuthbert. Some actual, physical details about his earthly life are there, but the writers are not directly concerned with them. There is no 'spirituality' there, if by that is meant the personal mental activities of Cuthbert when he prayed or when he taught. What the *Lives* do contain is a series of pictures of real events presented for their significance in relation to God. There is no way of stripping these stories of their piety in the hopes of finding a familiar and accessible figure at the centre. The anonymous and Bede do not write in that way. They use passages of the Scriptures that Cuthbert himself knew and by which he lived to illuminate the whole man. What they show, like all Christian hagiography, is that the words and deeds of this human being were gradually entirely filled, transfigured, with the presence of God in Christ reconciling the world to himself. A Christian saint is not remembered as wise or great or righteous but as a humble and sinful human being who learned, through who knows what agonies and darknesses, so to walk in faith in Christ through his daily life that at the point of death he revealed to others, if not to himself, that underneath are the everlasting arms. The hagiographer is one who shows this life of discipleship to readers for their encouragement and imitation. In the three passages examined from the *Life of St Cuthbert*, I do not at all suggest that the events did not take place, but that in each case the meaning of them is revealed by the use of Scripture: at Melrose, it is not Cuthbert's education linked to miraculous prophecy that is presented, but the whole basis of his life is shown to have been set by an acceptance of the faith that does the works of love; by the North Sea at Coldingham, Cuthbert was no animal-lover out for a walk, but the new Adam in whom the right ordering of creation was restored; and on Farne, the writers do not give a picture of a busy bishop longing to get away from it all to a lovely island with nature and scenery: they bring the reader into the presence of a man crucified with Christ, alone and keeping silence as he accepts death.

Such was the force of this love in this human being that after death his flesh continued to shine with wholeness and his living presence on the other side of Christ continued to be a refuge, the shadow of a mighty rock within a weary land. At the place where his body lay, in the sure and certain hope of a glorious resurrection, the poor and needy and terrified continued to find peace. It seemed ominously appropriate to Bede that when Cuthbert died the monks of Lindisfarne were singing psalm 60: 'O God, thou hast cast us out and scattered us abroad', and he tells the reader to note how the whole of that psalm was fulfilled afterwards.[31] But when he ended his prose *Life of St Cuthbert* he used a different psalm, a psalm not of judgement but of mercy and blessing, and that is surely the final message of Cuthbert, who did not leave his humble successor on Farne, Felgild, to endure deformity and pain, but cured him so

[31] *VCP* 40, pp. 286 – 7 (Anglican ps. 60 is Vulgate ps. 59).

that 'his face had always been free from this affliction, through the grace of Almighty God, who in this present age is wont to heal many, and, in time to come, will heal our diseases of mind and body; for he satisfies our desire with good things and crowns us forever "with loving kindness and tender mercies".' (Ps. 103 (102): 4)[32]

[32] *VCP* 46, pp. 304 – 7.

XI

Theodore of Tarsus: a Greek archbishop of Canterbury

Let us now praise famous men and our fathers that begat us [. . .] *their bodies are buried in peace but their name liveth throughout all generations*

The body of Theodore of Tarsus, the Greek monk who became seventh archbishop of Canterbury, was 'buried in peace' in the church of St Peter's one thousand three hundred years ago. He had died at the age of eighty-eight, after an episcopate of twenty-two years. The fact that his name still 'lives' as distinct from merely being recalled, is due almost entirely to the Venerable Bede, who first applied the above verse from Ecclesiasticus to him, adding that 'the English churches made more spiritual progress while he was archbishop than ever before'.[1]

It is 'spiritual' progress that concerned Bede, not worldly success or earthly event, and his account of Theodore needs to be read with that in mind. Bede's descriptions are never superficial. He wrote theological history, seeing the events of this world under the aspect of eternity for the spiritual benefit of his readers in his own time, a method which he experienced first of all in the pages of the scriptures, seeing 'divine Spirit through the letter's veil'. His *Ecclesiastical History of the English People,* where he gives his account of Theodore, was written in the same way: 'should history tell of good men and their good estate, the thoughtful listener is spurred on to imitate the good'.[2] His picture of Theodore, therefore, was not a collection of mere antiquarian facts, but a piece of spiritual insight into past events, and one of immediate relevance to the present.

This does not mean that Bede's facts are untrustworthy. On the contrary, this first and greatest of English historians took great care with the literal text of the scriptures before he explored the words for spiritual meaning: he used the same method with more recent history. First he assessed the 'trustworthy testimony of reliable witnesses' for the 'historical truth' of what he recorded. Then he reworked it according to its inner significance in the pattern of the whole.

His account of Theodore on one level is easily summarised and is as accurate as he could make it. Bede believed him to have been a native of Tarsus in Cilicia, a Greek a monk living in Rome before 668 and a friend of the African monk, Hadrian, abbot of a monastery near Naples. He was 'well-trained in secular and divine literature, both Greek and Latin'.[3] Chosen as archbishop of Canterbury by the

Illustrations on pp. 49 & 52 omitted in this reprint.

pope, Theodore was consecrated in Rome. He then travelled to England by slow stages in company with abbot Hadrian and the future founder of Bede's own monastery, the Northumbrian Benedict Biscop. He arrived in his see on the second Sunday after Pentecost 669, and began his work by visiting the churches throughout England. With Hadrian, he established and taught in a school at Canterbury; he called two major councils of the English bishops, one for discipline and organisation, the other for doctrine (Hertford 673 and Hatfield 680). When he died in 690 he was buried in St Augustine's with the other archbishops of Canterbury. Part of the inscription on his tomb ran:

Here lies a holy bishop's mortal frame
In Grecian tongue is THEODORE his name
A great high priest was he, the church's head,
Who with sound doctrine his disciples fed [. . .].
September was the month, the nineteenth day
When from the flesh his spirit took its way,
Climbing in bliss to share new life and love
With angel citizens of heaven above.[4]

Theodore and Bede

Such facts have only a mild interest for readers, and one must take a much closer look at Bede's text in order to discover why Theodore should be remembered more than a thousand years later with living affection and affinity.

First of all, Bede had personal knowledge about Theodore. Their lives overlapped and it is almost certain that he had both seen and heard him. How closely he was linked to Bede's own life, however, can be seen at the end of the *Ecclesiastical History,* where Bede summarised the dates in his account which seemed to him of outstanding significance. Each date has only one entry for the year, but five years, 664, 678, 680, 716, and 731, were notable for more. In particular, the middle one, 680, has three notable events: '[In the year 680], a synod was held about the catholic faith on the plain of Heathfield, Archbishop Theodore presiding. John, an abbot from Rome, was present. In this year Abbess Hilda died at Whitby'.[5] All three events touched Bede nearly. For they involved Hilda, the Northumbrian princess and abbess, a great Northern lady and saint, hostess to the council of Whitby, whose abbey was of the Celtic monastic tradition so much admired by Bede; John, the archchanter of St Peter's in Rome, the teacher of chant for Bede himself at Wearmouth; and Theodore, the friend of Benedict Biscop, presiding over the synod the proceedings of which proved to be one of the earliest works of the scriptorium with which Bede himself was to be associated. Hilda, John and Theodore form a group reflecting some of the main interests of Bede's life. Furthermore 680 had a more personal significance for him as the year in which the seven-year-old Bede was given to the abbey of Wearmouth and into the care of Benedict Biscop.[6]

Theodore was the archbishop of Bede's youth. He died only the year before Bede was ordained deacon at the hands of John of Hexham — a man trained in the school of Hilda and also at Canterbury. As the friend and companion of Benedict Biscop, Theodore no doubt visited Wearmouth on his visits to the north. There he would consult with the man with whom he had spent the years when he was preparing for his work in England.

Theodore was essentially a man of the universal Church, a part of the patristic tradition which Bede made his own. But the Greek learned to respect the simple and hard-working style of holiness of the Celtic monks, especially Chad of Lastingham, whom he knew to be 'a man of great sanctity'.[7] He was also an admirer of Cuthbert of Lindisfarne (for Bede the great saint of the north and repeatedly the subject of his loving description). Perhaps Theodore recognised in such men the simplicities of the deserts of Egypt, the origin of his own monastic tradition. Certainly with both Cuthbert and Chad, Theodore behaved as the bishops of the fourth century had to the desert Fathers. He wanted to draw these eccentric holy men into the framework of the Church's ministry. He did so by forcibly taking Cuthbert from his hermitage on Farne and making him a bishop. He also insisted that Chad abandon his custom of walking, like the apostles, about his diocese, to such an extent that the archbishop 'lifted him onto [a] horse with his own hands'.[8]

Such a combination of reverence for the sanctity and sincerity of the English with a concern for the right ordering of Christian life became a central theme in Bede's writings. As a child and a young monk, Bede saw the great archbishop welcomed at Wearmouth by his beloved abbot, and heard him speak, when he 'gave instruction on the ordering of a holy life and the canonical custom of celebrating Easter'.[9] This was a man to trust: while engaged in urging the English to improve the practical working of the Church here was a man of the Church universal who yet admired and revered the northern modes of sanctity and asceticism.

The schools of the day

Theodore was for Bede a man from outside the insular world of the English. He belonged to the central tradition of Christian learning. Not only did he read and speak Greek, he commented on the scriptures in the manner of the Fathers, with particular care for the literal meaning of the text. Both Theodore and Hadrian were 'extremely learned in sacred and secular literature' and for this reason

> they attracted a crowd of students into whose minds they daily poured the streams of wholesome learning. They gave their hearers instruction not only in the books of Holy Scripture but also in the arts of metre, astronomy and ecclesiastical computation.[10]

These subjects also formed the curriculum at Wearmouth and in Bede's own school at Jarrow. Some of Theodore's and Hadrian's students were alive in his own day, being equally competent in Greek as in Latin. Among them were Tobias, bishop of Rochester, Albinus, abbot of St Peter's, Canterbury and Oftor, who went from Hilda's school at Whitby to study with Theodore. Alcuin of York praised the school at Canterbury, while Aldhelm of Malmesbury both obtained the basis of his own massive learning there and recommended it above the Irish schools:

> Why, I ask, is Ireland, whither assemble the thronging students by the boatload, exalted with a sort of ineffable privilege as if here in the fertile soil of Britain teachers who are citizens of Greece and Rome cannot be found who are able to unlock and unravel the dark mysteries of the heavenly library to the scholars who are eager to study them?

'Britain' he added, with a flowery eloquence that is perhaps a deliberate travesty of the inflated style of the Irish, 'has Theodore as its sun, Hadrian as its moon'. Theodore among his students was 'like a savage wild boar checked by a snarling pack of hounds, repelling them with the filed tooth of the grammarian'. He was an archer, 'using the arrows of argument against the shield-wall of arrogant stupidity'.[11] It is a picture of a fierce and argumentative Mediterranean teacher, far from the more contemplative style of Bede himself, but of a most lively and popular one. It was a school that produced teachers and pastors, rather than learned monks who would continue the tradition, since it seems that Theodore trained no academic successor for his school.

In another sense also it seems that the school at Canterbury flourished more in the time of Theodore than later. Where there are students there must be books. Thus, with the coming of Theodore and Hadrian, Canterbury no doubt collected a library to rival that amassed by Benedict Biscop at Wearmouth and Jarrow. But it does not seem that any books survive from the Canterbury library which Theodore built up for his students. Or was it he who brought to Wearmouth the great copy of Acts (Bodley, Codex Laudianus), a text set out in double columns of Latin and Greek which Bede himself almost certainly used in his commentaries on the texts? Perhaps Theodore's school was too personal a venture to last. But in its time it was a wonder. Bede, as a student in the quieter northern monastery, may have regretted that he had not had the high excitement of the international group at Canterbury. There is perhaps a wistfulness in his comment on Theodore's school: 'all who wished for instruction in sacred studies had teachers ready to hand'.[12]

Why chosen as archbishop?

To return to Bede's account of Theodore: there are several points in it which deserve closer consideration beside the obvious admiration of Bede for a learned and catholic man. In Bede's estimation Theodore's greatness did not lie primarily in his accomplishments, but in the fact that he was chosen, indeed chosen contrary to human plans. For the choice of Theodore as archbishop of Canterbury was by no means obvious. It was made in a setting of need and suffering. At the death of Archbishop Deusdedit, the first Englishman to be archbishop of Canterbury, the kings of Kent and of Northumbria had agreed to send Wigheard, a monk of St Peters in Canterbury, to be consecrated in Rome. This Englishman was chosen by Egbert and Oswey as the discreet choice after the delicate union achieved concerning the date of Easter at Whitby. In his *History of the Abbots of Wearmouth-Jarrow* Bede says that his knowledge of English was considered to be of prime importance:

> Egbert [. . .] considered that if he had a bishop of his own race and language he and his people would be able to enter more deeply into the teachings and mysteries of their faith, since they would receive them at the hands of someone of their own kin and blood and hear them not through an interpreter but in their own native language.[13]

Wigheard and his companions reached Rome. But before he could be consecrated, he and all the members of his group died there of the plague in 664.

Pope Vitalian took time to consider whom he should appoint in his place, quietly assuming that it would be he who would now choose the archbishop, and not the English kings. His first choice was the young and able African, Hadrian, who was abbot of a monastery near Naples, a monk who had already travelled in Gaul and had therefore some contact with the north. Hadrian refused the appointment and suggested Andrew, a man with a reputation for sanctity who was chaplain to a convent in Rome. When Andrew's age and health prevented him from agreeing, Hadrian suggested an exile in Rome, the monk Theodore. This was a man of sixty-six who was both able and strong. He was a scholar and a linguist: above all, he was someone who stood right outside the Easter controversies of the English Church. The pope agreed, but only on condition that Hadrian would go with him. This was partly because of his contacts in Gaul, partly as a check on any possible misunderstandings of Theodore's thought. It was also as an economy move: he had 'an adequate number of followers'.[14]

It was not a very glorious beginning. Theodore, far from being the obvious man, was appointed only as fourth choice. Moreover he was sent with a watch-dog. The papacy did not even fit him out with his own retinue; nor was he the Englishman the kings had wanted. But in spite of hesitation, Vitalian had chosen with some awareness of the English scene. Not only did Theodore come to the English situation without being burdened by the Easter controversy: he gained also from being the pope's own choice.

In another matter the sensitivities of the English Church were also considered. Theodore was given a new haircut. Bede says that Theodore had 'the tonsure of St Paul', presumably a shaved forehead such as it is possible to see in icons of St Paul, who shaved his head because of a vow. Such a tonsure could easily have been mistaken for the shaved band of the Irish, who wore their hair in the fashion of Roman slaves. It was a matter of some importance and the subject of division in the English Church, an external sign of great significance in a semi-literate society. Theodore waited four months and was tonsured with a shaved crown, the tonsure of St Peter. It was the shape, they said, of the crown of thorns.

It is likely that Bede noted other indications of Theodore's suitability. This was the seventh archbishop, a sacred number in itself, what Aldhelm called the number 'sacred from the very beginnings of the new-born world'. Furthermore he bore the same name as his predecessor: a Theodore replaced a Deusdedit, 'God's gift' in either case.

Early days

Bede gives us the outline of Theodore's journey to Canterbury. It was by no means the eager rush of an apostolic messenger. Chosen reluctantly, he was to make his way to England without pomp. Four months after his election, Theodore was consecrated as bishop. This was at Pentecost. He left Rome the next day with Hadrian and his retinue. With them went Bede's future abbot, Benedict Biscop, the Northumbrian thegn who had recently made monastic profession at Lérins and was in Rome on a pilgrimage to St Peter. Benedict had been directed by the pope to accompany the new archbishop to England, partly as a guide, partly as an interpreter but also as a native of Northumbria, the kingdom of Egfrid. The party went by sea for the first part of the journey to Marseilles and then by land into Gaul. At Arles they were received by Archbishop John on the recommendation of the pope. There the web of Merovingian politics closed round them and they were detained. However Ebroin (the mayor of the palace under Theoderic III) eventually gave them permission to move on. The party split up and Hadrian travelled to visit his friends at Sens and at Meaux. There he was to be embroiled once more in the machinations of Ebroin: the latter suspected him of being an agent from the Byzantine emperor Constans II on route to England with offers of alliance against Gaul. As a result it was two long years before Hadrian and his retinue were free to travel on to Canterbury.

Theodore went more privately with Benedict Biscop to visit Agilbert, the bishop of Paris, with whom he stayed for the winter. Here Theodore moved definitively into English-oriented circles. Agilbert, a Gaul by birth, had been a student in Ireland and was well-learned in the scriptures. He had become bishop of the West Saxons under Cenwealh, a friend of Benedict Biscop. But the king 'who knew only the Saxon tongue grew tired of his barbarous speech and foisted upon the kingdom a bishop named Wine who [. . .] spoke the king's own tongue'.[15] Agilbert had been highly offended when the king divided his diocese and gave him the less prestigious part. He left his see and went north to the court of Oswy of Northumbria. There he ordained Wilfrid priest and was present at the council of Whitby. As spokesman for the Roman side at the council, Agilbert once more found himself handicapped by his lack of linguistic skill and when asked to present the arguments for the Roman calculation of Easter, he proposed Wilfrid as his deputy because 'he can explain our views in the English tongue better and more clearly than I can through an interpreter'.[16] Immediately after the council Agilbert had returned to Gaul and become bishop of Paris.

He was therefore someone well aware of the major problems of the English Church. He had been deeply involved in the paschal controversy. As a friend of Aldfrith of Northumbria and of Cenwal of Wessex he knew the politics of at least two kingdoms. He had experienced at first hand the division of his diocese by a king: therefore he knew the particularly close link between kings and bishops, and the problems this posed in the English political situation. Moroever, he had twice had bitter experience of the limitations placed on someone unable to learn the language of the local kings. No doubt Theodore and Agilbert discussed their common interest in scripture commentary. But during that winter it is possible that Theodore, an accomplished linguist, and one who, by his origin, was party to a tradition in which wide use was made of the vernacular, took the opportunity to learn some dialect of English. No doubt he also absorbed the picture both Biscop and Agilbert could give him of his future home.

In the spring, Egbert of Northumbria sent his reeve Raedfirth to Paris to escort the bishop to England. But Theodore was yet to be humiliated by another delay, this time because of illness at the port Quantavic. At last, at the end of May 669, more than a year after his consecration, Theodore came to Canterbury. Like his predecessor Augustine, he had shown no great zeal to arrive in this country on the edge of the world and had taken time in civilized Gaul to equip himself for his work there. It was a humble beginning, lacking in glory and assurance.

'An able and energetic pastor'

When Bede described Theodore's work as archbishop, he was speaking of what seemed to him a golden age. It was an age, moreover, which was closely connected with his own monastery and friends. The picture he gives is of an able and energetic pastor, ready to discover all about his responsibilities, travelling widely and consulting with bishops and kings. Two matters chiefly concerned Theodore: the first was educational, the second organisational and pastoral.

For education, the school he established at Canterbury was not made out of simple love for learning. Above all, the English needed guidance how to think. He himself carefully explained in his commentaries on scripture many foreign objects and customs for the edification of this eager but insular race of warriors and farmers. Since he himself had been concerned with matters of doctrine, Theodore was anxious that no heresy contaminated his diocese during his rule. In 679 he called a council on the matter of doctrine at Hatfield, to which the pope sent a representative specifically to check the theology of Theodore's Church, and carefully recorded the agreement of the bishops with him on all points of doctrine. It is not necessary to suppose that Theodore held some specifically 'Greek' theological position. The chief matter that needed clarification was contained in the decrees of the first Lateran council of 649, where Pope Martin had opposed the heresy of Monothelitism. In the process he had become the last of the popes to die in exile as a martyr. This was some eighteen years before Theodore's consecration as archbishop. Theodore had taken part in the discussions of Monothelitism when he was still in Rome, and he was probably alert to the need for precision in the expression of doctrine.

Theodore understood, but deplored, the insular custom of the English kingdoms, where the facts of conversion had made each king regard the bishop as his man. The bishops were for the people of the king, whether Northumbrians, West Saxon, Mercians or Kentish. While this was workable in the case of a small group of converts with their leaders, the partisanship involved was regrettable. Furthermore there were too few bishops for a rapidly expanding Church. Theodore, like Gregory the

Great, proposed a division of bishoprics, by which the number of bishops should be increased to meet the needs of the people, while yet retaining income sufficient for their needs. At the council in 673 at Hertford, the ninth heading for discussion was 'that more bishops shall be created as the number of the faithful increases'. It met the fate of so many proposals in committee: it received 'general discussion, but at that time we came to no decision on the matter'.[17] Theodore was not deflected, and used every opportunity to divide dioceses and appoint more bishops to smaller groups under the novel impression that bishops were not status symbols and royal advisors but pastors of people: where you had more Christians you needed more bishops. He was neither entirely successful nor invariably right. In the tangled matter of the right of Wilfrid to the vast see of York, for instance, Theodore was clearly wrong. Though he received the support of Rome for his arrangements, in the end he had to restore the same Wilfrid whom he had earlier deposed.

In these matters Bede learned much from Theodore. At the end of Bede's life he wrote a letter commenting on contemporary problems in the English Church in 735. It both echoes themes from Theodore's episcopate and shows that his changes still needed to be applied. Like Theodore, Bede deplored the lack of pastoral bishops in the Church:

> for who indeed cannot see how much better it would be to divide such a great weight of ecclesiastical government among several? [. . .] The holy pope Greogry decreed that twelve bishops were to be ordained here after the faith had been accepted, among whom the bishop of York should receive the pallium and be a metropolitan.[18]

Like Theodore, he urged the clergy to take great care of their flocks, to spend time with good and learned companions, to meet frequently in synods for mutual support. He also suggested a much closer link between the monasteries and the bishops. In other words, like Gregory the Great and Theodore, Bede was adamant that a bishop was a man of God and not another political figure among others.

Limitations

There were other opinions about Theodore beside that of Bede. Eddius Stephanus, the biographer of Wilfrid, thought Theodore not only misguided in his treatment of Wilfrid, but corrupt. He suggested that he took bribes from King Egfirth and his queen to act against Wilfrid:

> contrary to the will of God [. . .] they summoned the archbishop Theodore with the aid of bribes to help them in their madness [. . .]. When the archbishop had come they explained to him what they intended to do to bring about Wilfrid's humiliation and he consented to condemn him unjustly [. . .] for no crime whatsoever.[19]

In view of everything else known of Theodore and of Eddius Stephanus' over-zealous partisanship for Wilfrid, it is difficult to accept this suggestion. But it is interesting to note that Eddius Stephanus' view of the rightness of Wilfrid's cause was shared by the great twelfth-century historian William of Malmesbury. Though prepared to respect Theodore in other ways, William found his conduct towards Wilfrid reprehensible.

Bede was well aware of the limitations in Theodore the man. But such criticism as that of Wilfrid's biographer found no place in Bede's portrait. For him Theodore was more than a prelate. His account of Theodore is subtle and detailed, and it is significant that he placed it at the beginning of the fourth book of his *Ecclesiastical History of the English People*. Bede saw the history of the world in a quite specific framework, in which the life in Christ of the English was part a world view leading into and surrounded by the ages of eternity. In several places in his works he outlined his scheme of world history.

Bede's scheme of epochs

There were six human ages, the sixth being now; and running consecutively with this sixth age was the seventh: this involved the rest of the saints in heaven. Both living and dead were awaiting the eighth age, the fullness of times, when 'He shall have put all things under his feet' and 'God shall be all in all'. The first age began with the expulsion of Adam from paradise, the beginning of time. The second age was from Noah and the flood to Abraham; the third from Abraham to David and the fourth from David to the deportation to Babylon. The fifth age extended from there to the nativity of Jesus Christ. To this plan Bede added five ages of man, an infancy, childhood, youth, maturity and old age.[20]

It seems to me that this is the historical framework Bede had in mind also for his account of the English Church. The first book described an expulsion from paradise and then infancy of the English Church under Augustine, the second the childhood and growth of the Church, the third book the valiant youth of the Church and the fourth its maturity under those princes of the Church, Theodore, Wilfrid and Cuthbert. A fifth age of decline followed in book five, while Bede himself wrote in the continuing sixth age, surrounded by the saints of the seventh age. These together, with all mortals, awaited the eighth day of God.

The fourth age had its David in Theodore. Like David, he had not been the first choice for his office but was a most unlikely candidate. Like David, also Theodore cared about music and aimed to organise a peaceful kingdom. The heroes of book four are Theodore, Wilfrid and Cuthbert, each in his own way a prince of the new kingdom of God: Theodore, the chosen and anointed one, Wilfrid, another style of prince-bishop, while Cuthbert showed only the royalty and glory of prayer and suffering love.

'A sinner born to die'

Theodore's last years were marked by thoughts of his impending death. Eddius Stephanus is more explicit than Bede and says that, like King David, he was deeply penitent: 'being troubled by frequent infirmity, he summoned to London the holy bishops Wilfrid and Eorconwold. When they had come the archbishop prudently and frankly revealed to them the whole course of his life, making confession before

God'.[21] It is not necessary to believe that this took the form of the grovelling apology to Wilfrid which Eddius Stephanus' partisanship suggests. But it is entirely in keeping with Theodore's life that he should be a penitent at its end. One of the works associated with his name is, after all, a Penitential. A Northumbrian disciple had written down Theodore's replies to the many questions put to him by the English about sin and repentance through Eoda the priest: among the mass of information the Penitential contains there is a constant theme of personal repentance, a life of constant turning towards God, of penance as a medicine for the soul rather than a legal penalty for offence. 'This', he wrote, 'is carefully to a be considered in all penance; the length of time anyone remains in his faults; with what learning he is instructed; with what passion he is assailed; with what courage he stands; with what tearfulness he is seen to be afflicted'.[22] After a day spent in the house of Lords, John Wesley was later moved to ask, 'What is a lord but a sinner born to die?' Of Theodore the prince of the Church, that could equally be asked. From the beginning, his career was marked with trials and cross-like tribulations. From a city which had fallen into the hands of the Persians, he was a refugee in Rome. There he had become a dubious and late choice for an archbishopric on the edge of the civilised world. He was already beyond retiring age when he left for Canterbury. He needed all his courage to respond to this call as he walked and at times stumbled along the strange and barbarous half-Christianised rulers of the English. As he tried to draw them into a more viable pastoral life, he met with resistance and setbacks. He himself acted at times with impatience and lack of understanding. But he persisted in doing what he could, and that was his glory. He did not withdraw, and he never gave up, even though he must sometimes have remembered with longing the quiet of his former monastery where he was not yet responsible for anyone else.

It has been said that what Theodore was trying to do came too late for the English. Already they had compromised too much. Even a hundred years later, they were still in the same position: hence Bede's insistence that the English bishops should stop thinking about money and position in order to devote themselves to the gospel and the people of their land. Nevertheless Theodore laid down the basis of church organisation. In particular, he provided the framework for the regular consultation of the clergy in synod. This was in itself a major achievement.

However, it was not learning or correct doctrine, nor was it a wider view or a better organisation that was the best gift offered by this Eastern monk to England. Far more significant is the fact that this clever but ordinary man survived in alien circumstances as a servant of Christ, teaching by word and by example. For here was an example not of greatness, but of humble service. In this respect, also, his name lives on 'throughout all generations'. As his twentieth-century successor, Michael Ramsey, insisted, each generation in turn has its part to play. And he concluded a Lindisfarne sermon on Theodore's contemporaries, Aidan, Chad, Oswald and Cuthbert with the words:

The glory of us children is our fathers; remember them, thank God for them, imitate their faith. And the mighty purpose of God will move forward, and instead of our fathers there shall be our children, princes of Christ in our own and every land.[23]

1. *Bede's Ecclesiastical History of the English People,* ed. and tr. B. Colgrave and R.A.B. Mynors (Oxford 1969), p.475 (hereafter *Bede*).
2. *Bede,* p.3.
3. *Bede,* p.331.
4. *Bede,* p.475.
5. *Bede,* p.565.
6. *Bede,* p.567.
7. *Bede,* p.337.
8. Ibid., *loc. cit.*
9. *Bede,* p.333.
10. *Bede,* pp.333, 335.
11. Alhelm, *The Prose Works,* tr. M. Lapidge and M. Herren (Cambridge 1979), p.163.
12. *Bede,* p.335.
13. Bede, 'Lives of the Abbots of Wearmouth and Jarrow', trans. J.F. Webb in *The Age of Bede* (Harmondsworth 1965), p.187.
14. *Bede,* p.331.
15. *Bede,* p.235.
16. *Bede,* p.301.
17. *Bede,* p.353.
18. Bede, 'Letter to Archbishop Egbert', tr. J.A. Giles in *English Historical Documents* ed. D. Whitelock (Oxford 1979), p.804.
19. Eddius Stephanus, *The Life of Bishop Wilfrid,* ed. and tr. B. Colgrave (Cambridge 1927), p.49.
20. Bede, 'De Temporum Ratione', ed. C.W. Jones in: *Corpus Christianorum Series Latina* CXXIXXB, p.49.
21. *Life of Bishop Wilfrid,* p.89.
22. Theodore's 'Penitential', tr. M. Deansley in: *The Pre-Conquest Church,* (London 1961), p.128.
23. Michael Ramsey, 'Lindisfarne', in: *Durham Essays and Addresses* (London 1957), p.105.

XII

BEDE AND THE CONVERSION OF THE ANGLO-SAXONS

The Ecclesiastical History of the English People was completed by the Venerable Bede in "the year of our Lord 731," a chronological calculation for which he himself was responsible, and which was to have a more lasting influence on European thought than even his histories and biblical commentaries. Living as a simple monk in a monastery in the north of that *alter orbis,* Britain, which seemed to the men of the Mediterranean world the very edge of civilization, in a land with no tradition of learning, whose people had been converted to Christianity only fifty years before, Bede nevertheless became the most learned man of his age and the first, and perhaps still the greatest, of the historians of England. His reputation among his contemporaries was as a commentator of the Scriptures. Boniface, writing to England with requests for books to help in the conversion of Germany half a century later, asked for the works of "that keen investigator of the Scriptures, the monk Bede"[1]; "... a spark," as he called him, "from the light of the Church which the Holy Spirit has kindled in your land."[2] And Bede himself says of his own life, "I have spent all my life in this monastery, applying myself entirely to the study of the Holy Scriptures."[3] His fame later was, and is, as the inventor and popularizer of the dating of our era by the year of grace A.D., from the Incarnation of Christ, thus giving a framework to our consideration of past and present which underlies all our thought. But it is Bede's historical work, the *Ecclesiastical History of the English People,* which is today the most popular of his works and the most widely read. The work of a very great historian, whose critical standards would be admirable in any historian of today, it provides the main source for the early history of England, and is unique in its scope and accuracy as well as in its readability. It is a great and rich work, within which I will draw attention to two aspects only: first, the interaction of religion and politics in the world Bede describes, and secondly, the extent to which paganism remained close to the surface in this newly baptized people.

The conversion of the Anglo-Saxon invaders of Britain to Christianity as seen by Bede a generation later is a remarkable story, full of life and vigor. In it, the interweaving of religion and politics is so close that it is impossible to treat them separately, a fact to bear in mind, incidentally, when considering the history of the Church in England later. There were two main areas of missionary activity to begin with: the Italians in Kent and the Irish in Northumbria. In both cases, the preaching of the missionaries, indeed their very presence in the island, was dependent on the good will of the kings. Even where, as in Kent, the missionaries had the friendship of the queen, already a Christian, the good will of the king was vital before they could stay and live in his territory at all. In 496, Augustine landed in Kent and was given by the king, Ethelbert, "a dwelling in the city of Canterbury, the chief city of all his dominions"[4] with freedom to worship and to preach. But Ethelbert himself did not receive baptism until some time later (June 597 seems to be the most likely date[5]) and then not alone but with others, presumably some of his great men and advisors. In Kent, therefore, baptism, marriage, and politics were intimately intertwined: through Bertha, great-granddaughter of Clovis, Ethelbert heard of and learned to respect Christianity, through a marriage primarily undertaken to cement his contacts with Gaul and Rome—a mixture of elements which appears in various ways in the conversion of other Anglo-Saxons.

In Northumbria, a similar situation soon developed: Ethelbert's daughter, Ethelburga, was, like her mother Bertha, a Christian princess who was involved in the conversion of a kingdom. Edwin, the king of Northumbria, sent ambassadors to her brother Eadbald (who had himself been a pagan and had received baptism not long before) to ask for a marriage alliance between the kingdoms. Eadbald insisted that his sister should have full liberty to practice her religion in the pagan court and accordingly she went north with bishop Paulinus, one of the second group of monks sent by St. Gregory from Rome, thus introducing Christianity into the northern royal court.[6] As in Kent, foreign alliances and the political motives of kings combined with the presence of a Christian wife, but these were not sufficient for conversion. Edwin, like Ethelbert, allowed the Christians to preach, but did not himself receive baptism until he had conferred with his thanes and obtained their agreement to the change. It is significant that both Bertha and Ethelburga needed to be urged by the pope to try to convert their husbands more firmly; clearly, marriage to a Christian was in itself only a factor towards conversion and should be seen as part of a complex of influences, secular and sacred.[7]

The importance of consultation before a king's conversion is brought out in the situation of Redwald, king of East Anglia. Redwald received baptism alone while he was in Kent during the lifetime of Ethelbert, but when he returned home, he was unable to implement this without the support and agreement of his family and his thanes: "on his return home, he was seduced by his wife and by certain evil teachers and perverted from the sincerity of his faith."[8] He compromised and had a Christian altar alongside a pagan altar in the same building. If Redwald is indeed the king for whom the Sutton Hoo Ship-Burial was prepared, the artifacts there illustrate this ambivalence.[9]

Later, when Edwin of Northumbria was in exile and as yet unbaptized, he took refuge at the court of Redwald, and Redwald's wife was again influential in persuading her husband to support the young man. The sons of Redwald became Christian: one, Sigebert, incurring his father's anger and fleeing to Gaul, the other, Eorpwald, being persuaded to baptism by Redwald's previous guest, Edwin.

Marriage alliance was linked with conversion and politics in the pagan kingdom of Mercia also. Here, Penda remained a pagan all his life but permitted the preaching of Christianity and indeed was said to dislike nominal Christians: "He hated and despised those who, after they had accepted the Christian faith, were clearly lacking in the works of faith."[10] His daughter Cyneburgh, was married to Aldfrid, son of Oswy, the Christian king of Northumbria, a friend of Bishop Wilfrid, and active in church affairs, for instance at the Council of Whitby.[11] Penda's son, Peada, who was also sub-king under his father in the Midlands, asked for the hand of the Christian princess, Alhflaed, the daughter of Oswy and the sister of Aldfrid. Oswy made it a condition of the marriage alliance that Peada should become Christian, and Aldfrid, a friend of Peada, "earnestly persuaded" him to do so. Peada was baptized by Bishop Finan "together with all his thanes and gesiths."[12] It seems that Christianity became well-established in Peada's kingdom and flourished particularly under Wulfhere, the younger son of Penda and Peada's successor. It is ironic to note that Peada himself was murdered by his wife, the Christian princess for whom he had accepted Christianity "during the very time of the Easter festival."[13] Presumably her loyalty to her father's house exceeded her loyalty to her husband—an indication, of which there are many in Bede, of the strength of the pagan and political ties above those of the new religion.

In addition to this pattern of conversion through politics and marriage alliances, in which often the kings involved stood godfather to one another, there was the factor of exile. Anglo-Saxon kings ruled smaller or larger groups of men and were continually fighting one another. They were subject also to the blood-feud. In such a situation, in an island newly settled by the invaders and with the unalterable limits of its coast line, it is not surprising that so many of the leaders, and probably lesser men also, spent so much time in exile. Sigebert and Edwin were in exile before they became kings; and at various times Oswald, Owsy, and Aldfrid in Northumbria and Cenwalh and Ceadwalla in Wessex went abroad. When Oswald took over the realm of Northumbria, the queen Edwin had taken from Kent fled back there with her bishop, Paulinus, and thought it prudent to send her children to the court of her friend, King Dagobert in Gaul.[14]

Exile ensured that all kings recruited into their service men from other kingdoms; it gave them experience of other and older cultures than their own, and in many cases it was while they were in exile that they were baptized. Oswald, for instance, one of the sons of King Aethelfrith of Northumbria, spent the whole of the reign of Edwin, Aethelfrith's enemy and successor, in exile with his brothers "among the Irish or the Picts" where, Bede tells us, "they were instructed in the faith as the Irish taught it and were regenerated by the grace of baptism."[15] This Irish connection was to be as influential in England in the north as was that of Italy and Gaul in the south. Oswald sent for missionaries from Ireland, and eventually Aidan was sent who, with his companions, and in close association with the king, became the apostle of Northumbria. The influence of Irish learning and love of letters came with these monks, just as in the south the school system of Gaul was introduced into East Anglia, where Sigebert who had been in exile in Gaul because of the enmity of Redwald, had both received baptism and admired the schools: "with the help of Bishop Felix . . . he established a school where boys could be taught letters."[16]

With this story of the enormous vigor and ambition of the Anglo-Saxon kings, with their continual wars and rivalries, their political alliances and inevitable betrayals, their return to paganism and their greed for gold, Bede presents the growth—the amazingly strong and quick growth—of Christianity, gradually penetrating even the warrior ideology, until at the end of his account he could write with something more than rhetorical wishful thinking, "this is the state of the whole of Britain at the present time, about 285 years after the coming of the Anglo-Saxons to Britain, in the year of our Lord 731. Let the earth rejoice in his perpetual kingdom and let Britain rejoice in his faith and let the multitude of the isles be glad and give thanks at the rememberance of his holiness."[17] For Bede one sign of the thorough conversion of the English was the fact that many of the "both noble and simple have laid aside their weapons and taken the tonsure, preferring that they and their children should take monastic vows rather than train themselves in the art of war."[18] Many pages of the *Ecclesiastical History* are concerned with monks: the Irish at Iona and Lindisfarne, at Whitby and Lastingham, and the Roman monks at Canterbury, Ripon, and Jarrow. Monks came from Rome and monks from Ireland, and combined their influence with that of monastic Gaul, where some Britons had gone, since they could not find monastic training initially in England. The Irish monks, such as Aidan and Columba and Chad were highly respected for their austerity and zeal; the Roman monks, such as Augustine, Mellitus, Laurence, Justus, and later the Greek Theodore, for their life of ordered prayer and worship.

The influence of the kings was as important to the establishment of monastic life as it was to conversion. At Canterbury, the Abbey of St. Peter and St. Paul (now St. Augustine's) was the burial place of the kings of Kent; in the north, the Abbey at Whitby was the sepulchre of the royalty of Northumbria.[19] Kings sometimes renounced their authority for the cloister[20] and queens and princesses frequently became nuns. The best known of these is Hilda,[21] a princess of Deira, and cousin of King Edwin; her sister became queen of the East Angles and Hilda was succeeded as abbess of Whitby by Elfleda, the daughter of its founder Oswy. Jarrow, Bede's own monastery, was founded by Benedict Biscop, a Northumbrian nobleman and a retainer of Oswy. At twenty-five he obtained a land grant from the king and began to travel widely abroad, becoming a monk and eventually building the monasteries of Wearmouth and Jarrow, filling them with treasures from Rome and Gaul, and above all with the books which gave Bede the opportunity to become the greatest scholar of his age.[22]

With such involvement of the aristocracy in monastic life a tension of ideals was set up which Bede himself noted and deplored. In the *Ecclesiastical History* he underlines this tension in, for instance, a story of Bishop Aidan and King Oswin, the unfortunate brother of Oswy, who was murdered by his most Christian brother's orders. Oswin gave Aidan a horse, in the traditional manner of an Anglo-Saxon king, the gift-giver, whose favor was given along with the gift. Aidan, a monk, with very different patterns of behavior in mind, gave the king's gift to a beggar. The king protested and Aidan defended his action in the great hall where the king "who had just come in from hunting stood warming himself by the fire with his thanes," emphasizing the unimportance of worldly goods and kingly patronage compared to the needs of the poor. The story, as vivid as possible from the hands of such a superb story-teller as Bede, concludes with the realization by the king of this different scale of values. "At once he took off his sword and gave it to a thane and hastening to where the bishop sat, threw himself at his feet and asked his pardon."[23] Bede ends the story with a touch which contains a wealth of social comment: Aidan began to weep while the king went back to sit down to the feast, and when another

Irishman asked him, (in Celtic) why, he said, "I know that the king will not live long, for I never saw before a humble king."[24]

The tensions involved between monastic values and those of a warrior class were not always so simply resolved. Bede also tells the story of Sigebert, the son of Redwald who was baptized while in exile in Gaul. He resigned his office as king and became a monk. When Penda of Mercia attacked East Anglia, his countrymen asked Sigebert to return and help fight the pagan king; Sigebert refused and was dragged unwillingly to the field of battle, where he was killed and the army destroyed.[25] Bede does not comment favorably on this and it seems that here he deplores the failure of a king in not doing the proper work of a king, in contrast to Oswald, the saintly king of Northumbria whom Bede presents as a great war-leader and also a Christian saint who died willingly in battle at the hands of the same enemy.[26]

Bede was himself a monk and therefore had no illusions about the value of monastic life in itself; and it is not surprising to find, in his letter to Egbert, that he wrote with despondency about the many English monasteries of his day which were aristocratic clubs rather than strongholds of the life of the spirit.[27]

Bede stresses the importance for the conversion of the Anglo-Saxons of the interpenetration of Christian values and the structures of aristocratic society, yet he himself found the social structure of little lasting value. As a monk this greatest of the historians of the conversion of a barbarian nation was not interested in barbarians; he was interested in their end, that is, the kingdom of heaven. It is tempting, however, to see Bede too much as a Doctor of the Church, a man whose greatness and goodness is transtemporal and immediate, and also as a historian who would be entirely at home with modern critical study of texts. This view has its value but it is instructive to look also at

Bede in his own day, a man within his own times and of those times. We know Bede through his own many writings, through his own account of himself, through the comments of contemporaries, and especially in an account of his death drawn by an intimate disciple. He was born in 672 in Northumbria, just after the death of Oswy, while Theodore was archbishop of Canterbury and Wilfrid was pursuing his tempestuous career at York, and when even Mercia could boast of a Christian king. He says nothing of his parents, and this is in accord with his conviction as a monk that earthly parentage is of no importance compared with life in the kingdom.[28] He was given as a child to the monastery of Jarrow, newly founded by Benedict Biscop as a twin monastery with the monastery of St. Peter at Wearmouth, and spent all his life there: "From that time I spent all the days of my life in the said monastery,"[29] until he died sixty-three years old in 735. The offering of small children to monasteries was a common practice and one which is mentioned more than once in the *Ecclesiastical History,* most strikingly perhaps in the case of Elfleda, the daughter of King Oswy, who was dedicated by her father at the age of one ("scarcely a year old") in the monastery of Hartlepool where Hilda was abbess, as a thanksgiving for his victory in the battle of Winwaed.[30] The anonymous account of the *Lives of the Abbots* of Bede's monastery mentions a small boy who, with the Abbot Ceolfrid, alone survived a severe onslaught of the plague there,[31] and it may be that this boy was Bede. His admiration for Ceolfrid and for the other abbots is apparent in Bede's own *Lives of the Abbots.*[32] It is unlikely that Bede ever went further from his monastery than Lindisfarne and possibly York; he never became an abbot or bishop and had no direct influence on church or state. He described his own life thus: "I spent all the days of my life in the said monastery, applying all my study to the meditation of holy Scripture and observing the discipline of the rule and the daily task of singing in the church; it has always been my delight to learn or to teach or to write."[33] The monk Cuthbert who wrote an account of Bede's death assures us that his concern for his pupils continued when he was dying—he occupied his last days in completing a translation of St. John's Gospel into English, a noteworthy part of his concern with those of the English who did not know Latin, and with a selection of passages from Isidore *On the Wonders of Nature*, the most influential book for natural history in the early Middle Ages because, he said, "I cannot have my children learning what is not true, and losing their labor on this after I have gone."[34] Bede was known in his own time as a great commentator on the Scriptures and clearly that is how he wished to be known—his commentaries drew together those of the Latin Fathers of the Church in a "library of the fathers" and Bede expanded them with his own allegorical interpretations of the Scriptures. In this he was of his own time and in the tradition of St. Augustine and St. Gregory the Great, to whom he constantly refers. Of his own times, also, were his books on chronology, which remained the classic authority in Europe until the sixteenth century. Even today we feel the influence of Bede as a chronologer since he adopted and made fashionable our present calculation of years within the Christian era, but it is also true to say that the kind of calculations involved were of more interest to his contemporaries than to ourselves.[35]

To stand in the ruins of the monastery of Jarrow today is to be far from the world of Bede, further than when reading his works. The once-busy monastery, with its rich endowments and the spoils of the Mediterranean world in its walls and windows, in its ornaments and in its library, open to the visits of kings, open also to the poor, full of news of the world from visitors who generally found their way to the cell of Bede, this lively monastery is reduced to silent stones in a grey landscape with industrial Yorkshire on the horizon. Bede died there on the Vigil of Ascension Day, a contented man: "I have not lived so that life among you now would make me ashamed, but I am not afraid to die either, for the God we serve is good."[36] "Not afraid to die": that is to come to the place which Augustine of Hippo recommended to his dying friend Nebridius. "There is need of much withdrawal of oneself from the tumult of the things that are passing away in order that there may be formed in man . . . the ability to say, 'I fear nought.'"[37] This peace of heart fills that *Ecclesiastical History* which Bede wrote towards the end of his life, placing the rivalries, political machinations, greed, valor, and tumult of the Anglo-Saxon kings and nobles within the light of the coming of the kingdom of God; it shows up their limitations and it shows even more the working of the mercy of God within those limitations. At the end of the book, the most vivid of all accounts of a barbarian society in the process of conversion, Bede added his own prayer, as the heir of this tale of nobility, treachery and conversion:

> And I pray thee, merciful Jesus, that as thou hast graciously granted me sweet draughts from the Word which tells of Thee, so wilt Thou of Thy goodness, grant that I may come at length to Thee, the fount of all wisdom, and stand before Thy face forever. Here, with God's help, ends the fifth book of the *History of the English Church.*[38]

NOTES

[1]*The Letters of Saint Boniface,* trans. Emerton, XXXI *Records of Civilization, Sources and Studies,* (Columbia, 1940). Letter LXI (70), p. 134.

[2]*Ibid.*, Letter LIX (75), p. 133.

[3]Bede's *Ecclesiastical History of the English People,* ed. and trans., B. Colgrave and R. A. B. Mynors, (Oxford, 1972), (hereafter referred to as *EHEP*), p. 566.

[4]*Ibid.*, I, 55, p. 74.

[5]*Ibid.*, I, 26, p. 76. No precise date is given by Bede for the conversion of

Ethelbert; for a discussion of the date 597, see Nicholas Brooks, *The Early History of the Church of Canterbury*, (Leicester, 1984), pp. 8-9.

[6]*EHEP*, 2, 9, p. 162.

[7]*Ibid.*, 2, 11, pp. 172-174, for the letter of Pope Boniface to Ethelburga. Letter of Pope Gregory to Queen Bertha, Ep. XXIX, trans. *Epistles of Gregory the Great*, trans. J. Barmby, *A Select Library of Nicene and Post-Nicene Fathers* (Second Series) Vol. XIII, Book XI, letter XXIX, pp. 56-57.

[8]*EHEP*, Bk. 2, 15, pp. 188-190.

[9]The ship-burial at Sutton Hoo has been widely discussed; a thorough analysis can be found in R. L. S. Bruce-Mitford (with others) *The Sutton Hoo Ship-Burial*, 2 vols., 1975, 1978.

[10]*EHEP*, III, 21, p. 280.

[11]*Ibid.*, III, 25, pp. 294-308. For an alternative account of the Council of Whitby, see Eddius Stephanus, *The Life of Wilfrid*, trans. J. F. Webb, edited with introduction by D. H. Farmer in *The Age of Bede*, (Penguin Books, 1965).

[12]*Ibid.*, III, 21, pp. 278-290.

[13]*Ibid.*, III, 24, p. 294.

[14]*Ibid.*, II, 20, p. 204. It is clear that Ethelburga placed no reliance on the Christianity of King Oswald, and removed her family before he could destroy them as possible rivals.

[15]*Ibid.*, III, i, p. 212.

[16]*Ibid.*, III, 18, p. 268.

[17]*Ibid.*, V, 23, p. 560.

[18]*Ibid.*

[19]*Ibid.*, III, 24, p. 292, for the burial of Edwin at Whitby; cf. *The Earliest Life of Gregory the Great* by an Anonymous Monk of Whitby, ed. and trans. B. Colgrave, (Kansas, 1968), p. 104.

[20]*Ibid.*, III, 28, pp. 266-268.

[21]*Ibid.*, IV, 23, pp. 404-414.

[22]Benedict Biscop's life is described by Bede in *The Lives of the Abbots of Wearmouth and Jarrow*, trans. J. F. Webb, in *The Age of Bede*, ed. D. H. Farmer, (Penguin Books, 1965), pp. 185-211.

[23]*EHEP*, III, 14, p. 258.

[24]*Ibid.*

[25]*Ibid.*, III, 28, pp. 266-268.

[26]*Ibid.*, III, 2, pp. 214-218.

[27]Letter to Egbert, archbishop of York, by Bede, trans. D. Whitelock, in *English Historical Documents*, Vol. I, c. 500-1042, (London, 1955). For an instance of the decline in monastic standards see *EHEP* IV, 25, pp. 420-426, in the case of the nuns of Coldingham.

[28]Cf. H. Mayr-Harting, *The Venerable Bede, the Rule of St. Benedict and Social Class*, Jarrow Lecture, 1976.

[29]*EHEP*, V, 24, p. 566.

[30]*Ibid.*, III, 24, pp. 290-292.

[31]*History of the Abbots* by an anonymous author, Latin text ed., Plummer (1896), cap. xiv. Trans. English Historical Documents, vol. I, pp. 758-770.

[32]Bede, *Lives of the Abbots of Wearmouth and Jarrow*, trans. J. F. Webb, ed., D. H. Farmer, (Penguin Books, 1965), *Age of Bede*, pp. 185-211.

[33]*EHEP*, V, 24, p. 566.

[34]Cuthbert's letter on the Death of Bede, *EHEP*, pp. 580-586.

[35]Bede's works on computation are edited by C. Jones, (1943).

[36]Cuthbert's Letter on the Death of Bede, *EHEP*, p. 582.

[37]*Letters of St. Augustine of Hippo*, X, to Nebridius; trans. M. Dods, (Edinburgh, 1872), p. 24.

[38]*EHEP*, V, 24, p. 570.

XIII

A CONVERTING ORDINANCE

Some reflections on the hymns of Charles Wesley in the light of medieval biblical commentary.

> If anyone wants to be converted to the Lord, let him pray from his heart that the veil of the letter might be taken away and the light of the Spirit come, as it is said, 'we all behold with open face as in a glass the glory of the Lord and are changed into that image from glory to glory even as by the Lord the Spirit'.[1]

This sentence is not from John Wesley's 'Preface to a Collection of Hymns for Use of the People Called Methodists', though it sounds very like it. It is, in fact, from Origen's *Commentary on the Book of Genesis*. John Wesley introduced the hymns of the Methodist Hymn Book in the eighteenth century with much the same approach to the essentials of Christian life as Origen in the third century. It is this similarity of *approach* that I would like to examine rather than a direct influence, though John Wesley thought well of Origen and other church fathers: 'I reverence their writings because they describe true, genuine Christianity and direct us to the strongest evidence of the Christian doctrine'. His respect for the fathers of the church was not, however, without reservations: he remarked briskly of a list of fathers he had read which contained not only Origen but also Irenaeus, Clement and Cyprian: 'Some of these had not strong natural sense'. It is a typically eighteenth century caveat, but in fact both John and Charles Wesley had much in common with those early fathers, especially in the way they regarded the Bible.[2]

I do not want to show that the Wesleys were directly influenced by reading the fathers in their attitude to scripture; that is certainly true, as Henry Bett and others have shown. Nor do I want to establish a link between Charles Wesley and ancient or medieval traditions of hymnography, which seems extremely unlikely. What I would like to illustrate is a rather simple point: that the hymns of Charles Wesley are a part of the ancient Christian tradition of biblical exegesis and as such they are examples of a common Christian attitude which arises spontaneously in different parts of the divided church. To do this, firstly I will analyse three of Charles Wesley's hymns in detail relating them to the early traditions of Bible study. Secondly, I will draw attention to the words of the hymns in relation to the scriptures and to the early exegesis of those passages which they so faithfully reflect. For this I will often make use of the commentaries of the Venerable Bede, partly because he sums up the tradition of the fathers as well as contributing to it in a very marked manner, partly because he is the first and greatest of English commentators on the Bible, and also because to do so indicates the continuing tradition of commentary through the Middle Ages, even in that '*alter orbis*', England. I will for convenience talk about 'medieval' biblical exegesis, though, of course, that was formed by patristic exegesis, in order to underline the fact that for more than a thousand years of Christian history this tradition was as central in the West as in the East.

For the Middle Ages, the key to understanding the scriptures lay in the Gospels themselves. In the Gospel of St Luke, in the story of the disciples on the road to Emmaus (Lk. 24.26–7), they read: 'Beginning at Moses and all the prophets, he expounded unto them in all the scriptures the things concerning himself'. The claim that Christ himself used the Old Testament to illuminate the New produced three convictions about exegesis: firstly, the words of the scriptures could be used as the surest interpreter of themselves; they were seen as the words of one writer, the Holy Spirit, and different parts of the scriptures were therefore used together with complete assurance that they would illuminate one another. Secondly, since Christ had used the scripture to show 'the things concerning himself' this led directly to what came to be called the spiritual, doctrinal meaning of the scriptures, that is, the conviction that every part of the scriptures contained some kind of Good News about the person of Christ, though such meaning was often hidden. That is exactly what Origen meant in the passages already quoted when he talked about the 'veil of the letter' being removed so that, quoting St Paul, 'we may see . . . the glory of the Lord'. Thirdly, the early commentators also understood from this passage that such study was indeed a '*converting ordinance*':

'Did not our heart burn within us, while he talked with us by the way, and while he opened to us the scriptures?' (Lk. 24.32). This gave them what they referred to as the 'moral' meaning of the text, that is, how it applied to the reader in his own relationship with Christ, what Origen calls being 'converted to the Lord'. As Bede says, to read the scriptures is to receive the Word of God through both a deeper understanding of the mystery of Christ and its application to mankind:

> by breaking the bread which He gave to His disciples, the Lord designates the secret meanings by which the world was to be nourished unto perpetual salvation.[3]

Most of all, it was in the verse, 'Ought not Christ to have suffered these things', that ancient writers found their key to the Bible. In commenting on the book of Esdras, Bede sees in the rebuilding of the Temple a detailed pattern of redemption, and exclaims, 'by the Lord's passion the vast abyss of the Scriptures has been laid open to us'.[4]

The hymns of Charles Wesley are most clearly understood as forming a part of this tradition. In them the two Testaments are constantly used to interpret one another. They draw from the text of scripture meditations on the person of Christ, leading to conversion of the heart. Again and again it is this double sense of the scriptures which is instinctively taken up and turned into poetry and music, for both private meditation and congregational singing. Here of course is another way in which Charles Wesley's hymns belong to the medieval and, in fact, monastic tradition of praying the scriptures. Throughout the Middle Ages, the text of scripture was not regarded as well read unless it was read in two ways: first, proclaimed by Christians together in a liturgical context with participation of each by voice and action; and secondly, used by Christians in private for *lectio divina*, in such a way that the individual could be penetrated by the divine Word. The great mass of biblical learning, that intense stretching of the mind and intellect which is so notable throughout the Middle Ages was not divorced from life and practice: learning had one end, the study of the sacred page as food for the soul. Bede says about the scriptures:

> Sometimes it is food for us, sometimes drink, In the more obscure places it is food because it is broken as it were by explanation and it

is swallowed after chewing; but it is drink in the clearer places, because there it is absorbed just as it is found.[5]

To feed on the word of God for the early church was to read the scriptures as well as to receive the eucharistic elements. It was the same for the Wesleys; in his meditation on the Lord's Prayer, John Wesley gave as the primary meaning of 'daily bread', 'things pertaining to life and godliness' which included the daily feeding upon the scriptures in prayer, though he also interpreted it as meaning the eucharist:

It was the judgment of many of the ancient Fathers that we are here to understand the sacramental bread also; . . . highly esteemed, till the love of many waxed cold, as the grand channel whereby the grace of His Spirit was conveyed to the souls of all the children of God.[6]

In presenting three of Charles Wesley's hymns I would like to insist that they belong above all to this medieval tradition of liturgical meditation: they were meant to be sung and they were meant to be prayed, not expounded; any talk about them can only be a feeble suggestion of how they can be understood.

'And can it be'

Firstly, I want to look at the second of Wesley's conversion hymns, 'And can it be' (MHB 371), almost certainly by Charles though it has been attributed to John. It reflects very clearly the brothers' reaction to those moments which they regarded as definitive for their faith, when, to use Origen's words, they were 'turned to the Lord'. On May 21st 1738, Charles received an inward assurance of faith, and three days later his brother John also found his heart 'strangely warmed'–two moments which, may I suggest in passing, are illuminated when seen in the medieval tradition of 'compunction', the piercing of the heart by love and fear of God. A result of Charles's conversion was to release fully his latent gift for hymnody, which became the centre of his spiritual life. It issued at once in a hymn (MHB 361) marvelling at the grace of God:

Where shall my wondering soul begin?
How shall I all to heaven aspire?

and a few days later another 'thanksgiving for salvation' (MHB 371) was written at Little Britain. This more sophisticated hymn expressed in poetry of even greater appeal the experience of both brothers, giving it a universal and scriptural expression:

> And can it be that I should gain
> An interest in my Saviour's blood?

Charles begins, using a modern and daring image taken from a trade much respected in eighteenth century England, banking. The images are then mainly from the New Testament, above all from St Paul, which is in line with the *Commentaries* of Luther on Romans and Galatians which underpinned the conversion of both brothers. The first three verses combine Romans 5.8, 1 Peter 1.2, and Philippians 2.7, so that each illuminates the other and all are applied personally. The first verse both sets out the doctrinal meanings of texts of St Paul, that is, their spiritual sense, and applies it in the moral, that is, the personal sense. 'But God shows his love for us that while we were yet sinners Christ died for the ungodly' (Rom. 5.8) is restated with the reiteration of 'for me' throughout the verse:

> Died He for me who caused His pain?
> For me, who Him to death pursued?
> Amazing love! How can it be
> That Thou, my God shouldst die for me!

In the second verse, this mystery of love which gives itself for the salvation of sinners and which is described in 1 Peter 1.2 as 'things which the angels desire to look into' becomes

> In vain the first-born seraph tries
> To sound the depths of love divine.

The third verse makes personal the Christological poetry of Paul in Philippians 2.7: 'He thought it not robbery to be equal with God but emptied himself' (Phil. 2.6–7) becomes

> Emptied himself of all but love,
> And bled for Adam's helpless race.

The last verse applies this doctrinal understanding of atonement personally in an amazing combination of many key Pauline verses. Not only does Romans 8.1, 'Therefore there is now no condemnation to them that are in Christ Jesus' become

> No condemnation now I dread,

but 1 Cor. 15.22, 'as in Adam all die so also in Christ shall all be made alive' becomes,

> Jesus, and all in Him are mine!

The next line, 'And clothed in righeousness divine,' takes up a verse from the Old Testament, Job 29.14, 'I put on righteousness, and it clothed me: my judgment was as a robe and a diadem', and combines it with Romans 13.14, 'put ye on the Lord Jesus Christ', and Galatians 3.27, 'you have put on Christ'. The climax of the hymn,

Bold I approach the eternal throne
And claim the crown, through Christ, my own.

is a combinations of Ephesians 3.12, 'In whom we have boldness and access by the faith of him', and the great images of the book of Revelation, 'I will give him a new robe', 'I will give him a crown of life'. Such a combination of scriptural texts to illuminate one another for the believer is essentially patristic and medieval, but it is the fourth verse that used the early tradition of exegesis most markedly, in a personal application of the story in Acts 12.6–9, of Peter's delivery from prison:

Long my imprisoned spirit lay,
Fast bound in sin and nature's night;

Here the text of Acts has been applied to the individual in relation to redemption by Christ. The soul, like Peter, is held in a prison, which is sin and sinful nature, composed of the five senses and the four elements of the world, according to the interpretation of biblical numbers from the third century onwards. Like Peter, the soul is delivered by a messenger of God, that is Christ, the angel, the one who is sent, and the chains of habit fall off as he goes forward, set free.

Thine eye diffused a quickening ray–
I woke, the dungeon flamed with light;
My chains fell off, my heart was free,
I rose, went forth, and followed Thee.

Bede comments on this passage from Acts in the same way as Charles Wesley, connecting the 'deliverance' of the soul even more specifically with the Cross:

> The blow on the side [of Peter] is a reminder of the passion of Christ from whose wound salvation flowed. And to us also, held by binding chains, the apostle Peter gives consolation from this saying, Christ therefore suffered in the flesh and we should also arm ourselves in our thoughts.[7]

To trace such references, and they are by no means exhaustive, is to discover another medieval trait in Charles Wesley: he does not quote the scriptures but brings out of his mind what is there already. He reminisces, uses what is there, combining phrases and words by an instinctive Christian understanding; he brings, as did every medieval writer, 'things new and old' out of the scriptures simply by absorbing them into his being and then writing and speaking. It is a use of memory which was integral to the ancient world and to take apart any medieval text is to discover this; so it is with these hymns.

'Happy the man that finds the grace,'

Secondly, I want to look at a much less famous hymn, 'Happy the man who finds the grace,' (MHB 360). It is a careful exegesis of Proverbs 3.13–18, and here the commentary of Bede on Proverbs is very close in method and content to Wesley's poem. Like the former hymn, 'Happy the man' it is included in the *Methodist Hymn Book* among the hymns grouped under the heading, 'The Christian Life'; it is included in the part called 'Repentance and Forgiveness', and it is followed directly by the Wesleys' first conversion hymn. It is a tranquil hymn, a meditation on the peace of heart that comes from the experience of 'evangelical conversion'. The whole account in Proverbs of the blessings given to the one who loves wisdom is transferred in both Bede and Charles Wesley to the Christian, and the blessings of the chosen race are transferred to the Christian church, the new Israel, the New Testament illuminating the Old. Moreover, 'Wisdom' is presented as 'Christ, the wisdom of God', as Bede says of this verse of Proverbs: 'Wisdom clearly is Christ'. The last line of the first verse, 'the faith that sweetly works by love' is based not on Proverbs, but on Galatians 5.6, 'the faith that works by love' which, as I have shown elsewhere, was an important concept for Bede, as 'faith which does the works of love'. The second verse of the hymn summarizes again the experience of the Wesleys through their own 'evangelical conversion' with their familiar emphasis on personal salvation:

> Happy beyond description he
> Who knows: The Saviour died for me!

As John Wesley said, 'an assurance was given me that Christ had taken away my sins, *even mine*, and saved *me* from the law of sin and death'. In Proverbs, the verse that is relevant is 'understanding will guard you, delivering you, from the way of evil' (2.11–12). Verse three of the hymn,

Wisdom divine! Who tells the price
Of wisdom's costly merchandise?
Wisdom to silver we prefer,
And gold is dross compared to her.

is based closely on Proverbs 3.14, 'the gain of it is better than gain from silver and its profit better than gold' which Bede links with 'a greater treasure laid up in heaven' (cf. Matthew 19.21).

Her hands are filled with length of days,
True riches, and immortal praise,
Riches of Christ, on all bestowed
And honour that descends from God.

has as its basis Proverbs 3.16, 'long life is in her right hand and in her left are riches and honour', which Bede, like Wesley, sees as the promises of God in redemption:

> He bestows in perpetual light the vision of His Godhead to His elect and them in this present life He illuminates and strengthens by His sacraments and gifts. He gives to them who bought from him by selling all an hundred fold in this life and life eternal in the age to come.[8]

The next verse

To purest joys she all invites,
Chaste, holy, spiritual delights;
Her ways are ways of pleasantness,
And all her flowery paths are peace.

is based closely on 'her ways are ways of pleasantness and all her paths are peace' (Prov. 3.17), Bede takes this verse as prophetic of the peace of redemption: 'everything which He bore in the flesh for reconciling man to God, for making peace between angels and men, for showing how God ought to be served, is for us both peace and longing love', surely a meaning contained within the otherwise rather bland phrases of this verse.[9]

The last verse of the hymn makes poetry of the practical injunction of Proverbs, reiterated again and again to 'keep Wisdom', and combines it with the phrase of St Paul, 'Christ the power of God and the wisdom of God' (1 Cor. 1.24). Bede speaks of 'the wisdom of God that is Christ gives life to the church now through the flesh and blood received and in the future blessedness in His presence.' and contrasts the 'pointless praises of men in this life' with the 'praise by Wisdom in the future', the same link between Christ and Wisdom and heaven as in Charles Wesley's last line, 'Wisdom and Christ and heaven are one.'

'Thou Shepherd of Israel and mine'

The third hymn on which I want to comment is a hymn so deeply part of the mystical commentary on scripture that John Wesley at first disapproved of it for public worship. This is 'Thou Shepherd of Israel, and mine,' (MHB 457), a meditation based on the Song of Songs. The first line shows the double interpretation placed on the scriptural text throughout: the 'shepherd' is Christ; and he is not only the shepherd of Israel, that is, the church, but also shepherd of the soul of the reader, a use of the doctrinal interpretation of the scriptures intricately combined with its personal, moral application. The phrase from Psalm 80, 'Hear, O Thou Shepherd of Israel', combined with 'He shall feed his flock like a shepherd, (Isa. 40.11), and 'The Lord is my shepherd (Ps. 23.1), have been applied to Christ from earliest times, on the basis of his own claim in John to be 'the good shepherd'. The lines of the hymn,

> The pasture I languish to find
> Where all, who their Shepherd obey,
> Are fed, on Thy bosom reclined,
> And screened from the heat of the day.

are derived from Isaiah 40.11, 'he shall gather the lambs in his bosom', and the Song of Songs 1.7, 'where thou liest at noon day'. This idea is carried straight into the second verse,

> Ah! show me that happiest place,
> The place of Thy people's abode,

where the same verse of the Song of Songs, 'Show me where thou feedest thy flock', is turned into a direct link with the Passion of Christ, an interpretation common to the fathers which is given full expression in the next lines

> Where saints in an ecstasy gaze,
> And hang on a crucified God;

The idea of the pierced side as the place of the heart of Christ and so the centre of the love of God which is heaven is completed in the final couplet,

Concealed in the cleft of Thy side,
Eternally held in Thy heart.

Bede in his commentary on the Song of Songs also gives both a Christological and a personal interpretation to this passage:

> He who pastures his sheep lies down among them at midday within the hearts of his faithful ones, lest the fire of temptation kindle in them; he refreshes them with the remembrance of the sweetness of heaven and remains there graciously among them.[10]

The great commentator, however, on this passage and one even closer to Wesley than Bede is Bernard of Clairvaux in his sermons based on the Song of Songs where he says,

> O my dove that art in the clefts of the rock . . . the literal meaning yields us not much but . . . the clefts of the rock are the wounds of Christ . . . the rock is the refuge of the conies and where indeed is there more complete security and rest for us frail men save in the Saviour's wounds?[11]

It is an amazing tour de force by Charles Wesley to have bound together in a hymn for popular use so much of the mystical and liturgical interpretation of the church fathers.

Two final points occur to me in thinking about these hymns of the Wesleys within the tradition of medieval scriptural exegesis. Firstly, they are not emotional and sentimental instances of enthusiasm connected with a moment of personal experience; they are the controlled and redirected use of emotion combined with a very strong doctrinal understanding, which is instinctively within the main lines of Christian tradition. Like Bede and all other commentators of the early church, the Wesleys were concerned with the exact and literal meaning of the words of scripture and would use their Greek Testaments to correct where necessary the English version whose balanced cadences they loved. The grammatical sense was as important to them as to their predecessors; and like them, the Wesleys studied the words of scripture closely. But the meaning of the texts was for them not confined to the meaning the words had for their human authors. When Charles Wesley wrote his hymn about Bible study (MHB 310)

When quiet in my house I sit,
Thy Book be my companion still,

he saw the scriptures not as historical documents, but as 'the records of Thy will' to be 'searched . . . till every heartfelt word be mine', and every medieval commentator would have agreed with him. Study of the Bible was a part of prayer in the ancient world, which had no separate concept of 'theology' and 'spirituality' but simply the 'study of the Sacred Page' which included what later ages divided out. The pages of the early commentaries on the scriptures read like homilies, turning the text into living prayer in all its aspects. In the same way, thankfulness and praise mark the hymns of Charles Wesley as much as those other traditional parts of prayer: repentance and intercession; indeed, the desire that all men may come to the love of God filled each hymn, from the first amazed moments of the brothers' conversion which produced in their first conversion hymn (MHB 361) the line 'Come, O my guilty brethren, come'.[12]

Secondly, the hymns of Charles Wesley were composed for private meditation, but most of all, they were intended for singing as part of the services of the church. They were a kind of devout Christian meditation upon the texts of the Bible made living within liturgical gatherings of the people of God. In this they provide a rare instance of non-scriptural material used in worship. Long before the Reformation the Western tradition of worship saw the text of the Bible as almost the only source for words used in the church, but the hymns of Charles Wesley are, instinctively, part of another tradition of worship. In what other church is there such freedom about the use in worship of the poetic meditation of the Christian spirit on the words of scripture, turning both doctrine and personal involvement into song? Certainly in the Orthodox church, especially in the Odes used at its Offices. In Orthodox Mattins, for instance, for the Feast of the Annunciation, the theological understanding of redemption which Irenaeus found in St Paul finds poetic expression as

> The Son of God becomes the Son of man, that, sharing in what is worse, He may make me share in what is better. In times of old Adam was once deceived: he sought to become God, but received not his desire. Now God becomes man, that He may make Adam God. (*The Festal Menaion*, trans., Mother Mary and Kallistos Ware, Faber and Faber, p. 460)

A hymn of Charles Wesley (MHB 568) takes up the same exegesis and applies it to the singer himself:

Heavenly Adam, Life divine,
Change my nature into Thine;
Move and spread throughout my soul,
Actuate and fill the whole;
Be it I no longer now
Living in the flesh, but Thou.

Every example I have used from the hymns of Charles Wesley could be paralleled in Orthodox worship, but more striking than details of exegesis is the similarity of understanding in two parts of the Christian poetic tradition; they have the same way of looking towards Christ and expressing it in music. The fathers saw the human body as the harp of the Spirit, and interpreted the last verses of the psalter in just that way: to be stretched out like the strings of a harp or cithern is to be stretched, they said, like Christ on the wood of the Cross; the body wholly given as the Spirit breathes over the strings:[13]

Come, Thou everlasting Spirit,
Bring to every thankful mind
All the Saviour's dying merit,
All His sufferings for mankind:

Come, Thou Witness of His dying;
Come, Remembrancer divine,
Let us feel Thy power, applying
Christ to every soul, and mine, Amen. (MHB 765)

It is the central tradition of Christianity and one in which Charles Wesley was clearly at home.

This talk was given originally at the St Theosevia Centre for Christian Spirituality in Oxford on 12th March 1988.

NOTES

All hymns are quoted from *The Methodist Hymn Book*, London, 1933.

Quotations from the Scriptures are from the Authorised Version of the Bible.

The Latin text of Bede's commentaries on Scripture will be found in the editions of *Corpus Christianorum Series Latina*, Turnholt 1960–1962, vols CXIX, CXIXa, XXX, hereinafter refered to by the titles of: Bede's commentaries with page numbers to these editions: the English translations are my own.

1. Origen, *Homilia in Genesim* 6:1, ed. with French translation A. Doutreleau, *Sources Chrétiennes* 7 (Paris 1976).

2. John Wesley, 'A Plain Account of Genuine Christianity, 1753' in *John and Charles Wesley: Selected Writings and Hymns* ed. Frank Whaling, Classics of Western Spirituality, Paulist Press/SPCK 1981, p.133.

3. Bede, *In Marcam* p.611.

4. Bede, *In Ezra et Neemiam* p.352.

5. Bede, *In Lucam* p.272.

6. John Wesley, 'Sermon on the Mount VI', in *John and Charles Wesley: Selected Writings* op.cit. p.116.

7. Bede *On Acts* XII: 7.

8. Bede *In Proverbia Salomonis* p.42.

9. ibid. p.42

10. Bede *in Cantica Canticorum* p.200.

11. Bernard of Clairvaux, *On the Song of Songs* 11:14; Sermon 61.

12. John Wesley, *Journal* 'I began to pray with all my might for those who had in a more especial manner despitefully used me and persecuted me' op.cit. p.107.

13. cf. Augustine of Hippo, *On the Psalms* on Ps.CXL1X:4.

XIV

TRANSLATOR'S CHARITY

For I have translated in the charity, which makes things better,
and so I trust that I shall be translated myself at the last.
Christopher Smart, *Jubilate Agno*

❦ It is often supposed that the mention of 'charity' in connection with academic or literary work automatically leads to a lessening of truth and accuracy. In theory, of course, the reverse should be the case; God who is truth is also and equally love. There is, in the end, no question of priorities:

There we shall be still and see; we shall see and we shall love; we shall love and we shall praise. Behold what shall be in the end without end![1]

The art of the Christian translator rests in both 'seeing' with the clear eye of truth and 'loving' at the same time, in the light of the 'end without end'. There is a long tradition of 'charitable' translation, in the sense of Christopher Smart's 'in the charity', which enhances rather than lessens accuracy and truth. This is not to suggest that Christian translators have any kind of monopoly of charity about their work; clearly, an honourable translator does his work because he loves both the text and its transmission, and the basis of that love is a concern for accuracy and truth. For the translator of Christian texts, the obligation to seek truth through accuracy is underlined and not contradicted by the equal obligation to charity. It is in fact more astringent because most Christian literature, above all the Bible, is not translated for antiquarian or aesthetic purposes but for practical utility in the work of prayer. The translation therefore must be transparent for the orginal inspiration to shine through clearly, but also made available for the reader to use as a way to God for himself, without the distraction of thinking about the text as a translation. It is not meant to be a literature for casual curiosity. The author of *The Cloud of Unknowing*, for instance, insists in his prologue that

whoever you may be who possess this book, . . . you should, quite freely and of set purpose, neither read, write nor mention it to anyone, nor allow it to be read, written or mentioned by anyone unless that person is in your judgement really and wholly determined to follow Christ perfectly.[2]

Presumably that same stricture would apply to the same author's translation of the *Mystica Theologia* as *Dionise Hid Divinite*. Christian literature is designed for the purpose of aiding conversion of the heart towards God, and the demands of truth and love in conveying it from one language to another are part of the process. It is, of course, easy to corrupt such a pragmatic approach and make it a political one, and at once examples leap to mind of tendentious translations of Christian literature, where the translator is determined to support his own ideas about right thinking through his text, but this is always at the expense of truth. It is the balance of love and truth that 'makes things better', not either one without the other. This ideal is not an easy matter to write about; nevertheless it is an ideal, and one related to a concern of all Christian scholars, the pursuit of learning and the desire for God.

Christians were concerned with translation from the start. The Old Testament was used by the early Church not in Hebrew but in the Greek translation known as the Septuagint, simply because Christians in the Greek-speaking world did not generally read Hebrew, and as Christianity spread among Latin-speaking converts, translations into Latin of both Old and New Testaments were not so much desirable as essential. Even so fine a scholar as St Augustine seemed reluctant to read Greek where Latin was available. He was certainly aware that the young Christians of north Africa would be more accustomed to using translations into Latin of the New Testament than reading the text in Greek. The best way, of course, and this is always so, was for them not to need translations, and when St Augustine provided directions about reading in *On Chrisian Doctrine*, he says at once that some knowledge of Hebrew and Greek at least should support the use of the second-best way of using translations:

> The sovereign remedy [against being misled] is a knowledge of languages, and Latin-speaking men, whom we have here undertaken to instruct, need two others for a knowledge of the Divine Scriptures, Hebrew and Greek, so that they may turn back to earlier exemplars if the infinite variety of Latin translations gives rise to any doubts.[3]

Like any modern university teacher, St Augustine had to set his sights low; he knew, as we all do, that very few would actually know enough Greek and Hebrew to read the Scriptures regularly in the original languages. But he was alert to the dangers of translations and required his students at least to be able to check. Accurate knowledge of what the authors actually wrote is his first requirement for the Christian scholar. Some words, he says, are in fact untranslatable and he cites 'amen', 'alleluia', 'racha', and 'hosanna'[4] as instances of this. But it is not for this that he recommends a working knowledge of two languages; it is for checking words and phrases when confronted with a wide variety of divergent translations, since, 'in the early times of the faith anyone who found a Greek codex and thought that he had some facility in both languages attempted to translate it'. Clearly the pitfalls for translators as regards accuracy were no different in the fourth century. A poor knowledge of either language could wreck translation: 'many translators are deceived by ambiguity in the original language which they do not understand so that they transfer the meaning to something completely alien to the writer's intention'. In a long passage St Augustine takes a practical stance about what is possible for the average student who cannot check faulty translations for himself. To these, he recommends the use of 'those who translate word for word, not because they suffice but because by means of them we may test the truth or falsity of those who have sought to translate meanings as well as words'. Literal, word-for-word translation is not sufficient to convey the content of the text, but it is helpful in determining meaning.

Grammar, then, for St Augustine, mattered; the meaning of the original writer must be understood as accurately as possible; it should then be conveyed to the reader as clearly as possible in his own language; and a translation should be regarded as a way into the text, not a substitute for it. But St Augustine surrounds this basic, fundamental demand for accuracy with another kind of hard work for the scholar: the first section of *On Christian Doctrine* is about a preliminary requirement: the love of God, charity: 'It is to be understood that the plenitude and the end of the Law and of all sacred Scriptures is the love of a Being which is to be enjoyed'.[5] And after his instructions on the necessity for careful attention to the text, St Augustine asserts again the primacy of charity in its interpretation:

> Thus when the tyranny of cupidity has been overthrown, charity reigns with its most just laws of love for God for the sake of God, and of one's self and of one's neighbour for the sake of God. Therefore in the considera-

tion of figurative expressions a rule such as this will serve, that what is read should be subject to diligent scrutiny until an interpretation contributing to the reign of charity shall be produced.[6]

Love and truth cannot be in opposition; what is true will also be charitable, and what is charitable will also be true.

St Augustine does not mean by 'charity' a woolly kind of niceness that will distort the text. He has already defined charity as 'the motion of the soul towards the enjoyment of God for his own sake and enjoyment of one's self and of one's neighbour for the sake of God'.[7] If a translation does not promote this desire for and enjoyment of God, then it cannot be the true meaning of the text. For St Augustine, charity is the context as well as the content of a translation. Translation must be accurate, and part of that accuracy is to discover charity towards the writer and towards the readers, and towards God within the text. It must also be then a truth transmitted in words appropriate to the truth. Here St Augustine was dealing with a matter which is not quite the same in translations into English, though the principle is applicable. Latin versions of the Scriptures in the fourth century were for reading aloud, and the pointing and stress of the language could help or hinder its intelligibility. Thus, while St Augustine takes a brisk line with those who worry about pronouncing '*ignoscere* . . . with a long or a short syllable', when their concern should be with 'asking God to forgive . . . sins',[8] he is equally sure that correct and even elegant language should be used in the reading aloud of a text; the speaker must 'teach, delight and persuade';[9] if he does not take care to make the form of his discourse attractive, he will simply not be heard at all. Nor is this idea of 'enjoyment' a mere trick of pedagogy; for those who love the true God in all things, St Augustine speaks in the language of desire and enjoyment from his own heart:

> I have learned to love you late, Beauty at once so ancient and so new! I have learned to love you late . . . I tasted you and now I hunger and thirst for you. You touched me, and I am inflamed with love of your peace.[10]

Enjoyment of language for its own sake is not a concern of St Augustine. Beneath the work of the translator there is always the fact of utility and service rather than aesthetics. The transmission of the true meaning of a text through another language is not primarily for the enjoyment of the translator, who is after all well able to read the original. To undertake translation is in itself a part of charity. It is primarily when there is widespread ignorance of the original language that those who do understand it must undertake translation. It is a service, a way of offering treasure to others. This primary motive of charity towards those less well equipped for reading has been a constant motive in translation from other languages into English, just as it was for St Augustine from Greek and Hebrew into Latin. The difference is that translators into English have rarely supposed that their translations would lead readers towards the original languages; in fact, rather the contrary. Translations, it is true, have often been treated in England as cribs, and therefore to be outlawed and confiscated presumably because of a hidden certainty in the minds of preceptors that children will not go to the trouble of learning a language if they can get the meaning out of a text in any other way. Nevertheless, it is not as cribs but as new texts that translations have been most popular with the English, and this began very early indeed in our history. Two Englishmen in the early middle ages in particular exercised this charity towards others by providing translations of ancient texts, and both followed the ideals and precepts of St Augustine in doing so. The first of these was Bede (*c.* 673–735).

Bede himself wrote primarily in Latin, the literary language of the newly formed Church among the Anglo-Saxons. He was however concerned that the Gospel should be understood by those who knew no Latin, in fact, the vast majority of the new converts. In the *Ecclesiastical History of the English People*, he notes with approval that King Oswald of Northumbria acted as translator for the Irish monk, Bishop Aidan, when the latter preached to the English:

> While the bishop, who was not yet fluent in the English language, preached the Gospel, it was most delightful to see the king himself interpreting the word of God to his ealdormen and thanes; for he himself had obtained perfect command of the Irish tongue during his long exile.[11]

For Bede, translation was necessary for the ignorant, and it should therefore be the duty of the translator to work carefully in order not to mislead those who were made completely vulnerable by their ignorance. He says that he himself corrected and clarified 'a book on *The life and sufferings of Saint Anastasius*, which had been badly translated from the Greek, and worse amended by some unskilful person'.[12] And the monk Cuthbert described how Bede continued to work at translations into English on his death-bed:

TRANSLATOR'S CHARITY

He translated into our language, for the profit of the church of God, from the beginning of St John's Gospel to the place where it is said, 'but what are they among so many?' and some extracts from the works of Bishop Isidore, for he said, 'I would not that my children should read a lie and labour therein without fruit when I am gone.'[13]

In a letter to Bishop Egbert, Bede had insisted that the teaching and prayers of the Church should be made available to 'those who are acquainted with no language but their own'.[14] He had himself taught the Lord's Prayer and the Creed in English to both laymen and priests. Significantly, his purpose was neither academic nor artistic but practical:

For thus is it brought to pass that every band of the faithful may learn how to be faithful, by what steadfastness they ought to fortify and arm themselves against the assaults of the unclean spirits; and that every choir of suppliants to God may understand what especially should be sought from the Divine clemency.[15]

As for St Augustine, translation for Bede was part of the greater 'charity' of a whole life turned towards Christ.

The task of translation was taken up two hundred years after Bede by another Englishman, in the same spirit of service for the use of those otherwise cut off from the Latin past. King Alfred the Great, occupied, as he says, in a great many other tasks, still found time for translation. In his preface to his first translation, that of St Gregory the Great's treatise for the use of bishops, *On Pastoral Care*, Alfred says that he translated

sometimes word for word, sometimes sense for sense . . . I translated it into English as best I understood it and as I could most meaningfully render it; I intend to send a copy to each bishopric in my kingdom.[16]

It was meant to be a useful book, to help bishops care for the Christians in their churches, not an academic exercise for the literate. Alfred allowed himself more liberty with the text than either St Augustine or Bede. Like Queen Elizabeth after him, he also translated the *Consolation of Philosophy* of Boethius into English, and gave a freer rendering than in his work on St Gregory, rearranging the order, re-casting it as a dialogue between the inquirer's mind and the personification of Wisdom, and giving personal reflections on God and the world in place of some of the more autobiographical sections. His translation of the *Soliloquies* of St Augustine were still more free, but in his translation of the first fifty psalms into English, a text above all meant for prayer, he returned to a literal yet readable rendering of the text. These royal translations, the work of a busy man, were not for ornament but for use. They were for those who could 'derive very little benefit from [Latin] books because they could understand nothing of them since they were not written in their own language'.

Both Bede and Alfred, like St Augustine, translated in order to transmit to others poorer than themselves the riches of the past, and each had also the intention of increasing charity for others as well as for themselves by so doing. The whole man, mind and body, was to be brought into the service of Christ, and the living word of the Scriptures was to reach everyone for their response. By translation, other Latin writers who had commented on the text of Scripture or given advice about the conduct of Christian life were also to be opened to the ignorant present. For those undertaking this task three things were needed: first, a thorough knowledge of the original text; then the humility which stands back and allows what was written by someone else to be transmitted; and thirdly a command of the new language so that readers could appropriate the text and use it for the extension of the kingdom of God which is the reign of love.

The late middle ages and pre-eminently the Reformation saw the flowering of English translation, most of all in 'Bibles fair and old', and in particular that monument to the translator's art, the King James version of the Bible. But in the nineteenth century, English churchmen seriously undertook this task of charitable translation again, and for very much the same reasons as their predecessors. The Oxford Movement was primarily concerned with the revival of religion in England, where its members saw an alarming growth of secularity, which they called 'liberalism', in all parts of the Church. Against such 'liberalism' Pusey, Newman and Keble decided to set the zeal and purity of faith in the early Church. Themselves excellent classical scholars, and members of the senior common room at Oriel, their acquaintance with the ancient Latin and Greek fathers was fluent and easy. They naturally read the Scriptures in Hebrew and Greek, and Pusey at least was well acquainted with many other languages too. Yet they were aware, and it surprised and pained them, that there were many other members of the Church of England, even among the clergy, who could read only English. There must, therefore, be translations as well as editions of texts. The series which occupied their energies they called 'The Library of the Fathers', a phrase first coined by Bede. It was a project of translation undertaken for a purpose as missionary-orientated as that of St

Augustine, Bede or Alfred. Like them, they bowed down their proud and scholarly necks before the yoke of translation for the ignorant, like them they insisted on the highest standards of accuracy, and like them also they had in mind no mere antiquarian effort, but a living contact with the tradition of the Church. Unlike their predecessors, however, their work was undertaken in a new scholarly atmosphere, for both texts and translations. The critical editions of ancient texts had been undertaken already, and the editions of the Maurists[17] provided far more texts and alternative readings of the Church Fathers than were available to any one person in the whole of the ancient or medieval world. Moreover, the work of translation was already being discussed as an art, most notably in Matthew Arnold's essay *On Translating Homer*. The Tractarians were well aware of the critical gaze their colleagues turned upon their enterprise, which gave to their translations the edge of debate as well as the content of devotion. Newman at once disagreed with Arnold's plea for 'translation from poesie into poesie', and urged, in his *Reply*, verbal exactness above all. The translation of the Fathers of the Church, Tractarians and classicists all agreed, should be above all accurate; but a division arose between Pusey and Newman about the amount of freedom to be allowed translators in turning Latin or Greek into readable English. Pusey was in favour of exact literal translations, which preserved the Latin sentence structure as far as possible; Newman, for all his opposition to Arnold, feared the unreadability which was already a characteristic even of Pusey's original writings in English, and therefore cautiously suggested a certain measure of idiomatic English. In a letter to Pusey, Newman wrote:

> I do not like diffusive translations. Unliteralness is no more diffuse than the contrary; I only meant not word for word. *Placet mihi* may be Englished 'it pleases me' or 'I please'. Here, what is least literal, whether better or not, is shorter. All I meant was idiomatic translation.[18]

Pusey replied that while he agreed with Newman on 'the principles of translation, I think that one might even sacrifice idiom, if one may call it so, to retain the effect of the original'.[19] His own translations were in a rigid style, as indeed were those of John Keble. But for the direction of those who undertook translations for the series he eventually wrote to Keble:

> My instruction to translators is a clear, nervous, condensed unparaphrastic style, and thus as free and as like the original, and idiomatic as may be.[20]

In his Preface to his translation of St Augustine's *Confessions*, Pusey set out his theory of translation more fully:

> The object of all translation must be to present the ideas of the author as clearly as may be, with as little sacrifice as may be of what is peculiar to him; the greatest clearness with the greatest faithfulness.[21]

Any paraphrase he suspected as changing the meaning of the original, interpreting it for the reader, so that it became no longer a translation but a commentary on the text.

Pusey and Keble preferred literal translations and at the expense of their English style. Newman, however, and his younger contemporary John Mason Neale, sat more lightly to the precise order of the ancient languages. Newman, a superb stylist in English, and Neale, a storyteller and novelist, as well as a translator of liturgical texts for use in church, regarded translations of ancient texts as vehicles for right doctrine, but even more as means by which men would learn to pray. Neale wrote novels and short stories based on events and persons of the past to stimulate devotion, as well as translating with a free genius which at times extended to downright invention; while Newman, whose translation of St Athanasius was as pedantic as Keble's version of St Ireneus, also produced edifying novels in an attempt to make the past available in English prose. They both went a step further in translation than either Pusey or Keble in making one text in particular available for private meditation. This was the *Preces Privates* of Bishop Lancelot Andrewes, a seventeenth-century divine, who himself prayed as easily in Greek and Latin as in English. In Newman's translation and in the further selection which Neale later translated, Andrewes's compilation from the ancient languages flowered into original compositions in English. The original copy of Andrewes's book, now lost, was stained and tattered and 'watered with his penitential tears',[22] evidence that the prayers were used constantly and with deep emotion. Andrewes arranged the material as a series of devotions for each day of the week, drawing mainly on the Scriptures and the liturgy, in Hebrew, Greek and Latin, but set out as personal prayers of adoration, thanksgiving, confession and intercession. Newman translated the main part in No. 28 of *Tracts for the Times* (1840) and Neale added the rest in an equally fine version. Neither Newman nor Neale needed a translation to use Andrewes's book of prayers. Their undertaking was entirely for the use of others poorer than themselves; and it is noteworthy that the pedantry of the Newman of the *Reply* to Arnold is here replaced by something that could well be seen as 'poesie into poesie'. It is a rare thing for a translation to become a new and excellent work in its own right, but that is what these two achieved. In this work, the charity of the past became the charity of the present in its most direct and personal form; it is the finest example I know of the combination of truth with love in the process of translation into English.

The main virtue of a translation of any ancient text is that it should be a translation and render the original meaning clearly. But the art of the translator is rather more than an attempt at transliteration, as a comparison between the translations of Pusey and Newman shows. The past is to be placed in the hands of the present, and it is here that the translator of Christian texts about or containing prayer has a particularly delicate job. Penguin Classics have presented this kind of material in, for instance, translations of English mystics, the *Prayers and Meditations of St Anselm of Canterbury*, Helen Waddell's *Mediaeval Latin Lyrics*, and, in some sense, in Betty Radice's own translation of *The Letters of Abelard and Heloise*. The aim of such translations is to be transparent, but also readable and usable. The transparency comes first, but where 'charity' is applied this does not cloud but clarifies the sense; as Charles Williams put it, 'accuracy is fruitfulness . . . it is the first law of the spiritual life'.[23] In the quotation given at the beginning from Christopher Smart, as fine a classicist as any, the comma after 'better' is not an accident; the second clause is not related to the word 'charity' but to the whole preceding phrase. Smart does not claim, nor does any true translator, that he has used charity in his work in order to make what he translates more acceptable to the reader; he claims that he has translated in the charity which is Christ, and it is this fact that 'makes things better'. So, like St Augustine, Bede, Alfred, or the Tractarians, Christopher Smart can conclude with the longing of the Christian translator for his own salvation also: 'and so I trust that I shall be translated myself at the last'.

NOTES

Translator's Charity (pp. 206–15)

1. St Augustine, *City of God*, translated by Henry Bettenson (Penguin Books, 1984), p. 1091.
2. *The Cloud of Unknowing*, translated by Clifton Wolters (Penguin Books, 1978), p. 51.
3. St Augustine, *On Christian Doctrine*, translated by D. W. Robertson (Oxford, 1958), Book II, XI, p. 43.
4. ibid., p. 43.
5. ibid., p. 30.
6. ibid., p. 93.
7. ibid., p. 88.
8. ibid., p. 46.
9. ibid., p. 142.
10. St Augustine, *Confessions*, translated by R. S. Pine-Coffin (Penguin Books, 1961), pp. 231–2.
11. Bede, *A History of the English Church and People*, translated by Leo Sherley-Price (Penguin Books, rev. ed. 1968), III, 3, p. 145.
12. ibid., V, 24, p. 337.
13. Letter of Cuthbert, quoted by C. E. Whiting, 'The Life of the Venerable Bede', in *Bede: Life, Times and Writings*, ed. A. H. Thompson (Oxford, 1935), p. 34.

14. Letter to Egbert, in *English Historical Documents*, vol. 1, ed. D. Whitelock (Oxford, 1979), p. 801.
15. ibid.
16. From *Alfred the Great*: Asser's *Life of King Alfred* and other contemporary sources, translated by Simon Keynes and Michael Lapidge (Penguin Books, 1983), p. 126.
17. The work of the Benedictine monks of the Congregation of St Maurus in editing texts is discussed by David Knowles in *Great Historical Enterprises* (London, 1963), pp. 35–62.
18. H. P. Liddon, *The Life of Edward Bouverie Pusey* (London, 1894), vol. 1, p. 422.
19. ibid.
20. ibid., p. 423.
21. *Confessions of St Augustine, Revised from a former translation by Rev. E. B. Pusey D.D.* (Oxford, 1838), preface, pp. xxxi, xxxii.
22. *The Private Prayers of Lancelot Andrewes*, ed. H. Martin (London, 1957), introduction, p. 9.
23. Charles Williams, *The Figure of Beatrice* (London, 1943), p. 133. I am grateful to Dr Barbara Reynolds for drawing my attention to this remark.

ꟽIDDLE AGES: ELEVENTH TO FOURTEENTH CENTURIES

XV
ANSELM OF CANTERBURY
A MONASTIC SCHOLAR

IN THE YEAR 1109, on the Wednesday in Holy Week, the Archbishop of Canterbury lay dying. His friends, knowing that they were at the death-bed of a saint, were ready to improve the occasion: 'My lord and father,' they said, 'we cannot help knowing that you are going to leave the world to be at the Easter court of your king.'[1] But Anselm was not to be caught by pieties and sentimentalities. His reply is the key to his life and a way to begin to understand him: 'And indeed,' he replied, 'if His will is set upon this I will gladly obey His will. However, if He would prefer me to stay among you, at least until I can settle a question about the origin of the soul which I am turning over in my mind, I should welcome this with gratitude, for I do not know whether anyone will solve it when I am dead.'

There is in this reply first the obedience of the monk—a joyful love of whatever might be God's will for him. And secondly a true estimate of his own intellectual powers as a scholar, without false humility; a mind still employed to its utmost in understanding the things of God for the sake of the people of God. From that starting point I would like to make some comments on Anselm as a monastic scholar and man of prayer in the belief that his way of doing theology is relevant to our own situation. But before proceeding to his ideas, perhaps I should fill in the background of his life since it is essential to my argument that his monastic life cannot be separated from his ideas and theology.

Seventy-six years earlier Anselm had been born in Aosta in northern Italy. As a young man he left home and came north into the turbulent, changing society of eleventh century Europe, eager to learn and equipped with one of the most powerful and original minds of the age—or of any age. For three years he seems to have wandered about northern Europe, presumably visiting the great centres of monastic and liturgical life, at Cluny and Fleury, as well as the monastic schools which were still centres of intellectual experiment before the rise of the secular schools and universities.

Eventually, says his biographer and disciple, Eadmer, 'he went to Normandy, to see, to talk to, and to stay with a certain master by the name of Lanfranc.'[2] This was the beginning of Anselm's association with the monastery of Bec, where Lanfranc was prior. He left it thirty-four years later to become Archbishop of Canterbury. It was during these years as monk, prior and abbot of Bec that Anselm began to write, and his first works were by no means immature or experimental. It was then that he wrote the *Prayers and Meditations*, the *Monologion* and, above all, the *Proslogion*. Later, as Archbishop of Canterbury, Anselm wrote only 'in great tribulation of heart'. The greatest of his theological works does indeed belong to that period, the *Cur Deus Homo?*, but it was completed only in the peace of exile, not in the constant pressures of controversy and bickerings at home. As archbishop he was an administrator first, a scholar perforce second, and he was regretfully aware of this. To his monks at Canterbury he said: 'Just as an owl is glad when she is in her nest with her chicks and . . . all is well with her . . . so it is with me. For when I am with you, all is well with me, and this is the joy and consolation of my life. But when I am separated from you, and my ways lie among men who are in the world, then I am torn this way and that by the onrush of disputes of many kinds and I am harassed by secular disputes of many kinds which I hate.'[3] His words leave no room for doubt about where his preference lay, but that does not mean that he did his work as archbishop grudgingly. As far as the 'secular disputes' were concerned he had one very simple expedient for dealing with them 'for', says his biographer, 'when he was in a crowd of litigants, while his opponents were laying their heads together . . . he would compose himself, in the sweet quietness of a pure heart, to sleep.'[4] As archbishop, however, he was alert and discerning in all that pertained to church affairs.

Anselm was to occupy a central place in public affairs in England in the second half of his life, but it was the cloister that had really set free his most creative abilities. At Bec he was the spiritual master, the monastic scholar *par excellence*, and it is in the writings of that period that it is easiest to see what it meant for Anselm to be a monk and a scholar, with the entire commitment of the monastic life combined with the integrity of scholarship of the highest kind.

II

Eadmer tells us that Anselm noticed the similarity of the two disciplines from the beginning. As a pupil of Lanfranc, Anselm 'wearied his body with late nights, with cold and with hunger because of his studies, and so he began to think that if he became a monk he would not have to put up with anything more severe than he was now suffering, nor would he lose the reward of his labour.'[5] This is not, of course, the highest possible motive for religious vocation, and the fact that Eadmer records it points to his having heard of it from Anselm, who was never one for illusions about himself. The account of his choice of Bec must similarly have come from the saint himself: not, he decided, Cluny, where liturgy would prevent him from studying; and he was dubious about Bec 'because there the outstanding ability of Lanfranc will condemn me to insignificance.'[6] Again, not a pious outlook, but with all its imperfections one which showed his basic honesty; he knew he could never play second fiddle in intellectual matters, and he could admit it plainly.

It is interesting to note in passing that Anselm did not immediately choose the monastic way of life of the great Benedictine house. He hesitated; and the alternatives he considered are symptomatic of that age. He thought first of becoming a hermit, one of the major attractions in the next hundred years; and then of becoming a secular land-holder on his estates, serving the poor—a remarkable anticipation of later forms of Christian life and devotion.

In the end he settled the matter in a way which was typical of him: he acted under obedience to another, and obeyed implicitly what his adviser (Lanfranc) told him to do—he became a monk at Bec. Within three years Lanfranc had gone to Caen, and Anselm was appointed prior; and at the death of the abbot and founder, Herluin, Anselm became abbot. Thus for thirty-three years he lived at Bec under the Rule of St.Benedict as interpreted in a Norman monastery of the eleventh century with the full weight of liturgical observance. During that time he wrote the *Prayers and Meditations*, his most directly spiritual work; the *Monologion*; the *Proslogion*, one of the greatest of all philosophical works; *De Grammatico, De Veritate, De Libertate Arbitrii, De Casu Diaboli* and the *Epistola de Incarnatione Verbi*—about half of all his works. And he wrote them not in spite of but because of his monastic commitment.

How did all these writings form part of his monastic life? The clue I think is in the *Vita Anselmi* in which Eadmer says: 'From that time on he gave himself up entirely to being a true monk, and to understanding the rational basis of the monastic life and expounding it to others.'[7] These three points seem to form the ground of Anselm's understanding of his vocation as a monk and scholar and I would like to take them in turn.

First: 'he gave himself up entirely to being a true monk.' Anselm's concept of monastic life has to be gleaned from his statements in his letters, in records of private conversations, and from some of the *Prayers*. The most important of the letters in which Anselm discusses the monastic life is the one he sent to the monk Lanzo at Cluny in 1072. He himself considered this letter to contain his true opinion of monastic life, later recommending a monk of Canterbury to read it, while Eadmer quoted it in the *Vita* as typical of Anselm's position on monasticism. It is the letter of a monastic conservative *par excellence*; there is no trace of discontent with the intellectual and spiritual atmosphere of monasticism as he experienced it. 'Let him rejoice at finding himself where he can at last remain for the whole of his life, not unwillingly but voluntarily, driving away all thought of removal so that he may quietly give himself up to the exercises of a pious life . . . let him refuse to pass judgement on the customs of the place even if they seem useless.'[8] And more directly to Lanzo: 'Devote your whole strength to attaining peace of mind . . . which is not attained by any monk without constancy and forbearance . . . or without a studious and devout observance of all the customs of the monastery, even if their purpose is not clear.'

This is the framework out of which came ways of thought and of prayer which revolutionised medieval theology and devotion. And they did not come out of it as a protest but as a natural and right growth. Anselm loved being a monk; accepting and being formed by monastic ways was to him a matter not only of duty but of joy. To Helinandus he wrote of monastic life as *'pondus cantabile'*–a weight that is borne singing. The monk, he insisted elsewhere, is the man who instead of being able to give God merely the fruits of a tree has given him the tree itself.

Anselm's concept of the monastic life was a part of his general way of thinking, not an exception to it as though he had never tried to apply his mind to monastic life. It is in line with his other ideas, for instance, his idea of truth as that which corresponds to what really and objectively is, rather than to the thought in the mind of the speaker. His concept of freedom is similar: freedom does not lie in the ability to choose between good and evil but in the ability to choose always what is right. 'The ability to keep uprightness of will (*rectitudo*) for its own sake is the complete definition of freedom of choice.' Likewise, for Anselm, sin is not to be assessed by a psychological standard but by a theological one: 'How can any sin be called small', he asks, 'when it is an offence against God?'

His definitions are always vertical, not horizontal. They define man in relation to God, and have as much to do with theories of similitude and likeness, image and symbol, as with theories of cause and effect. So, in relation to monastic life, authenticity was not to be judged by personal approval or disapproval of monastic customs; 'even if their purpose is not clear' the customs are to be followed. They are seen, in fact, as converting ordinances by which a man will be changed and shaped. It is, as we shall see later, the same encounter that he suggests in the *Proslogion*.

Like the Greek Fathers, Anselm believed that man is created in the image of God, and his whole purpose is to have this image restored so that he can again perfectly reflect this truth that is in God. But the image is not reflected truly in man; it has been distorted by sin. And for Anselm the monastic life is the way of restoring that image defaced by the disobedience of sin. In the 'Prayer to St John the Baptist' Anselm says: 'You fashioned your gracious image in me, and I superimposed upon it the image that is hateful . . . refashion the face I have spoiled, restore the innocence I have violated.' This is the key to Anselm's approach to monasticism, which seems at first sight far from our way of thinking. He would not have said, for instance, that the monastic way of life is the expression of an individual's understanding of God's call to him, or that its authenticity depends upon the external actions being the direct fruit of that understanding. For Anselm, monastic life, like other things, existed in its highest degree in the mind of God, and was reflected in man who is God's image. But the image was marred by sin, and so there is a gap, a discrepancy between the ideal and the actual which can be remedied only by a continuing experience of the detailed reality of monastic life which can remove and remedy the deformed image. The monastic life is an ideal to which the monk is to be conformed. This leads Anselm to lay great stress on the externals of religious life, especially upon the habit. To his mind no one who had worn the habit, even if they had never intended to take vows, could leave the monastic life without apostasy. This was clearly his opinion in his letters to the Princess Gunhilda and her cousin Mathilda, neither of whom had made religious vows, though they had worn the habit. He refers to them both as 'lost daughters' and sees every step away from the cloister as taking them along the road to damnation. The habit is to him sacramental: 'The black and heavy clothes remind the monk that he is a sinner; they cover him from head to feet to turn him to this thought from the beginning to the end of life; they present also the form of the cross and re-establish in him the passion of the Lord; the crown of hair left by the tonsure tells that the monk is both priest and king.'[9]

The monastic life was a practical affair for Anselm, a matter of actually doing certain things, not just thinking various thoughts. It was, as it were, an icon through which a man came to the reality it represented. An icon and not an idol, for he was equally aware that monastic customs were not an end in themselves. 'To wear the religious habit serves no purpose unless at the same time an effort is made to be interiorly what one appears to be.'[10] It is the way through, not the end. In his 'Prayer to St Benedict' this is also the theme: 'I profess to lead a life of continual turning to God, as I promised by taking the name and habit of a monk, but my long life cries out against me, and my conscience convicts me as a liar to God and angels and men.' 'I profess myself a soldier, a scholar, a monk, but my life cries out that I am a liar.' Again in the 'Prayer for any Abbot' he says: 'They behold me preceded like an abbot but I do not behold that I live like an abbot.' The monk for Anselm was '*peccator monachus*'—a sinner in need of the mercy of God. This sense of shortcoming, of sin, of alienation, is present in all the prayers and the solution in each is to turn towards the mercy of God. By coming gradually into relation with God the image is restored, and then the truth perceived by the heart and expressed by the lips will fully correspond to the truth as it really is in God.

III

For Anselm, an essential part of this process of conversion was an intellectual one. The intellect is an integral part of man's created being and needs, as much as the rest of him, to be brought into contact with God for restoration and cleansing. 'To discover the rational basis of the monastic life' is the second part of Eadmer's statement about Anselm's concerns. 'The rational basis'—what did Anselm mean by '*ratio*'? To find out one looks rather at the *Monologion* and the *Proslogion* than at the *Prayers*. The first title Anselm gave to the *Monologion* was '*De ratione fidei*', an ambiguous title which he soon dropped. More appropriate for what he was trying to do was his sub-title, '*Fides quaerens intellectum*', for the *Proslogion*—that treatise in which prayer and intellectual thought are most wonderfully combined. It is here that we can see what Anselm meant by '*ratio*', and how it formed part of his prayer.

The *Proslogion* begins as a meditation:

> Come now, little man,
> turn aside for a while from your daily employment,
> escape for a moment from the tumult of your thoughts.
> Put aside your weighty cares,
> let your burdensome distractions wait,
> free yourself awhile for God
> and rest awhile in him.
> Enter the inner chamber of your soul,
> shut everything out except God
> and that which can help you in seeking him,
> and when you have shut the door, seek him.
> Now, my whole heart, say to God,
> 'I seek your face ,
> Lord, it is your face I seek.'[11]

It is clear that the major part of the *Proslogion*—twenty-one chapters out of twenty-five—is a meditation, a prayer reflecting upon the nature of belief in God. But to look only at those is to side-step the issue, for the early chapters contain a philosophic statement about the existence and nature of God more exciting than any produced in a monastery before or since and which has, more than anything else, given to Anselm—mistakenly—the title 'Father of Scholasticism'. It is a demonstration which has aroused, and continues to arouse, lively interest among philosophers and theologians, including Descartes, Kant, Hegel, Leibnitz and Barth. Indeed, one might almost say it takes giants to misunderstand a giant, and it is interesting to note in this connection that R. W. Southern in his book *Saint Anselm and his Biographer* says: 'It may be claimed that a share of philosophical naïvety is an aid to understanding his [Anselm's] thought . . .'

'God is that than which nothing greater can be thought.' It is important to see this in context and not in isolation, and especially in the context of its first expression. At Bec Anselm was exercising all the abilities of his mind to discover 'the rationale of the nature of God as the true faith holds it to be', when suddenly 'one night during mattins the grace of God shone in his heart, the whole matter became clear to his mind, and a great joy and jubilation filled his whole being'.[12] It was a matter of illumination about what was already believed, and it is this that provided the starting point for his arguments, not the reverse. It happened in the middle of a monastic service, and the whole setting of it is a prayer of longing and desire for God which is entirely monastic in tone. There is a joy and excitement which is far removed from the logical demonstrations of scholasticism and closer to the mystical experience of prayer. Anselm was not constructing a logical structure and imposing it upon God; nor was he proposing to discover by logical argument the existence of God as the end term of his own propositions. His fundamental way of doing theology was to bring all the powers of his mind to bear upon what he already believed, and this experience at Bec produced the gift of understanding more.

It has often been said that the 'proofs' of the *Proslogion* would never convince an unbeliever. For Anselm, theology is only true insofar as it corresponds to the being of God, and '*ratio*' for him is '*ratio dei*', the living word of God which is beyond all systems of human thought. Applying to the utmost all the powers of intellect and reason to 'seeking God', the basis is nonetheless a confrontation with God himself and his saving purposes, which will in itself clear the mind of its darkness and restore it to that contact with God in himself which can be described either as true theology or as prayer. To do this Anselm uses every kind of concept: the Scriptures, dogma, and credal statements on the one hand, the secular concepts of philosophy on the other. 'God is that than which nothing greater can be thought' affirms the impossibility of proving the unknowable essence of God by human reasoning. It is a way of knowledge that is apophatic; it is a demonstration rather than a proof. And from it Anselm explores whatever can be said or thought about God, using this first insight as the basis of his prayer and thought. 'Thank you, good Lord,' he exclaims, 'for by your gift I first believed and now by your illumination I understand.'

This encounter with God, which he calls 'illumination', is the attitude of a monk who having dedicated his entire being to God offers the whole of his mind, as well as his body, to knowing that truth which is beyond concepts, and to receiving it as a transfiguring experience. This is how Anselm understood the rational basis of the monastic life—not by looking for reasons to justify it, but by seeing the truth in God.

IV

The mystics tell us that no experience of God remains static or unused, it must communicate itself. This leads to the third of Eadmer's points about Anselm: 'He expounded it to others.'

Anselm was not primarily a teacher, a school-man, a pedagogue, although some of his advice, on education, for example, was not bettered until the late nineteenth century. He is concerned with his personal search for God and it is significant that he uses the dynamic word 'seek'. For Anselm prayer is not a static reception of something that can be passed on to others but an ardent and vigorous quest in which others may join him if they wish. The end of the *Proslogion* is his fullest expression of this attitude:

> God of truth,
> I ask that I may receive,
> so that my joy may be full.
> Meanwhile, let my mind meditate on it,
> let my tongue speak of it,
> let my heart love it,
> let my mouth preach it,
> let my soul hunger for it,
> my flesh thirst for it,
> and my whole being desire it,
> until I enter into the joy of my Lord,
> who is God, one and triune, blessed forever. Amen.[13]

He shared his way of prayer by sending copies of his own prayers to certain people and by giving some guidance about how to use them. It was a personal and individual matter, not the setting up of a 'school of spirituality'. But from this intimate communication between the few came a whole new concept of meditative, solitary prayer in the inner chamber. Some of Anselm's ideas about praying are found in the preface he wrote to the collection of *Prayers and Meditations:*

> The purpose of the prayers and meditations that follow is to stir up the mind of the reader to the love or fear of God, or to self-examination. They are not to be read in a turmoil, but quietly, not skimmed or hurried through, but taken a little at a time, with deep

> and thoughtful meditation.
>
> The reader should not trouble about reading the whole of any of them, but only as much as, by God's help, he finds useful in stirring up his spirit to pray, or as much as he likes. Nor is it necessary for him always to begin at the beginning, but wherever he pleases.
>
> With this in mind the sections are divided into paragraphs so that the reader can begin and leave off wherever he chooses; in this way he will not get bored with too much material but will be able to ponder more deeply those things that make him want to pray.[14]

He wrote in a similar way to the Princess Adelaide and the Countess Mathilda, and it is interesting to reflect in this connection on the important part played by great and noble ladies in the development of devotion. They had the time and the leisure as well as the inclination and ability for spiritual adventure and were in a position to put the ideas of their spiritual masters into practice.

The *Proslogion* was also a prayer, an '*exemplum meditandi*', and it was written, Anselm says, to share with others the joy he had felt in his experience of God. His concern is that everyone, even the 'fool', should be brought to some experience of God whose nature it is to desire to bring sinners to repentance. Anselm's teaching always has this connotation of enabling others to experience God for themselves. He was not, like Lanfranc, a master of the schools, attracting pupils from outside the monastery and teaching them according to a system. Anselm preferred to talk with his friends, with a few intelligent monks, with whom he could discuss ideas and communicate by talking rather than by teaching.

This small group of lively and intelligent minds recurs throughout Anselm's life, whether it is the monastic group of Lanfranc and Gundulf at Bec, or the international circle of eminent men like Hugh of Cluny, Peter Damian, Hugh of Grenoble, Pope Calixtus II, Anselm of Laon, or that other group of more personal friends in England, Gilbert Crispin, Eadmer, Ralph of Battle, the monks Baldwin and Alexander. It was in the small group exchanging ideas that Anselm was most at home, not in the debating hall. He was a great friend, as his letters also show, and it was as one sharing experience rather than as a master teaching disciples that Anselm communicated his knowledge. He talked with men 'so that they may form themselves in the image of the spiritual man', and as a spiritual father Anselm was pre-eminent.

This is a side of him which has left, of its nature, little record, but

Eadmer assures us it was for his spiritual wisdom and insight that Anselm was most valued both at Bec and Canterbury. In the monastery 'all loved him as a very dear father'; 'any with a private trouble hastened to unburden themselves to him as if to the gentlest of mothers.' Like Aelred of Rievaulx, Anselm could be called a mother as well as a father in his care of his community, and this mothering side of his nature reflected the contemplative, receptive, caring aspect, just as the brilliant intellect and clear thought belonged to his fatherhood—a parallel which he himself draws in detail in his 'Prayer to St Paul':

> Therefore you are fathers by your effect
> and mothers by your affection.
> Fathers by your authority, mothers by your kindness.
> Fathers by your teaching, mothers by your mercy.[15]

Outside the monastery 'he received all who came to him with a gracious readiness and replied helpfully to them all . . . his conversation drew all men to him in friendship and affection . . . everyone who could enjoy his conversation was ready to do so, for on any subject they wished he had heavenly counsel ready for them.'[16] This is surely the true monastic scholar who shares his insight with others as the fruit of his contemplation of God; he is one through whom a knowledge of God can be reached rather than someone wise in his own right.

V

The picture I have tried to present of Anselm as a monastic scholar is one which could only have emerged in this century—perhaps only in this decade. Within a few years of his death Anselm's work suffered in various ways. He left no school of disciples, only a few friends who had been influenced by him but who then went their own way. His greatest work, the *Proslogion*, seems to have been virtually unknown in the twelfth century, and Thomas Aquinas knew it only at second hand and in a distorted form in the thirteenth. Fashions of thought changed rapidly and the formation of scholasticism soon held the ground in Europe. It was only by careful selection, much later, that scholars could begin to look back and call Anselm the Father of Scholasticism, and by then his theology was seen through ways of thought alien to his own.

In the realm of devotion, the genuine prayers of Anselm were at once lost to sight among a vast amount of similar material, most of it inferior. The prayers generated a school of spirituality and so found countless imitators. The corpus grew, all of it going under the name of Anselm, until the vast collection was published by Migne in the last century. At the beginning of the present century the work of Dom André Wilmart, in testing the authenticity of the Anselmian writings, prepared the way for Dom Schmitt's definitive edition in the 1960s. The prayers which are now regarded as genuinely by Anselm number nineteen, the meditations only three, which enables a much clearer picture to emerge of Anselm as a spiritual writer and guide. It is possible now to ask certain questions about Anselm as a spiritual writer and to discover in what way the impact of his teaching can be described as 'the Anselmian revolution'. Having discussed the approach of Anselm to monastic life and learning, the remainder of this paper will concern Anselm's contribution to Christian spirituality, first in his own day and then among the masters of the spiritual life.

The ethos of prayer in which Anselm was formed had changed little in the previous two centuries. It was basically a monastic devotion, for people outside the monasteries as well as for the monks. The central part that monasticism played in Anselm's life has already been noticed, and it only remains to emphasise the way in which the details of monastic life under the Rule of St Benedict permeated Anselm's prayers. Take for instance, the Prologue to the Rule itself:

> Hearken, my son, to the precepts of the master and incline the ear of thine heart . . . by the labour of obedience return to him from whom thou hast strayed by the sloth of disobedience . . . and first of all whatever good work thou dost undertake, ask him with most instant prayer to perfect it . . . as we progress in the monastic life and in faith, our hearts shall be enlarged and we shall run with the unspeakable sweetness of love in the way of God's commandments . . . we shall share by patience in the sufferings of Christ, that we may deserve to be partakers also of his kingdom.[17]

The life of the monk is seen here as a perpetual conversion, a turning from the kingdom of sin and alienation towards the kingdom of God and union with him; the way is that behind all the devotions of Anselm and, as we shall see, the movement from sin and fear to love and desire through the sufferings of Christ is central to his thought. In the 'Prayer to St Benedict' and the 'Prayer for an Abbot', there are also clear echoes of the Rule. There are the same images, the shepherd and sheep, the master and disciples, the father and sons. There is also the figure of Christ behind the figure of the abbot; the weight of solemn duty carried out in the shadow of the judgement seat of Christ is exactly the picture St Benedict draws of the work of an abbot or monk. What Anselm adds is the personal note of awareness of insufficiency for the human being within the role, the feeling of being a hypocrite, of claiming things far above one's ability. This is a part of a self-awareness new in the twelfth century. As for St Benedict, so for Anselm, prayer was based on the Bible and the liturgy, and in each case it was expected that individuals would extend this for themselves. For both, 'mind and voice' were to be 'in accord';[18] prayer should be made 'with tears and fervour of heart;[19] 'in purity of heart and tears of compunction'.[20] But where St Benedict sees private prayer as being 'brief and in the oratory',[21] Anselm insists that one should withdraw to a solitary place and pray there as long as one desires.

Within the Benedictine life at Bec there was, secondly, the Divine Office, the Mass, and the para-liturgical ceremonies of the Customary. The Office according to St Benedict offers a framework of prayer based on the corporate recitation of the psalter, interspersed with readings from the rest of the Bible at various intervals during day and night. The accretions with which centuries had surrounded the Office were still mainly in the nature of extra psalms. The psalter was the prayer book *par excellence* of the monk; its familiar recurring phrases shaped the sub-conscious as well as the conscious mind, creating in the monk the attitudes of repentance and need, rejoicing and praise, of the Psalmist. It was also the prayer book of those of the laity who could read and were inclined for it; the psalms could equally be learnt by heart by the devout among the non-literate. Any great lord or lady would want extracts from the psalter if they were at all inclined to piety. It is significant that the earliest of Anselm's prayers were written as an appendix to just such a selection from the psalms made at the request of a great lady of pious habits. Other prayers were made at the request of monks as well as for secular friends. It seems therefore that the austerity of the psalter was already wearing thin for monks as well as for laymen; a movement towards the personal, the interior, the subjective, was taking place in the eleventh and twelfth centuries and its effect was felt on the use of the psalms.

The psalter is a difficult prayer book for Christians to use; Augustine had popularised a Christological interpretation of the psalms and the influence of his great sermons on the psalms made them acceptable. The use of the Gloria Patri at the end of each also reminded the worshipper of the Christian setting of the Jewish prayers. But the psalms are most easily used in an objective, corporate way–in fact, in recitation in choir. But already in the eleventh century the need was felt to draw out and make explicit their Christian application. This was often done by attaching brief, collect-type prayers to the end of each psalm which would take up one or more themes from the psalm and give it both a Christian interpretation and a personal application to those using it.

Anselm's prayers are full of the phrases of the psalms; he was formed by them; but the pattern of his prayers is along the lines of the psalter-collects, only drawn to great length. It seems to me that one might look for the source of this tendency in the hermit movement of the eleventh and twelfth centuries. Increasingly numbers of men and women were praying alone; and using the psalms alone in a cell is completely different from their corporate recitation in choir. It is at least significant that the stirrings towards this more personal prayer with the psalms comes from the hermit Orders in Italy–from Peter Damian, John Gualbert and, in a rather different sense, John of Fécamp.

Thirdly, for the monk of Bec, there was the veneration of the saints. The Kalendar provided a liturgy for the saints throughout the year. Here again, Anselm received a tradition and expanded it. The devotion of the Carolingians was to God through Christ in the Spirit; it was permissible to invoke the prayers of those saints known from the Gospel, above all St Mary. The austere phrases of the litany of the saints was the basis for this: 'Holy Mary, pray for us.' But already by the time of Anselm a warmer devotion was being felt towards the saints, in particular towards Mary as the one closest to the Lord. The grave, restrained prayers to her, basically the *Ave Maria*, were expanding into something more personal and expressive. The *O singularis merita* by Maurillus of Rouen is one instance of this. Anselm took up this approach to the saints and expanded it into a kind of devotional psychology of holy persons, entering into dialogue with them, displaying an interest in their history, eager for their understanding–in particular St Mary, to whom he addressed three long prayers, and the biblical saints, Peter, Paul, John, Stephen, and John Baptist. Also Nicolas, a saint of special interest in Normandy, and St Benedict, patron of monks.

Thus, the idea of prayers said aloud and in conjunction with others was already shaping itself towards the idea of prayers said alone and in the heart. Here the tradition was met by another ancient tradition of private meditation upon the Scriptures. The whole method of praying was being re-shaped. It is here that Anselm is most an innovator, though it is here also that he is closest to the masters before and after him. There is no analysis in Anselm of how to pray—that was left for the Cistercians and the Victorines. But Anselm did give a paragraph indicating how he expected his meditations to be used, and this directive is startling enough in its mixture of prayer with meditation and reading.

Meditation in the strict sense was learning the psalms or other parts of the Scriptures by heart so that they became part of the one praying and issued in prayer. It was the material that set the pace and shaped the meditation. For Anselm, the emphasis is not on the material used but on the person praying. He uses these things—place, time, the subject matter—in whatever way helps him to pray; they are arranged so that the reader can choose parts, and leave parts, so that he can 'ponder more deeply those things that make him want to pray'. It was a deliberate withdrawal from external things for a close, intimate exploration of one's own inner self. It is in this setting no longer enough for prayer to be brief and simple; it is a lengthy examination of oneself rather than of the Scriptures. The starting point is a mental one—a phrase from the Scriptures, a story, a person, a situation— and from it the whole of the person praying comes into a relationship which in its turn leads to the thresholds of prayer. Here there is scope for sighs, groans, tears; emotion as well as intellect is being deliberately used to make the whole of oneself become alert to pray. *Affectus* as a way of prayer has been given a new and dramatic meaning.

The older tradition had nothing like that. To pray had meant to say the psalter; to meditate was to learn the Scriptures. Moments of personal encounter or illumination were expressed briefly, if at all. The 'new' prayer has a great deal to do with a profound change at that time in the ways of self-expression and self-understanding; a major change of sentiment in the history of mankind which formed the key-note of the twelfth century. These were the prayers that were now wanted and appreciated. Anselm was asked to provide them. They circulated widely during his lifetime, and very rapidly received that most significant form of flattery—imitation. The prayers, and those based on them, have so formed the devotional temper of medieval Europe that one can hardly imagine how anyone prayed without them.

The development was not all gain; even in Anselm there is a vein of sheer sentimentality which was to be imitated by lesser men with dire results. Moreover, in other hands his style could be tedious; it is not everyone who can write our prayers for us. But Anselm shaped devotion into the channels of meditation on the humanity of Christ, on his mother, and on personal confrontation with the mysteries of the Christian faith, in an appeal to emotion, intellect and will in a new way. The proper end of this vein of devotion lies in the great devotional poetry of the late Middle Ages. The hymn by a Cistercian, *Jesu dulcis memoria*, takes up the theme of Anselm's first meditation; the *Stabat Mater* derives from his 'Prayer to Christ'; and the great rolling periods of the *Dies Irae* are in direct line with the third and the first of his meditations.

I have tried to show very roughly that Anselm inherited certain practical traditions about prayer and in what ways he changed them. Now I would like to see how Anselm stands in relation to the masters of the Christian spiritual or 'mystical' tradition.

VI

There is in the West a distinctive spiritual tradition and two major figures in it are Augustine and Bernard; between them stands Anselm, a major theologian and part of this same tradition of spirituality. He called himself *Augustinus minor* and saw Augustine, as much as he saw anyone, as his master. It is, I suggest, possible to see him also as *Bernadus prior*, a precursor to some extent of the type of devotion popularised by Bernard. Anselm was that rare thing, an original thinker; he was also a man to whom prayer was of central importance. It is to be expected, therefore, that he should have made some contribution to the tradition of prayer. But he wrote no treatise on prayer; he is not a systematiser, an analyst of the science of sciences, the art of arts. What is to be known must be discovered from his actual prayers and a few more explicit references elsewhere.

First: *Augustinus minor*. There is in the concept of prayer presented by Augustine a complete unity of knowledge and love; one is inconceivable without the other and both lead to and are united in the further concept of praise. In the last paragraph of the *City of God* this is perfectly summarised: 'We shall rest and we shall see; we shall see and we shall love; we shall love and we shall praise.'[22] Augustine uses the language of love, of desire, of longing to express his understanding of prayer. It is a matter of discovery, of self-discovery and of search: 'Late have I loved thee, O Beauty ever ancient, ever new; late have I loved thee. I tasted thee, and now I hunger and thirst for thee; thou didst touch me and I burned for thy peace.'[23] The initial vision of God which he describes at Ostia may have been a '*momentum intellegentiae*', but it was far more than a purely intellectual experience. In it feeling and knowing were not separate but parts of a single process: '*da mihi, Domine, scire et intellegere.*'

As the quotations have already shown, intellect for Augustine was not a mental activity of abstraction. In the tradition in which Augustine wrote, prayer was a recognised part of philosophical enquiry, and in the *Confessions* in particular he gives this full scope. Here there is an intense self-searching, an acute self-knowledge, a sensitive probing of the inner ways of the heart, in the form of a monologue addressed by Augustine to God or to himself in the presence of God. It leads to an extensive exploration of the nature of man and of God in which the analogy of mind, intellect and reason leads Augustine to the three Persons in one God of the Christian revelation. This intense personal involvement with the philosophical and anthropological concepts of Christianity is no abstraction; it strains upwards to God, pleads for help, for guidance, for cleansing and, above all, for full knowledge which is union. 'These were the stages of my pitfall into hell . . . My God, you had mercy on me even before I had confessed to you . . . you were deeper than my inmost understanding and higher than the topmost thought that I could reach . . . how infinite is your mercy, O my God.'[24] This quivering sensitivity, with its desire for reformation, for *metanoia*, for a total union with God ('O my late joy'), turns inward, to the discovery of God at the roots of being. This, for Augustine, in the loving knowledge of God, becomes the drive behind all action and thought.

It is clear that to some extent Anselm was the inheritor of that tradition. I have drawn attention elsewhere to the similarities between the *Confessions* of Augustine and the *Prayers* of Anselm.[25] Like the *Confessions*, the *Prayers* (and with them I include the *Proslogion*), are written in an intensely personal literary form. Instead of a monologue, however, they are a dialogue, between Anselm and a saint, or Christ, or all three. There is here the extreme of personal involvement with carefully held theological concepts. The *Proslogion* may hold the intricacies of philosophical argument in the celebrated chapters about the existence of God; but the whole prayer is basically a prolonged example of how to think about God the Trinity in order to love and attain to him. The philosophical insight itself was, like Augustine's vision at Aosta, a *'momentum intellegentiae'*, revealed in a flash during the most exacting of all spiritual exercises, the recitation of Mattins. It is faith in search of understanding, *fides quaerens intellectum*. 'Let me seek you by desiring you, and desire you by seeking you; let me find you by loving you, and love you in finding you.'[26] Love and knowledge, knowledge in the sense of *sapientia*, wisdom, a loving knowledge, are certainly there. But are they there in quite the Augustinian sense?

It seems to me that there is a change and that the change makes Anselm both *Augustinus minor* and *Bernardus prior*. For Anselm gives a different place to love and to knowledge in his prayers. Anselm takes a phrase, a word, an image, a person, a situation, or an idea. He sets himself to explore it to the full with his mind, thus extracting from it the maximum meaning, and he allows himself to react totally to it; the mind triggers the emotions towards deeper understanding and therefore deeper love of God. It is a series of leaps and recoveries. Like Augustine, Anselm is concerned with *sapientia*, knowledge which is love; like him, he believed that the more truly the mind knows, the more fully it will love. And the process from self-knowledge through repentance and fear, from the first compunction of terror and self-abasement to the second compunction of love and desire and longing, is the same route of *affectus* as for Augustine. But there is almost unconsciously a difference; the strand called love has been teased out from the strand called knowledge, and is applied at certain moments for a certain effect. It is this effect which is the aim of the prayers; they evolve into emotional situations, carefully constructed by words and word-associations in order to involve the person praying more deeply in the mysteries of the faith. Thus prayer becomes essentially 'personal' in a new sense: the intellect and the emotions alternate as ways into prayer. The moment that is said the difference between Augustine and Anselm becomes clear: for Augustine, the mind, the intellect, defined the whole man; Anselm goes a long way towards changing this anthropology and giving separate functions to mind, emotion and will.

In Anselm this is there to be seen in practice. In Bernard it undergoes a further transmutation which leads the pattern back to that of Augustine, though from a different aspect. Augustine presented a spirituality of knowledge which is love; in Bernard this became a spirituality of love which is knowledge. Bernard was the heir to Anselm's distinction between love and knowledge, and gave knowledge a new and minor place in his teaching on prayer. But it was no longer the *sapientia* of Augustine; it had been shrunk to the *scientia* of the schools. This is not to say that there is a major difference in essence between the spirituality of Augustine and Bernard; they saw loving wisdom, wise love, as the end and the way and the goal. It was one central dynamism, under whichever name. It is Anselm who is at a distance from both; it could be said that he is the catalyst, that without him 'Augustine' would not have become 'Bernard'. All three agreed that the goal of the Christian life is union with God in heaven in the perfection of knowledge and of love, and their language is similar: 'Then the soul will know even as she is known, she will love even as she is loved; and the bridegroom who is Jesus Christ our Lord, above all, blessed for ever, will rejoice over the bride, knowing and known, loving and loved.'[27] But while for Augustine, true knowledge becomes love; and for Bernard, the loving heart attains to perfect knowledge; in Anselm, it seems that the brilliant reasoning mind alternates with the emotions, held in tension, at times fragmenting, as he explores the realms of *caritas* and *sapientia* and the lesser ways of *affectus* and *scientia*.

CONCLUSION

In describing the attitude of Anselm as monk, scholar and man of prayer, I have tried also to see him as part of his own society and mental ethos. In all these spheres it seems to me that Anselm, perhaps even more than either Augustine or Bernard, has something to say about our present involvement with theology and with prayer.

As a monk Anselm understood theology to be the dynamic reflection upon mysteries already accepted and believed, by which the whole person, engaging in an arduous and totally demanding task—an *ascesis*—would be transfigured, receiving more and more of the light which is God. Anselm was a man of profound learning and alert mind who made his intellectual genius an integral part of his commitment to God as a monk. This is a monastic approach, but there is surely something here which is true of all Christian scholarship. There have been many such men throughout history: Cassiodorous, Bede, Anselm, Mabillon, Wilmart—and a host of quiet monks whose names are known only in a smaller sphere of scholarship.

Dom Damasus Winzen, writing of one such scholar, a nun—Dame Aemiliana Lohr—at the time of her death, reflects perfectly the whole tradition of monastic and Christian scholarship as Anselm represented it:

> In the work of a truly Christian scholar, historical and philological research become instruments of that basic humility that bids him leave the accustomed ways of his human thinking in the effort to come to a more faithful understanding of the divine realities handed down to him in the word of God and the tradition of the Church.

Fides quaerens intellectum, or, as Hilary of Poitiers said: 'Bestow upon us, O Lord, the meaning of words, the light of understanding, the nobility of diction, and grant that what we believe that we may also speak.[28]

NOTES

1. *Vita Anselmi* by Eadmer, II, lxvii. The references to this source, abbreviated as VA, are to book and chapter and may be found in R. W. Southern's edition, reprinted in Oxford Medieval Texts, 1972.
2. VA, I, v.
3. VA, II, viii.
4. VA, I, xxvii.
5. VA, I, v.
6. VA, I, v.
7. VA, I, xxi.
8. VA, I, xx.
9. *Liber Anselmi Archiepiscopi de Humanis Moribus per Similitudines*, chs. 92 and 93. In *Memorials of St Anselm*, ed. R. W. Southern and F. S. Schmitt, London 1969, p. 78.
10. Ibid. ch. 96, p. 79.
11. *Proslogion*. In *The Prayers and Meditations of St Anselm*, trans. into modern English by Sister Benedicta Ward SLG and published by Penguin Classics, 1973. This quotation from p. 239.
12. VA, I, xix.
13. *Proslogion*, pp. 266-7. (See n. 11.)
14. *Prayers and Meditations*, p. 89. (See n. 11.)

15. *Prayers and Meditations*, p.154.
16. VA, II, ix.
17. *Rule of St Benedict*, ed. Justin McCann (London 1952), Prologue, pp.7-13.
18. Ibid., ch.19, p.69.
19. Ibid., ch.20, p.69.
20. Ibid.
21. Ibid., ch.52, p.119.
22. Augustine, *The City of God*, trans. David Knowles (Penguin 1969), p.1091.
23. Augustine, *Confessions*, trans. R.S. Pine-Coffin (Penguin Classics 1961), p.231.
24. Ibid., p.55.
25. *Prayers and Meditations*, op. cit. p.44.
26. Ibid., p.243.
27. St Bernard, *On the Song of Songs*, trans. a Religious CSMV (Mowbrays 1952), p.256. I have discussed the relationship between the spirituality of Anselm and Bernard in more detail in 'St Anselm and the Development of Prayer', *Cistercian Studies*, Vol. VIII, 1973, pp.72-81.
28. Hilary of Poitiers, *On the Trinity*, trans. Stephen McKenna (New York 1954), Bk. I, p.34.

SUGGESTIONS FOR FURTHER READING

Eadmer, *Life of St Anselm*, edited and translated by R. W. Southern, Oxford, 1972.

R. W. Southern, *St Anselm and His Biographer*, Cambridge, 1963.

G. R. Evans, *St Anselm and Talking About God*, Oxford, 1980.

G. R. Evans, *Anselm*, London, 1989.

Prayers and Meditations of Saint Anselm, with the Proslogion, translated by Sr Benedicta Ward SLG, Penguin Classics, 1973.

XVI

The Place of St Anselm in the Development of Christian Prayer

"Jesus Christ, my dear and gracious lord"; "My Lord and my God, my joy and the hope of my heart"; "Jesus, Jesus, be to me Jesus"; "Let me seek you by desiring you and desire you by seeking you; let me find you by loving you, and love you in finding you".... it comes as something of a surprise that such ardent language should clothe not a sermon by St Bernard but the most brilliant and difficult philosophical essay of St Anselm. Most of these sentences are taken from the *Proslogion,* [1] which Anselm also called "Faith in Search of Understanding". It is famous most of all for the argument it contains for the existence of God: "God is that than which nothing greater can be thought", a theological consideration which has been called the point at which East and West met for the last time before the parting of the ways. [2] Much could be said about this aspect of the work, but the argument occupies only a small proportion of the whole. The rest could be described as a meditation on the nature of God and is in many ways best understood as one of Anselm's *Prayers and Meditations.* [3]

The *Proslogion* and the *Prayers and Meditations* were written while Anselm was a monk at Bec and are among the earliest of his writings. It is in these that the brilliance, the fervour and the originality of Anselm can

* Sr Benedicta, an Anglican nun, is the translator of the edition of St Anselm's *Prayers and Meditations* referred to in note 3.

[1] F. S. Schmitt, O.S.B., *Sancti Anselmi Cantuariensis Archiepiscopi Opera Omnia,* vol. I, *Proslogion,* vol. III, *Prayers and Meditations.*

[2] P. Evdokimov, "L'aspect apophatique de l'argument de S. Anselme", *Spicilegium Beccense* (Bec, 1959), pp. 233-58.

[3] An English translation of the *Prayers and Meditations* of St Anselm with the *Proslogion* will be published by Penguin Classics in May. All translations used here correspond to that version.

best be seen; and it is also in these that his links both with the theological inheritance of undivided Christendom on the one hand and with the new twelfth-century movements of devotion on the other can be assessed. It is with the latter that I am mainly concerned here.

It is only recently that it has been possible to consider Anselm properly as an aesthetic theologian. He wrote no treatise on prayer, indeed it would not have occurred to him to do so, but he was known to his contemporaries as a man of prayer, one to whom they could go for instruction and guidance. It is in a few lines in his letters to friends, in his Preface to the *Prayers and Meditations*, but most of all in the *Prayers and Meditations* themselves (and with them I include the *Proslogion*) that his teaching about prayer is to be found. Some years ago André Wilmart [4] distinguished nineteen prayers and three meditations as the genuine work of Anselm from the vast amount of spurious material that gathered about them within a few years of Anselm's death. More recently, the genuine collection of *Prayers* has been made available in a critical edition of Dom Schmitt; and it is from this distinct body of material that Anselm's pattern of prayer can be traced. One aspect of this is the similarity between Anselm's understanding of prayer and the Cistercian school of spirituality. Both, no doubt, have their roots in the same Christian tradition of prayer; but it seems useful to consider the parallels between their expression of it, and in particular, to see how the spiritual teaching that Bernard proclaimed and popularized had been articulated earlier by Anselm.

When Anselm came north from Aosta, he came into a world alive with change. It was the beginning of that critical period in the European history of which Bernard of Clairvaux was the later interpreter. Between them, Anselm and Bernard dominate this period, Anselm at the beginning from 1033 to 1109, Bernard at the end, 1090 to 1153. Although they never met and there is little evidence that Anselm exercised any influence on Bernard, the one cannot be understood without the other; before there could be a Bernard there had to be an Anselm. They were, of course, very different personalities, and their understanding of the monastic life they had both undertaken was correspondingly different: Anselm chose the conservative form of Benedictine monasticism and, rejecting his first ideas of a break with tradition by the hermit life or a monastic-apostolic form of life on his own estates, entered the Norman monastery of Bec. Yet it is notable that he also rejected the epitome of monasticism in the grand manner as represented by the liturgical life of Cluny, since "there all I have spent in study would

[4] A. Wilmart, *Auteurs spirituels et textes dévots du moyen âge latin*, Paris, 1932.

be lost".[5] Anselm was never the reformer of monastic ways that Bernard was, but there is between them a fundamental agreement about the monastic life, and this is so closely linked with their understanding of prayer that it forms as it were the basis of it.

They agreed first of all on the fundamental importance of an individual response to monastic life. It was not enough that a monk should simply endure his lot as a kind of endurance test, passive in a great cosmic conflict; there had to be a deliberate personal choice, a response made out of genuine love. Anselm called monastic life not a heavy burden but a "weight borne with singing".[6]

To lead the monastic life in externals only, without real conversion of heart is for Anselm the great hypocrisy: "I profess to lead a life of continual turning to God as I promised by taking the name and habit of a monk, but my long life cries out against me, as a liar to God, to angels and to men."[7] For Anselm as for Bernard the essence of monastic life is this personal conversion of heart according to the Gospel.

The Abbot of Bec and the Abbot of Clairvaux had also in common a concern for stability. In Anselm this was obvious and in accord with the Benedictine tradition; to Lanzo he wrote, for instance: "Whoever undertakes the vows of monastic life must study with the whole of his mind to root himself with the roots of love in whatever monastery he may have made his profession... let him rejoice at finding himself at last where he can remain for the whole of his life, not unwillingly but voluntarily, driving away all thought of removal."[8] Bernard was ready to countenance a change to the Cistercian way of life, but once a man was at Cîteaux or one of her foundations, he would no more countenance a change than Anselm, as his letter to Robert shows.[9] For both, the monastic life was a final and irrevocable commitment. The monk was a rebel against the standards of the world, or against corruption in monasticism, but once he was professed at Bec or at Clairvaux, to leave seemed to them apostasy; their love of God meant also a love of "the brethren and the place".[10]

---

[5] Eadmer, *Vita Anselmi*, edited and translated by R. W. Southern, reprinted Oxford Medieval Texts 1972, I, v.

[6] Ep. 101 To Helinandus: "Qui putat melius sibi esse in habitu clericali religiose vivere quam subire monachicae vitae pondus importabile; consideret per totum mundum quanta hilaritate utriusque sexui, omni aetati, omni generi hominum sit pondu illud cantabile."

[7] Prayer to S. Benedict: "Vitam namque sanctae conversationis, quam promisi nomine et habitu monachi, profiteor; sed ab hac vita longe exulando, mentire Deo et angelis et hominibus ipsa mea conscientia convincor."

[8] Letter 37.

[9] P.L. 182, col. 67-79.

[10] "Amator fratres et loci", a phrase used of early Cistercians.

This "love of the brethren" is another monastic concept shared by Anselm and Bernard. The great Cistercian doctrine of friendship was present in embryo in Anselm, especially in his early letters and in the Prayers. The letters contain expressions of passionate affection: "whatever remains of my life desires your company, so that my soul's joy may be full in time to come",[11] "you have come, you have set me on fire, you have melted and fused my soul with yours".[12] He had his own friends, and it is first of all for them that he prays in the Prayer for Friends: "those whom your love has impressed more clearly upon my heart".[13] In the Prayers, as in the letters, however, his love is not restricted to those he knows personally; he calls those "friends" who are joined to him by monastic or Christian profession; and he prays that any who hate him will also be called his friends one day. In the prayers that are addressed to the saints, he appeals to the friendship, the care, of the good and powerful friend who is also a friend of God—in the prayer to S. John the Evangelist this is the dominant theme, the love of John for Christ, of Christ for John, and the place of the one who prays within that circle of friendship. In the *Proslogion*, it is friendship that is the unchanging bond in heaven: "they will love God more than themselves, and each other as themselves".[14] This bond of friendship has for Anselm its origin and end in love of "dulcis et benignus Dominus Jesus Christus".[15] For Bernard this is equally true. He saw all love as based on the "friendship" between man and God. It is to be fully realized in the unbroken circle of love in heaven, but on earth the monastery should be a school of love, a "schola Christi", a claustral paradise opening onto heaven.

It is in the *Prayers and Meditations* that Anselm's understanding of monasticism most resembles the ideals of Bernard and the early Cistercians, and it is in them that a "way of prayer" may be discovered which can be in some tentative ways compared to the more detailed and full ways of Bernard. Anselm wrote the Prayers while he was a monk at Bec, within the context of the daily life of an eleventh-century Norman monastery. He was shaped by the recitation of the psalter, the reading of the Scriptures and the daily routine of life, in which life and prayer are brought into union, "let mind

---

11 Letter 120.
12 Letter 120.
13 Prayer for Friends: "Sunt tamen plures quorum dilectionem, sicut specialiter et familiarius cordi meo impressit amor tuus, ita ardentius bene desidero illis et devotius opto orare pro illis."
14 *Proslogion*, cap. xxv: "diligent Deum plus quam seipsos et invicem tanquam seipsos."
15 Prayer for Friends.

and heart accord".[16] His prayers grew out of the monastic setting. For instance—to take a very obvious example—the argument for the existence of God upon which the *Proslogion* depends was revealed to him during Vigils; "suddenly one night during matins the grace of God illuminated his heart and the whole matter became clear to his mind and a great joy and exultation filled his inmost being."[17] His prayers were at first, as we know from the letter to Adelaide,[18] an appendix to selections from the psalter but soon the psalms disappeared and the prayers stood on their own. This provided a new kind of material for prayer, breaking the monopoly exercised for centuries in the West by the Bible and the liturgy; the language and inspiration was still that of the Bible but the words were those of Anselm, and in no sense could they be considered liturgical prayers. They were long personal effusions, demanding both time and effort of the reader. It was the place that Anselm gave to private prayer, as well as the matter he provided, that was revolutionary: he saw it as demanding as much serious and sustained effort by individuals as the Cluniacs gave to their corporate liturgy.

The first stage in prayer for Anselm is withdrawal: "Come now, little man, turn aside for a while from your daily employment, escape for a moment from the tumult of your thoughts, put aside your weighty cares, let your burdensome distractions wait; free yourself awhile for God, and rest awhile in Him."[19] There, in the "inner chamber", the prayers were to be read "little by little, with attention and deep meditation",[20] as a preparation for God's gift of prayer. The prayers, he says,[21] are meant to produce compunction, tears, and compassion; they are a preparation for the act of God.

A pattern of prayer is discernable in Anselm's *Prayers and Meditations*; it is implied and taught simply by being used. In Bernard, the way of prayer is analysed and examined. However, it is possible to see similarities between the two. The basic similarity between Anselm and Bernard seems to lie in their understanding of the Christian teaching on "recapitulation", the restoration of the relationship between man and God. In the Prayer to S. John the Baptist Anselm makes this very clear, though in the other prayers there is the same beginning, way and end. Self-knowledge, self-abasement before

---

16 Rule of St Benedict, cap. 19: "sic stemus ad psallendum ut mens nostra concordet voci nostrae."
17 Eadmer, *Vita Anselmi* I, xix.
18 Letter 10.
19 *Proslogion*, cap. I.
20 Preface to the *Prayers and Meditations*.
21 Ibid.

God, is the first stage in prayer, the "first compunction": man, created in the image of God, is estranged from him by his own choice: "You fashioned your gracious image in me, and I super-imposed upon it the image that is hateful";[22] "Alas, what have I made of myself; what was I, O God, as you had made me, and how have I made myself again."[23] Such awareness of sin in himself is intolerable: "Alas, you cannot flee from yourself, nor can you look at yourself, because you cannot bear it."[24] This leads to tears, to compunction, the first piercing of the heart by God; in the Prayer to S. Mary Magdalene this is again the theme: "Give me, O Lord, in this exile the bread of tears and sorrow."[25] It is through this beginning in fear, sorrow and tears that it is possible to begin the way of restoration and to come to the other "compunction", of love and desire.

The doctrine of resemblance, the image of God in man, forms the keystone of Bernard's ascetical teaching also: "the soul, already like the Word in nature, shows itself to be also like him when she loves as he is loved."[26] The image of God is defaced by sin, but in the land of unlikeness it preserves a semblance of its likeness to God as a manifest sign of its divine origin: "the proof of the kinship is in the likeness that remains",[27] "the soul has not put off her native form, she has put on a strange form over it."[28] The first stage, for Bernard too, is for a man to know himself: "the more she [the soul] is disgusted with the evil within her, the more she yearns to realise the good which she also sees and to become what she was made."[29] For both Anselm and Bernard, the first stage in prayer is to stir the soul out of its apathy and make it realise its loss and its need. Bernard calls this "the kiss of the feet"—"the first kiss is the sign of a genuine conversion of life";[30] "let them prostrate with me at the feet of a most severe Lord."[31] He also uses the penitence of Mary Magdalene as a type of contrition: "lie down where the holy sinner lay down her sins";[32] "she wept bitterly,

---

22 Prayer to S. John the Baptist: "reformasti in me amabilem imaginem tuam, et ego superimpressi odibilem imaginem."

23 Ibid.: "qualem me feci, qualis eram, Deus; qualem me fecisti, et qualem me iterum feci."

24 Ibid.: "fugere te non potes; ne ergo aspicias te, quia non toleras te."

25 Prayer to S. Mary Magdalene: "Da mihi, Domine, in hoc exilio panem doloris et lacrymarum."

26 *Sermons on the Song of Songs*, trans. K. Walsh (Cistercian Fathers Series, 1971), 83, 3.

27 Ibid., 82, 7.

28 Ibid., 82, 2.

29 Ibid., 83, 1.

30 Ibid., 3, 2.

31 Ibid., 3, 1.

32 Ibid., 3, 1.

she sighed deeply from her heart, she sobbed with a repentance that shook her very being"; "the heavenly physician came with speed to aid her." Always with Anselm this is the essential beginning; and the fact that it is the beginning of each of his prayers seems to indicate that he knew it was always necessary to repent. This was not a stage to be left behind; it was rather a continual movement, like an Orthodox prostration, of repentance for sin and adoration of the Lord. Man's continual need of the mercy of God is the basis for his union with God. Anselm, and Bernard, did not see the Christian life as progressive enlightenment but as continual conversion of heart.

The second stage in this conversion, for both Anselm and Bernard, is devotion to the humanity of the Saviour. In the *De Diligendo Deo* Bernard describes this as the second stage of love: "we have begun to taste and see how gracious the Lord is." [33] The way on is in devotion to the man Jesus: "my own practice from the beginning of my conversion has been to gather for myself this little bunch of myrrh out of all my Lord's troubles and distresses... to know Jesus and him crucified is my philosophy and there is none higher." [34] Anselm and Bernard expressed this new warmth of affection, of concern, of human feeling in their prayers again and again. It had its focus for both in the sufferings of the Lord and in the name of "Jesus". The well known passage from the Song of Songs sets this out: "hidden in this name of Jesus, O my soul, as in a vessel, thou hast a sovran remedy against every ill.... When I name Jesus I call to mind a man meek and lowly of heart, generous and reasonable, pure, merciful... and at the same time in the same Lord Jesus I see Almighty God; as a man he heals me by his example; as God he strengthens me by his aid." [35]

The passage in Anselm that can best be compared with the fervour of Bernard comes in the First Meditation. After a long meditation on the Judgement and the terror of falling into the hands of the living God, the stern Judge, Anselm writes: "but he himself is Jesus; the same is my judge, between whose hands I tremble.... Jesus, Jesus, for your name's sake deal with me according to your name. Jesus, Jesus, forget the pride that provoked you, see only the wretchedness that invokes you. Dear name, name of delight, name of comfort to the sinner, name of blessed hope. For what is Jesus except to say Saviour? So, Jesus, for your own sake, be to me

---

[33] *De Diligendo Deo*, cap. xi; PL 182, col. 994.
[34] *Song of Songs*, 15, 5.
[35] Ibid.

Jesus."[36] In this kind of language Anselm was developing a new genre, the ardent, personal desire to know Jesus and his sufferings, and an imaginative and emotional involvement with the details of the passion. In the Prayer to Christ this sentiment is fully expressed, and it paved the way for the devotion of the later Middle Ages: "would that I with happy Joseph might have taken down my Lord from the cross, wrapped him in spiced grave-clothes and laid him in the tomb";[37] "why could you not bear to see the nails violate the hands and feet of your Creator?"[38] It is in this prayer also that Anselm summarises the pattern of prayer, through contrition to contemplation: "your goodness Lord, created me; your mercy cleansed what you had created";[39] "I am like an orphan deprived of the presence of a very dear father, who, weeping and wailing, does not cease to cling to the dear face with all his heart."[40] "I am mindful of your passion, your buffeting, your scourging, your cross, your wounds, how you were slain for me, how prepared for burial and buried; and also I remember your glorious resurrection and wonderful ascension. All this I hold with unwavering faith and weep over the hardness of exile, hoping for the consolation of your coming, ardently longing for the contemplation of your glorious face."[41]

In later writers this approach could turn into mere sentiment and emotion; in Bernard and Anselm this was never the case. Anselm's warmth of emotion sprang from serious theological convictions about the nature of salvation, as is clear in the last of the meditations, the Meditation on Human Redemption. This was a prayed version of Anselm's greatest theological work, *Cur Deus Homo*. As Eadmer says, it was "a sort of compendium of it",[42] written near the end of Anselm's life when he was in exile at Liberi. It places the atonement theories of Anselm in the perspective of prayer rather than that of argument. It could be called a prayer about the Paschal mystery, and combines the reasoning of doctrine with the ardour of vision: "this is the perfect and free obedience of human nature, that Christ freely submitted his own free will to God.... Because of that which was done on the cross, by the cross our Christ has redeemed us. Then whosoever wills to come to this grace with the love it deserves will be saved.... See, Christian soul,

---

36 Meditation 1.
37 Prayer to Christ.
38 Ibid.
39 Ibid.
40 Ibid.
41 Ibid.
42 Eadmer, *Vita Anselmi*, II, xliv.

here is the strength of your salvation, here is the cause of your freedom, here is the price of your redemption"... "Draw me to you, Lord, in the fullness of love. I am wholly yours by creation; make me all yours, too, in love." [43] Bernard once said, "give me a soul who loves God alone and everything for his sake"; [44] he would have found that soul perfectly in Anselm.

For Anselm, as for Bernard, the dear contemplation of Christ Jesus is not the end of prayer. The end is the last "compunction", the piercing of joy in the vision of God. This longing desire for heaven concludes each of the Prayers, and comes to its finest expression at the end of the *Proslogion:* after a meditation on the unity of eternal love in heaven, in the vision of God, Anselm prays, "let your love grow in me here and there let it be fulfilled, so that here my joy may be in great hope and there in full reality." [45] "Let my whole being desire it [the fullness of joy in the vision of God] until I enter into the joy of my Lord, who is God one and triune blessed forever. Amen." [46] This is the last "kiss" of Bernard, the "supreme kiss, the kiss of the mouth": "this kiss is the Holy Spirit for he is the unperturbable peace of the Father and the Son, their unshakeable bond, their undivided love, their indivisible unity." [47]

Both Anselm and Bernard followed the Rule of St Benedict and found within it that core of Gospel freedom which they, in accordance with the insights of their age, developed and expanded. In their approach to monasticism and to monastic prayer they belonged to a new age. Anselm and his contemporaries made the initial break-through into the expression of firmly held theological truths in the language of emotion and personal concern; Bernard took this way of prayer which Anselm had begun to articulate and formed it into a robust and immensely popular movement in devotion. The idea of personal conversion can never be far from any understanding of the Gospel, but Anselm and Bernard came to it from a starting point which was not that of their immediate predecessors, namely, the starting point of the emotions rather than the will. The inner movement of the monastic life was their concern, and it was this that Anselm and his circle of followers began to express in their prayers. Bernard and the Cistercians brought this warmth and inner movement into the wider sphere of monasticism, and

---

43 Meditation on Human Redemption.
44 *Song of Songs,* 69, 1.
45 *Proslogion,* cap. 26.
46 Ibid.
47 *Song of Songs,* 8, 4.

made it the basis of a great advance in devotion, perhaps greater than any other similar movement before or since.

Perhaps it is legitimate to go beyond the immediate parallels between Anselm and Bernard, seen as a matter of historical interest. There is no doubt that both were working in a tradition of Christian devotion common to both East and West. In this they discovered what was relevant to their own day without rejecting the past; they formed therefore a part of a living tradition. One of the aspects of the background of devotional life in their own age was the dominating idea of a transcendent God, as stressed in the austerities and glories of the Carolingian liturgy, with its impersonal, corporate nature, and its deliberate reflection of the power and majesty of heaven. This "otherness" is never the whole of the Christian Gospel, and with Anselm and Bernard this sense of transcendence was complemented by an intimate concern for personal relationship with the Saviour. This unity which they achieved would seem to be relevant to certain contemporary problems, in a situation where we have either so stressed the "otherness" of God that it seems that he is dead; or, on the other hand, have so emphasized the familiar and human side of "the man Jesus" that he seems no longer to be God. The way by which Anselm and Bernard in their prayer could integrate the transcendent and apophatic approach to God with an immediate and personal love for Jesus should give us matter for reflection.

XVII

'Inward feeling and deep thinking': The Prayers and Meditations of St Anselm Revisited

Imitation, it is said, is the sincerest form of flattery. If this is so, it is an attention which has been lavished upon one small part of the works of Anselm of Canterbury far in excess of that given to his main theological writings. From the first, the prayers were used and misused, collecting around them a host of lesser works which went under the name of Anselm. The separation of the genuine prayers from the rest was undertaken by Dom Wilmart, and the small nucleus of three meditations and nineteen prayers which survived was edited by Dom Schmitt in 1946. These prayers have, therefore, received a good deal of attention, perhaps more than is good for them, since they are at best early and minor compositions of Anselm, somewhat apart from the main body of his works. Yet, they were popular and entered the mainstream of medieval devotion. There can be no doubt that the element of emotion used in a particularly personal way as a goad for the will in prayer was a notable innovation by Anselm in these meditations. But the very novelty of it, now as then, appears to have obscured the full context in which such emotion is used, so that the true balance within Anselm's prayers has not been fully appreciated. The question which arises in looking at the prayers and the later imitations of them, is whether the latter represent a true continuation of the method of prayer espoused by Anselm, or whether they actually prolong and exaggerate only *one* element within his prayers, an element which appealed to a particular style of devotion, itself shaped by quite different influences. In order to demonstrate how the second of these possibilities seems to be true, I would like to give an example of the use made, in a different century and devotional climate, of Anselm's prayers, not through an imitation of his style but through translations of the genuine prayers themselves.

The example I have chosen is the Middle English prose treatise, *A Talking of the Love of God*,[1] a minor part of the body of mystical writing which evolved in England in the thirteenth and fourteenth centuries and found its greatest expression in the work of Richard Rolle, Walter Hilton, Julian of Norwich and the author of *The Cloud of Unknowing*. That the prayers of Anselm, and the method of prayer he recommended, were known to these writers is apparent from their writings. Julian, in particular, makes use of the three states of compunction which are found in Anselm's prayers and echoes many of his images and phrases in her writings,[2] and Richard Rolle has been seen as the author of a translation of

Anselm's first meditation.[3] The *Talking* is a composite treatise, and one of far less depth than the writings of these four mystics, but precisely because it is more popular, less weighty and less universal in its appeal, it shows more clearly the way in which the prayers of Anselm were understood and used in general. Moreover, one section of the *Talking* is a translation into English of several of the prayers: the prayer of St John the Baptist, the prayer to St Paul, the second prayer to St Mary and the third meditation, as well as the preface. It is, furthermore, of some interest to see how a translation into another language can also mean a translation into an altogether different style of prayer.

The complete text of the *Talking* is preserved in two manuscripts of the fourteenth century,[4] both of which contain many more devotional works of a similar nature, and which seem designed for use in private prayer for individuals. In that sense, they belong to the kind of prayer 'in cubiculum meum' which was proposed by Anselm. They are texts to be used as a way into prayer and they are meant to be read privately. The *Talking* itself can be divided into three sections with a preface: the first part is a free and somewhat enlarged version of an earlier meditation on Jesus Christ as the lover of the soul, *An Orison to God Almighty*,[5] and the last section takes its main theme from another earlier work, *The Wooing of our Lord.*[6] These are linked by a section based on several of the genuine prayers of Anselm, and the whole work is prefaced by a version in English of the Preface to Anselm's prayers and meditations in which is outlined the way in which the prayers were to be used.

The Preface to the *Talking* is recognizably a version of Anselm's Preface, but a comparison of the texts shows at once that a world of difference lies between them.

Orationes Sive Meditationes

Prologus

> Orationes sive meditationes quae subscriptae sunt, quoniam *ad excitandam legentis mentem* ad Dei *amorem vel timorem*, seu ad suimet discussionem editae sunt, non sunt *legendae in tumultu* sed *in quiete*, et *cursim* et *velociter*, sed paulatim cum *intenta* et *morosa meditatione*. Nec debet intendere lector ut quamlibet earum totam *perlegat*, sed quantum sentit sibi Deo adiuvante valere *ad accendendum affectum orandi*, vel quantum illum delectat. Nec necesse habet aliquam semper a principio incipere, sed ubi magis illi placuerit. Ad hoc enim ipsum paragraphis sunt distinctae per partes, ut ubi elegerit incipiat aut desinat, ne prolixitas, aut frequens eiusdem loci repetitio generet fastidium, sed potius aliquem inde colligat lector propter quod *factae sunt pietatis affectum.*

Heer is a Tretys.
A Talkyng of þe Loue of God.

þis tretys Is a talkyng of þe loue of God And is mad for to sturen hem þat hit reden to louen him þe more And to fynde *lykyng* and *tast* in his loue. Hit falleþ for to reden hit *esyliche* and *softe*. So as men may mest in *Inward elyng and deplich þenkyng sauour* fynden. And þat not beo dene But bi ginnen and leten in what þaas so men seoþ þat may for þe tyme ȝiunen *mest lykynge*. And whon men haþ conceyued þe maters wiþ redyng *Inward þenkyng* and *deoplich sechyng* wiþouten eny redyng vppon þe selue maters and of such oþere þat god wol senden. Hose wole sechen schal ȝiunen *in ward siȝt* and *felyng in soule*. And *swetnes wonderful* ȝif preyere folwe. But hose wole in Meditacion *swete fruit* fynden hit mot be taken in wone wiþ þreo poyntes þat folewen: Affyaunce, And continuaunce, And louh herte and clene þat he truste sikerliche to fynden þat he secheþ And þat his þouȝt beo harde i set And ful bisyliche I.kept And holden him self vn worþ out of godes ȝifte. And wlate on him seluen.þorw siht of his fulþe Men schal fynden lihtliche þis tretys in Cadence After þe bigynninge ȝif hit beo riht poynted & Rymed in sum stude To beo more *louesum* to hem þat hit reden.God ȝiue vs grace so for to rede þat we mowen haue heuene to vre Mede.Amen.

For Anselm, the aim of the prayers was to increase the ability of the reader to love and fear God and to know himself; for the author of the *Talking*, it was to love God more and enjoy this sensation. Both recommend that the prayers should be read thoughtfully, quietly and slowly, but the words and phrases used by Anselm in his prayer – 'quiet', 'slow', 'thoughtful', and 'meditative reading' – are transformed during translation and represented in the *Talking* as 'easily', 'softly', 'enjoyment', and 'inward feeling'. Both writers suggest that selections should be made in using the material in preparation for prayer, but while for Anselm the guideline in such selection is that the reader should use only as much as leads him to prayer, in the old tradition of *lectio divina*, the author of the *Talking* says he should choose what pleases him and holds his interest. Perhaps the difference can be summarized by saying that while Anselm himself writes in the tradition of ascetical prayer, the author of the *Talking* transposes Anselm's words into the tradition of mystical prayer.

Comparing the texts themselves, this difference is clearly apparent wherever there is a parallel between the prayers of Anselm and those in the *Talking*. I shall discuss three instances where this occurs. In the first case we shall look at that section of the *Talking* which is most closely based on Anselm's prayers and which uses his prayer to St John the Baptist. The whole of the prayer by Anselm has a clear and precise basis in the Bible, and revolves around the concept of John the Baptist's recognition of Christ as the Lamb of God, which is linked with the use of a phrase in the liturgy, the 'Lamb of God who takes away the sin of the world'. The prayer is presented as a conversation between three participants – Anselm, St John the Baptist and Christ. The theme of the prayer passes between these three and the reader goes through definite stages of prayer: self-abasement and grief at sin; the possibility of trust in the aid of the saint; and confidence and adoration of Christ as the saviour of the sinner who repents.

In the *Talking*, only one element of Anselm's prayer has been selected and the result is an intense and self-concerned monologue, in which the person praying dwells at depressing length on his own sins and condemnation. Those mighty Anselmian contrasts between the sin of Adam, or the sin of Lucifer, and the sin of those who have known redemption, appear in the *Talking* as the almost hysterical exclamations of a man concerned with his own unworthiness, as if the more sinful he makes himself sound the more he will merit help. The controlled use of emotion has here been distorted by being taken out of its context.

In the second example, it is this concern with personal emotion for its own sake and the attempt to arouse as much of it as possible in the reader which distinguishes Anselm's meditation on the Passion of Christ from the section on the Passion found in the *Talking*. It is not Anselm's 'Prayer to the Cross', an austere and beautiful prayer based on the liturgy, which is the parallel for the text in the *Talking* but his longer and more passionate 'Prayer to Christ'. This prayer might well be considered the most emotional of Anselm's meditations on a scriptural theme, but it is precisely here that the contrast with the 'inward feeling' of the fourteenth-century mystics is most apparent. Anselm describes with emotional intensity the details of the sufferings of Christ on the cross – the buffeting, the scourging, the wounds, the piercing with a lance, and the tears of the Virgin – but, in doing so, he does not go beyond the information found in the Gospels, and he gives the account reserve and dignity by placing the scene at a remove. 'Would that I with happy Joseph might have taken down my Lord from the cross', Anselm writes, and it is this passionate regret at *not* having been present at the crucifixion that gives the scene its reality and dignity while simultaneously adding, through the expression of his longing, an emotional dimension to the situation. Moreover, the meditation on the details of the Passion leads to an equally strongly felt apprehension of the resurrection of Christ and into a prayer, as in the *Proslogion*, to see the face of Christ in heaven.

In the *Talking*, what do we have? A direct involvement with the lurid details of crucifixion at first hand: limbs twisted in agony, joints wrenched apart, blood, wounds and pain. The difference between this and Anselm's own prayer is the difference between the crucifixion scene as portrayed in the St Alban's Psalter and the representation by Heironymous Bosch of the deposition of Christ from the Cross. Moreover, where the reaction provoked in Anselm by the scene is that of repentance, adoration and desire for greater apprehension of the mystery of God, in the *Talking* it is a very different matter. Here an overflow of what can only be called erotic emotion is released, involving leaping upon the cross and sucking blood from the wounds: 'I leap at him as a greyhound at an hart – I fold him in my arms – I suck the blood from his feet'.[7] This is neither the method of prayer devised by Anselm nor is it the theology of the *Cur Deus homo*. Again, emotion has been isolated and distorted through exaggeration.

A third example shows the same divergence. The *Talking* lists the qualities that all men desire: beauty, generosity, wisdom, courage, riches, noble birth and gentleness. The writer sees each one as finding its perfection in Jesus Christ, portrayed as the lover of the individual soul: 'Who would not love you, sweet Jesus? For within you are gathered all things that may ever make anyone worthy of another's love'.[8] The aim here is to stir emotion in the reader towards the person of Jesus, making him desired with the emotions of human affection. Where these qualities are evoked in the *Proslogion*, it is with a very different intention. At the end of the *Proslogion*, Anselm presents the same qualities as finding their full flowering in the vision of God in heaven: 'whatever you love, whatever you desire, it is there, it is there indeed'.[9] Beauty, generosity, wisdom, friendship, riches and pleasures – these are not set out as the attributes of a person who is to be desired because he possesses them, but as the fulfilment of all human qualities in the shared vision of God. The *Proslogion* represents a deeply felt expression of a profound theological truth about God and the purpose of Man, and its aim is to stir the reader to attain to that end throughout his whole life.

There, is then, a wide difference between the 'inward feeling' of the *Talking* and the 'deep thinking' of Anselm. Yet it is Anselm who provided the model for the later writer. In one of his very rare references to his sources, the name 'Anselmus' appears.[10] In this respect, the writer stands as one in a series of devotional writers who took this one isolated theme of emotion and personal involvement with the subject of prayer from Anselm, and produced thereby some masterpieces of a certain type of personal devotion, for example, the *Stabat Mater dolorosa*, or that treasure of Protestant hymnody, 'When I survey the wondrous cross'. But this should not obscure from our view the fact that Anselm's total approach to prayer, in those few prayers which are certainly his own, was different. There is in each of them a firm apprehension of theological and scriptural reality, and the use he makes of emotion is subservient to these themes. What is most significantly in Anselm but lacking elsewhere is the dimension of 'the others': whether it is St Mary Magdalene, St Peter, St Paul, or the whole company of the redeemed, he demonstrates in his prayers a continual awareness of others, of a 'great cloud of witnesses'. Where prayer, for the author of the *Talking*, is an intensity of personal emotion – essentially private and inward – for Anselm, it is never a private matter, even when conducted in the small inner chamber. That which is most personal to each is in some sense common to all, and in the perfection of charity he sees the emotions of each as a source of unity rather than divisiveness.

Let me end with two quotations which illustrate these differences between Anselm and his translator. The first is from the end of the *Talking*: 'Ah sweet Jesus, sweet love, my dear heart, love of my life, my death, my bliss, because you made me your dear lover, I place myself between your arms and embrace you. Now give me awareness of you for ever and keep me in your care, sweet Jesus, King of heaven, amen'.[11] The second concludes Anselm's prayer to the evangelist St John who has been pictured as pre-eminently the friend beloved of Christ: 'See, he [Christ] shows how much he loves me, he comes near to me so that I may love him. So I press on and hope not in myself but in him, for he listens to my desire who thus crowns my prayer. My heart and my flesh rejoice in him and love him and all that is within me blesses him, amen'.[12]

Perhaps all I have shown in this paper is that to translate is to betray ('traducere tradere est'), but perhaps I have also indicated the particular kind of betrayal which a partial appreciation of Anselm caused, and which led his name to be linked, in spirituality as in theology, with a tradition very far from his own understanding and faith.

NOTES

1. *A Talkyng of the Loue of God*, edited with introduction and notes by M. Salvina Westra (The Hague, 1950).
2. See Benedicta Ward, 'Faith seeking understanding: Anselm of Canterbury and Julian of Norwich', in *Julian of Norwich*, edited by A.M. Allchin (Oxford, 1973 ; reprinted 1978).
3. 'Here is a good meditation which Saint Anselm made', in *Yorkshire Writers: Richard Rolle of Hampole and his Followers*, edited by C. Horstman, 2 vols. (London, 1895-6), II, 443-5.

4. Oxford, Bodleian Library, MS Vernon 3938, ff. ccclxvii-ccclxxi; British Library, MS Simeon, Add. MS 22283, ff. 171v and 172.
5. *On Wel Swude God Ureisun of God Almihti*, edited by W. Meredith Thompson, Early English Text Society, O.S. 241 (London, 1958).
6. *The Wohunge of Ure Lauerd*, edited by W. Meredith Thompson, Early English Text Society, O.S. 241 (London, 1958).
7. Westra, *A Talkyng*, p. 60.
8. Ibid., p. 26.
9. *Ans.Op.Om.*, I, 118.
10. Westra, *A Talkyng*, p. 20. The actual words referred to ('Ah, sorrow and sighing, crying and groaning, where are you abundant if here you are absent? Where are you ardent if here you abate?') are not a direct translation of Anselm but a paraphrase of the kind of sentiment and phraseology the writer looked for in him.
11. Ibid., p. 68.
12. *Ans.Op.Om.*, III, 49.

XVIII

THE DESERT MYTH

Reflections on the desert ideal in early Cistercian monasticism

IT IS TEMPTING to see the flight to the desert of the early Cistercians as a repetition of the life and ideals of the Desert Fathers in the fourth century. It is claimed that this was first stated by the early Cistercians themselves, and elaborated by later historians of the order. Yet once the statement has been made, there seems to be a pause, a kind of awkwardness, a lack of breath; the idea is not given substance, nor does it receive close analysis, though it is clearly an idea very significant and precious among Cistercians; in one way, the present conference is founded on that very assumption, i.e. that the first Cistercians found inspiration in the life of Eastern monasticism and that those of today can do likewise. It is the purpose of this paper to see upon what foundation this first assumption is based; how far, in fact, did the first Cistercians know anything about Eastern monasticism and how much did they want to imitate or learn from it? I would like to examine what is said in some early Cistercian documents about the Desert Fathers (and this without entering into the vexed question of the early Cistercian documents themselves); then I would want to see how, if at all, this differed from what was said by their contemporaries; then, how this was elaborated by later writers; and what contact the Cistercians had with contemporary Eastern monasticism.

I would then, for the second half of the paper, like to examine a very different kind of material, which seems to me to illustrate both the similarities and the differences between the Desert Fathers and the Cistercians in another way. This last type of material is that contained in the miracle collections, and it has rarely been the subject of serious historical study. In some ways this is the very dregs of historical material, unverifiable by its nature, closer to romance than history, and yet it is here that the atmosphere of the early days can be most clearly caught as it was known to the monks themselves. Their expectations, their standards of holiness, their ideals, are, after all, as important as their charters or their formal theology. What did they look for in a holy man? What images did they use to externalize their temptations? What meaning and significance did they give to miracles? How did they distinguish between a vision and a delusion? Between Augustine and Aquinas there is no known major work on miracles, but medieval life was pervaded by miracle and sign. It was not only simple and uneducated people that were impressed, as the Victorian rationalists supposed; Anselm, the greatest of medieval philosophers, Bernard, the wisest of spiritual guides, Hildebrand, Peter Damian, Hugh of Cluny, all men of outstanding intellect in any age, told each other stories like these: "the bishop of Annecy died and lay all night in a church, ready for burial; at cock-crow the dead man sat up and began to speak. He said he had died and been taken before the judgment seat of God, where he was condemned for his sins; but the Mother of God intervened on his behalf, so that he was allowed to return to the body in order to do penance for his sins." [1] Peter Damian says he had this from the Cardinal priest Stephen, one of the most able of the papal legates, and he is repeating it in a letter to Desiderius of Monte Cassino, another assiduous collector of miracle stories. Others he had from the venerable Hugh of Cluny. These stories were being exchanged, therefore, by some of the most able and respon-

1. Peter Damian, *De bono suffragiorum*; P. 145:562-3.

sible people of the day; they cannot be dismissed lightly.

Here I would like to draw attention to a few such stories that were told in Cistercian circles, and which seem to show some similarity to Eastern ways of thought, and to be in some sense an expression of that underlying Greek influence which Professor Hamilton has so happily called, quoting William of St Thierry, *orientale lumen.* It is a common language for experiences held in common, and it is there that I would look for parallels with the experience of the Desert rather than in any direct contact or imitation.

First of all, however, what did the Cistercians of the first generation have to say about the desert ideal? According to the *Exordium Parvum* and the *Carta Caritatis,* nothing whatever. The *Exordium Parvum* uses the word *heremus* to describe the site of the new monastery and says of it: *nemoris spinarumque tunc temporis opacitate accessui hominum insolitus a solis inhabitabatur feris.* It was prized because it was inaccessible, because they would be safe there from interference; but their ideal, what they were going there to do was not "to imitate the Fathers of the Desert" but to "follow the Rule of St Benedict," *secundum regulam S. Benedicti deo servire cupientibus.*

There were two hints here upon which later writers were able to build: one was the Rule of St Benedict. In Chapter 73, *de hoc quod non omnis justitiae observation in hac sit regula consitituta,* St Benedict recommends those who desire perfection to read, *Colltiones Patrum, et Instituta et Vitae eorum, sed et regula sancti patris nostri Basilii.* Behind St Benedict lay the Desert tradition, and for those following the Rule faithfully, this was a decisive pointer. Then there was

2. P. McNulty and B. Hamilton, *Orientale Lumen et Magistra Latinitas: Greek Influences on Western Monasticism* [*900-1100*] (Chevetogne, 1963). *Orientale lumen* — William of St Thierry, *The Golden Letter,* cap. XI; PL 184:33.

3. *Exordium Parvum*, ed., J. B. van Damme, *Documents pro Cisterciensis Ordinis.* (Westmalle, 1959) cap. III, p. 7.

4. *Ibid.*, II, p. 6.

5. Rule of St Benedict, ed., J. McCann (London, 1952) cap. 73. p. 61.

also the fact that the first Cistercians were following a different observance of the Rule from that which was customary. They were "new" monks in the "New Monastery," and the whole point of their break with Molesmes was that they wanted a different kind of observance of the Rule. They would have said they wanted to observe the Rule *literaliter,* and so convinced were they of this that they could use the word "perjury" of their previous observance.[6] But this "new" thing was itself an interpretation; it laid the emphasis in different places, on ideals different from that "discretion" so prized by other monks, and, as the black monks were quick to point out, on ideals scarcely to be found in the Rule at all. The next generation had to justify this, and they turned in the direction St Benedict gave them, to the lives of the Fathers of the Desert, to justify the austerities and simplicities in their own times.

It is with William of St Thierry and St Bernard that the desert comes into the ideology of the Cistercians. They saw the Rule of St Benedict as crystallizing the ideals of an older and purer monasticism and were able to call upon what they knew of it to justify their interpretation of St Benedict. It is significant that it is in the *Apology*, a work of polemic rather than devotion, that St Bernard refers to the desert: he contrasts the present "slackness" of monks with the desert, *quis in principio, cum Ordo coepit monasticus, ad tantam crederet monachos inertiam devenire? O quam distamus ab his, qui in diebus Antonii exstitere monachi.*[7] Later, in defence of the austerities of Clairvaux against the dispensations of other monasteries, he says, *sic Macarius vixit? Sic Basilius docuit? Sic Antonius instituit? Sic Patres in Aegypto conversati sunt?*[8] This appeal to pre-benedictine monasticism indicates a new concern: St Bernard goes beyond an exact fulfillment of the letter of the Rule and articulates more clearly a concern

6. *Exordium Magnum Cisterciense*, ed., Bruno Griesser (Rome, 1961) Book 1, cap. XI, p. 63: *manifeste perjurii crimen se scienter incurisse dolendo fatentur.*

7. C. 9; OB 3:96.

8. *Ibid.*, C. 11; p. 100.

for an integral and authentic monasticism, appealing to the Fathers beyond St Benedict.

It was the austerities of the desert that St Bernard appealed to; and this was the case also with William of St Thierry. In his letter to the brethren of Monte Dei, he sees the Carthusians as introducing the fervor of the Desert Fathers into the West, and it is to them, not the Cistercians, that he is speaking in his references to *patres nostri in Aegypto et Thebaida*;[9] how well justified this was, will be seen later. But in his part of the *Vita Prima* he used the same language about the early Cistercians: when he first stayed at Clairvaux, *mansi autem indignus ego cum eo paucis diebus quocumque oculos vertebam, mirans, quasi coelos me videre novos et terram novam et antiquorum Aegyptiorum monachorum patrum nostrorum antiquas semitas, et in eis nostris temporis hominum recentia vestigia.*[10] Of St Bernard himself he says, *et primum quidem circa resuscitandum in monastico ordine antiquae religionis fervorem,*[11] the fervor in fact of the monks of Egypt.

Both Bernard and William are speaking about the life lived at Clairvaux under Bernard, and it is fair to see in them a development of the Cistercian ideal. With William there is surely also his special knowledge of and admiration for the hermit ideal among the Desert Fathers to be taken into account. Both are referring to the early monks for the example of their fervor in asceticism and the simplicity of their lives; in particular, manual labor, poverty and austerity are singled out as having their prototypes among the Desert Fathers. There were other sides to the desert monasticism that made no appeal to them or to their successors, and there were developments at Clairvaux and in the whole Order that were very different from the ways of the Thebaid; the whole liturgical life, for instance, and their concept of community, were unknown to the desert; and the whole social background

9. William of St Thierry, Ep frat; PL 184:332-4.

10. *Idem.*, *Vita Prima*; PL 185:247.

11. *Ibid.: col. 251.*

of the new Order was unbelievably different from Egypt: the phrase, *vir eximiae sanctitatis, nobilis quidem genere sed morum nobilior fuit*[12] occurs again and again in descriptions of the early Cistercians; it could never have been used of Macarius the smuggler, Moses the highwayman, or Pachomius, Antony or Amoun.

In practical ways, then, the "return to the desert" was tentative and selective; in theology the case was different, as other writers will show. In monastic life itself, it was a literary ideology, based on readings in Cassian and the *Vita Patrum,* as seen through the Rule of St Benedict, and seems to have been brought in by the second generation of Cistercians to support their ideals of a more primitive monasticism than that of St Benedict. These hints were taken up and solidified by the next generation. In the *Exordium Magnum Cisterciense*[13] we meet the myth of the desert in its full formulation: Conrad of Eberbach traces the fundamental monastic spirit to Jesus Christ and John the Baptist, making it revolve round the words *paenitentiam agite.* In Book I, chapter III he traces this spirit to the desert: *Antonius, Pachomius, Basilius,* are specially mentioned; and after them, *Macharius, Paphnutius, Pambo, Ysidorus,* and the monasteries of Egypt and the Thebaid. He refers to the "Rule of St Antony," and "Rule of St Pachomius" and, more understandably, "the Rule of St Basil," the latter being the only "Rule" which he says was written down, *scripsit monachorum regulam.* The virtures of these monks, he says, was summed up in St Benedict and transmitted by him to the West. This definite statement that the Rule of St Benedict is to be seen in the light of a more primitive monasticism leaves the way free to trace the distinctively "new" Cistercian customs back to the Desert fathers, and to claim their authority for them. To have the best of both worlds, Conrad also inserts a chapter on the *Vita Apostolica,* the life of the primitive church in Jerusalem, which he tries to fit into the

12. *Exordium Magnum*, Bk. 1, cap. XXXII, p. 89.
13. *Exordium Magnum,* Bk. 1, cap. 1-5, pp. 48-54.

scheme of pure monasticism; in using both ideals he is not unique, but the developments of the Cistercians on the one hand and the Augustinians on the other were to prove that these were two very different patterns and not at all the same thing.

The other writer who asserts that the primitive ideal of Cîteaux was concerned with the desert, right from the beginning, is Ordericus Vitalis. In the third book of the *Historia Ecclesiastica,* he gives an account of the beginnings of the Cistercian movement and puts this information in the form of a dialogue between Robert and the monks at Molesmes. Vitalis was a monk of St Evroul, a black Benedictine, writing at the time when feeling between the Orders was beginning to run high, yet he admires the Cistercians, and presents arguments in their favor. He sees Robert as the leader and inspirer of the movement, urging a more primitive form of monasticism, against the arguments for discretion from the other monks at Molesmes. There are other imaginary debates in Vitalis' *History,* such as that between William and his chaplain, Samson of Bayeux,[14] and there is no reason to believe they are anything other than interesting and lively pieces of writing, reflecting opinions that were current, not accounts of actual dialogues. This would seem to be the case with this passage about the Cistercians: Vitalis is giving a vivid account of a conversation which appears in no known source for Robert or the Cistercians, and presents the ideals and arguments for the Cistercian reform in his own day, putting them into the mouth of the supposed founder. He sees Robert as reading the sources—*perscrutatus est*[15] —the Rule of St Benedict and *aliorum sanctorum documentes Patrum perspectis,* and then exhorting his monks thus: *manibus nostris non laboramus, ut sanctos Patres fuisse legimus...legite sanctorum Antonii, Macarii, Pacomii, et ante omnes aliis, doctoris gentium, Pauli apostoli.* It is manual

14. Ordericus Vitalis, *Historia Ecclesiastica*, ed., Marjorie Chibnall, Oxford Medieval Texts (1972) vol. III, bk. IV, p. 300-302.

15. *Ibid.*, Part III, bk. 8, cap. XXV; PL 188:637.

work in particular that he is shown as choosing out of the early monastic customs. In reply, Vitalis sees the monks giving two kinds of answers, both common-place in Benedictine polemic of his day: first, the ways of St Benedict and other abbots were approved by God by miracles and signs, *quorum vita evidentibus miraculis insignita manifeste refulsit,*[16] *quorum santitatem Deo placitam in vita et post humationem refulsit;* and secondly, that the Egyptian monks acted as they did from necessity, in a barbarous and non-Christian situation; to which Robert is said to have replied, *inimitabilem Aegyptiorum Patrum vitam ad informationem commemoro. Sed inde nulla nobis violenta imponitur exactio imo salubris proponitur persuasio, verum ad tenendam per omnia Sancti Benedicti Regulam vos invito.*[17] *Paulus et Antonius aliique plures, qui primitus eremum expetierunt, et in abditis deserti locis monasteria sibi construxerunt, timore paganorum...illuc complusi, arctam nimis vitam elegerunt, et cooperante gratia Dei, necessitatem in voluntatem transmutaverunt.* The role that Vitalis assigns to Robert is at best controversial, and the references to the desert do not agree with any other early Cistercian account of the beginnings. It is perhaps useful to cite here another account by a contemporary of Vitalis of the same matter, to see how differently two writers handled it, according to their own ideals. In the *Gesta Regum Anglorum,* William of Malmesbury describes the early Cistercians,[18] and here the hero is Stephen Harding, *noster puer,* and the example of the desert finds no mention. He records only that monks were appointed to examine the Rule, *ita duo fratres electi, in quibus scientia literarum cum religione quadraret, qui, vicaria collatione, auctoris regulae voluntatem inquirerent, inquisitam aliis proponerent.*

It seems, therefore, that the connection of early Cîteaux with the ideals of the desert was a myth which grew up in the

16. *Ibid.*

17. *Ibid.*

18. William of Malmesbury, *Gesta Regum Anglorum,* IV; PL 179:1287.

second and third generations of the life of the Order. What connection there was came through the Rule of St Benedict and literary sources such as the *Vita Patrum* and the *Conferences* and *Institutes* of Cassian. It is worth noticing, in passing, that the *Vita Patrum*, along with miracle stories of all kinds, formed the staple of instruction in the Cistercian novitiate, if we are to believe the stories about Achard, who was novice master at Clairvaux, and the statements of Caesar of Heisterbach at the beginning of the *Dialogus Miraculorum*. It remains to see if the first Cistercians had any knowledge of contemporary Greek monasticism.

It seems probable, it seems almost inevitable, that they knew of the Greek monastic foundation of St Nilus; that they had met and talked with Greek monks in Italy; but evidence of this is wholly lacking. Much could be said about the emigrant Greek monks, individuals and communities, who had settled in the West in the previous century. Symeon of Trier, for instance, was a monk from Mount Sinai, who settled at Trier in the early eleventh century, edifying all by his complete enclosure, his long fasts, great austerities, and his combat with demons —*per noctis enim audiebat rugitus leonum, ululatus luporum, grunnitus porcorum, cetetarumque duras infestiones ferarum*[19]— in the best tradition of the Thebaid. Constantine, *quid monachus Graecus,* settled at Malmesbury in 1030 and planted a vineyard there — *cibi sobrius, potus parci et paene nullius.*[20] Like Symeon, he was renowned for manual work, silence, fasting and prayer. The West was made aware of the austere traditions of Eastern monasticism through such men, but their connection with Cîteaux has not yet been proved, and by the twelfth century this kind of contact was very greatly reduced.

There is one reference in the *Exordium Magnum Cisterciense* which shows the kind of hearsay knowledge current in the West in the twelfth century about Greek mon-

19. "Symeon of Trier," *Acta Sanctorum*, 1 June, 88-101.

20. William of Malmesbury, *Gesta Pontificum*, ed., N. E. S. A. Hamilton (Cambridge, 1870) V. 415-6.

asticism: Conrad quotes Anselm of Havelburg,[21] a friend of St Bernard, and his observations of monasticism when he visited Constantinople. In the *Dialogues* written later, he claimed to have seen nearly 500 monks living according to the Rule of St Pachomius at Philanthropou, 700 monks at Pantocrator, under the Rule of St Antony, and *vidi quamplures congregationis sub regula beati Basilii Magni.* Although Anselm claims to be *avidus explorator et diligens inquisitor diversarum religionum,*[22] doubt has been cast upon his accuracy. The numbers seems greatly exaggerated, eighty being more possible for Pantocrator, and forty at most at Philanthropou.[23] But his main impression is clearly of a great many monks living a devout life in great monasteries, and Conrad of Eberbach quotes him as evidence of the continuity of the desert ideal to the present day. It is an exaggerated and confused impression that emerges, of a wide-spread and venerable kind of monastic life, no distinction being made between eremitic and cenobitic life, associated with great names, and seen through the Rule of St Benedict. The appeal is to something that seemed to the Cistercians very like the kind of life they were themselves evolving, and, uncritically, they claimed their reform as a return to this more primitive monasticism.

There were other "new" Orders at the beginning of the twelfth century that also claimed the Desert Fathers as their predecessors. St John Gualbert and St Romuald saw their hermit foundations in this light, and St Romuald, says Peter Damian, deliberately modelled his practices in fasting and vigils on what he read in the *Vita Patrum.*[24] St Bruno's biographer also says that he took the Desert Fathers as his example in very practical ways, *et exemplo beati Pauli eremitae, beatorum Antonii, Arsenii, Evagrii, aliorumque*

21. *Exordium Magnum*, Bk. 1, cap. III, p. 51.

22. Anselm of Havelburg, *Dialogues*, ed., Gaston Salet (Paris: Cerf, 1966) Bk. 1, p. 101.

23. *Ibid.*, See note on p. 101; ref. to R. Janin, *Le Siège de Constantinople et le Patriacat Oecuménique* t. III, Les Eglises et les monastères, p. 503, 540.

24. Peter Damian, *Vita S Romualdi,* cap. 8; PL 144:962-3.

sanctorum cum beato Joanne Baptisto antra deserti quaeramus in montibus nos salvos faciemus.[25] William of St Thierry, as has been noticed, saw the Carthusians as fulfilling the ideals of the desert in a special way, and this ideal of hermit life seems in fact much closer to the desert than that at Cîteaux. It was, it would seem, common practice in the twelfth century, to claim the Desert Fathers as the example for changes in monasticism, as belonging to a purer form of monasticism, to which the Rule of St Benedict was the antechamber.

But there is another way in which the early Cistercians were in fact closer to the desert than in actual imitation or contact. The evidence of the miracle collections and the stories told about the first Fathers of Cîteaux point to a deep similarity of experience and understanding.

There were hermits among the early Cistercians whose austerities and experiences recall the life of the Thebaid. Peter Tolasano,[26] for instance, *habitavit in solitudine ieiuniis et laboribus multis* and faced the attack of demons: of *innumera bella temptationum a spiritibus maliginis.* There was also the hermit William,[27] who was visited by an angel disguised as a pilgrim, who came to rebuke him for breaking his fast. And here is the first instance I want to give of the difference between the stories of the Thebaid and those of Cîteaux, as well as noticing their similarity: the story of an angel visiting a hermit to correct him for breaking his fast sounds like a typical story of the desert, but in two important respects it differs. First, any Desert Father would have inquired very closely indeed into the credentials of an angel;[28] and secondly, the desert rule was to place hospitality and charity before rules of fasting, eating cheerfully with guests.[29] The changes in this Cistercian version of the story seem to be

25. *Vita Antiquior.* PL 152: 484-5.

26.. *Exordium Magnum,* Bk. 3, cap. XV. p. 180.

27. *Ibid.,* cap. XVI. p. 183.

28. *Apophthegmata Patrum,* Abba Zacharius; PG 65:336.

29. *Ibid.,* Abba Poemen. col. 457.

due to a concern to prove the divine approval of both the fast and the Cistercian-hermit life, by the rebuke and by the visit itself.

The theme of temptation which occurs with these hermits is more wide spread in the accounts of the Cistercians than is the theme of their solitude; devils and the conflict with demons is a main theme throughout the *Exordium Magnum* and the *Dialogus Miraculorum.* In this the Cistercians were in the desert tradition. The withdrawal of the Desert Fathers had not been simply a flight from the unattractive conditions of late Roman society, and the Cistercian withdrawal was more than a flight from ecclesiastical interference. The Great Old Men of the fourth century saw themselves going into a desert crowded with demons, with whom they were to do battle. The Desert Father was the heir of the martyrs, the warrior of Christ, engaged in unseen warfare. At Cluny, Peter the Venerable[30] described the corporate monastic life in just these terms, and it is a recurring theme in monastic literature, East and West. Cassian, St Benedict, St Gregory, all thought of the monk as the spearhead of resistance in supernatural conflict, and this imagery is there in the Cistercians. The outcome of the conflict is, naturally, assured, but the battles have to be fought. *Quisquis ad aeternum cupiens pertingere vitam / Currere felicem monachi contendis agonem,*[31] begins the verse preface to the *Exordium Magnum,* and this *agon* was no other than the *agon* of Christ.

When St Bernard brought a repentant thief, Constantius, back to Clairvaux, it was for *diuturno cruciatu et morte longissima mori...cruci affixum per annos plurimos faciam in poena iugiter vivere et pendere.*[32]

This similarity with the desert cannot be pressed too far. The conflict with devils, the noises, attacks, delusions, temptations of the desert had been the common heritage of Europe since Athanasius published his *Life of St Antony.* There is

30. Peter the Venerable, *de Miraculis*, cap. 12; PL 189:876.

31. *Exordium Magnum,* Prologus, "Sequentis Operis Versifice," p. 45.

32. *Ibid.*, Bk. II, cap. XV. p. 109.

hardly a saint in medieval Europe whose temptations and battles with the devil are not modelled on those of St Antony. The idea of the monk as a holy man who had special powers, both against the demons and with God, the one who could claim access to the divine, is not a Cistercian discovery. Men had lived under the shadow of the Last Judgment for centuries and knew what they looked for in a holy man. Perhaps the significant difference here is that with the Cistercians, although they revered the great men who did battle in that way, it was predominantly the Order and not the individual that saved. To remain in the Order assured salvation, to leave it was apostasy; to belong to it gave you access to God and power over the demons at death; to make light of its least customs was perilous; to keep them in humility and obedience was a sure way to heaven. Not the great individual fast, the feat of endurance, but the rule of abstinence from flesh meat, the custom of not eating after the grace at meals — these were the things that counted at Cîteaux. As at Cluny, it is the ordered round of the monastery that keeps the devil at bay.

The authority of the *Life of St Antony* was parallelled for them by another book, the *Dialogues of St Gregory*, with its accounts of holy men and miracles in Italy. Very close to the Eastern understanding of such things, it is nonetheless the miracle book of the Black Benedictines. It showed, in the miracles of St Benedict, God's approval of their way of life. There can be no doubt that a desire to emulate this lay behind the books of miracles produced by the Cistercians. They saw miracles as divine confirmation of their way of life, and with the example of St Antony and St Benedict, and behind them the vast authority of the Bible miracles, they had the pattern that formed their expectations. They had already read what happened when God approved of a way of life. They knew God would approve of them, and they looked for the signs. The whole way of life at Clairvaux especially made for miracles: the plain white-washed walls, the lack of exterior ornament, the concentration on the inner life, deadened the senses to the commonplace and made the monks, especially the unlettered lay brothers, unusually aware of the strange or peculiar circumstance. A presentiment, a coincidence, a ray of sunlight in an unusual place, might suggest a miracle for which there were a dozen parallels. Angels walked with St Benedict, and they filled the choir at Clairvaux: *cum ymnus Te Deum Laudamus cantaretur, vidit sanctos angelos multa claritate fulgentes, ...qui utrumque chorum percurrentes modo hunc, modo illum excitabant.*[33]

But here, in the details of this last miracle, is another major difference between Cîteaux and the desert: the liturgical life. The Desert Fathers scorned it: "It belongs to monks to weep," they said, and kept to their cells with the psalter. At Cîteaux, it was central. Many miracles show the divine approval of the choir, and the immense importance of the night office. Again, the place of the Eucharist was very different, and another miracle illustrates both the likeness and the differences: Symeon of Trier represents the authentic Eastern tradition in his dream: a devil appeared to him as an angel and tried to persuade him to celebrate Mass; the saint refused and held the whole matter to be a diabolic suggestion — he dispersed the vision by prayer and the sign of the cross.[34] But when the lay brother, Walter, at Clairvaux dreamed, he was sure it was an angel who spoke to him, and he learned the Mass of the Holy Spirit from him in his sleep. Moreover he still knew the words when he awoke, to the edification of all.[35] Another lay brother similarly learned to read Latin in his sleep.[36] Clearly, the expectations and desires of the Cistercians were not those of the desert: liturgy, learning, and priesthood are revealed in these stories as desirable goals, not temptations of the demons.

Lastly, what did the Cistercians expect of a holy man? In the Desert, this was quite clear: he was the athlete of Christ, the one who was near to God by the whole conduct of his life,

33. *Ibid.*, cap. IV. p. 101.
34. *Symeon of Trier, op. cit.*, cap. 7, col. 90.
35. *Exordium Magnum,* Bk. IV, cap. XV, p. 240.
36. *Ibid.*, Cap. XVII. p. 242.

and especially by his humility and prayer. This was true also at Citeaux. The theology of transfiguration, of the restoration of the image of God, will be dealt with in other papers; here it is sufficient to notice that it colored the miracle stories of the holy men. Fastrad, abbot of Cîteaux, was seen to be so filled with the Holy Spirit that *vultu angelico radiabat ut vix posset fidelium aliquis desiderabili eius aspectu satiari, praesertim qui puritatem animi eius et sinularitem manseutudinem cogitabant quam in exteriori homine velut in proprio sigillo divinitus impressam esse cernebant.*[37] St Bernard seems to see this transfiguration as the ground of the power to work miracles. It is to him a part of manhood redeemed by Christ, rather than a working of divine power in itself. This at least seems to me to be the meaning of his words to Anselm of Havelburg, who asked him to cure him, *si eadem haberes fidem quam habent mulierculae, posset tibi,*[38] and his insistence, when his message to sick persons "come and I will cure you" was changed by the messengers to "come and God will cure you through me," that the first version was correct.[39]

Bernard himself was a thaumaturge, a holy man with power to heal sickness of body and to cast out demons. Such powers were attributed to some of the Desert Fathers likewise, and although in this Bernard was not typical of the early Cistercians, in himself he stands in the desert tradition in this respect. What is more general, however, is his attitude to miracles, which is in line both with the teaching of the desert monks and the rest of his own Order. Miracles were, according to Cassian, second class; they were not the primary thing. "We should not ask of a man whether devils are subject unto him, but whether he possesses love;"[40] and that was Bernard's own teaching: only three things were worthy of wonder, *deus et homo, mater et virgo, fides et cor*

37. *Ibid.*, Bk. 1, cap. XXXII. p. 91.
38. *Vita Prima;* PL 185:384.
39. *Ibid.*, col. 356.
40. Cassian, *Collationes XV*, cap. VII.

humanum.[41] In his account of St Malachy of Armagh, he extols Malachy's virtues, and then says, *quidne coelitus missa crederentur quae tot caelestia confirmant miracula? et ut fidem dictis faciam, perstringam nonnulla paucis.*[42] The miracle, the sign, is secondary; conversion of heart is first; the signs follow where this is indeed true.

Bernard himself was also in the tradition of the desert by his insight into souls, which was so great it seemed miraculous. Also, like Antony, he was called into the Councils of the Church to combat heresy, and his place in politics is essentially that of a holy man, an outsider, and therefore an arbitrator, though it must be said that his actual participation in Church affairs far exceeded that of any desert saint.

It remains to ask, what of ourselves? The relationship between the monasticism of the desert and early Cistercian monasticism seems to present both differences and similarities. The Cistercians do not, either in a formal way or in the ways of inspiration, seem to have copied the desert. They found in it rather a familiar way of thinking and acting, a sense of friendship and similar thinking. They adapted their own ways to the demands of their own culture realistically, and in no spirit of archaism, yet the desert myth remained with them: demons, angels, cures, dreams, signs and wonders, tales that could have been told in Egypt or in Clairvaux. Some of the tales came directly from the East, of course, and were generally known in Europe long before the Cistericans, especially in the Mary miracles. Others seems to show a family likeness between Clairvaux and the Thebaid. The Fathers in both places would have been unsurprised; they would perhaps have said, "Where the life is truly lived, these are the signs that will follow." And is that perhaps the question they would still ask today: you have shown us your

41. *Sermo in nativitate Domini 3*, OB 4:257-262.

42. *Vita S. Malachi*, cp. 6; OB 3:314.

ideas, your methods, your theology; now show us your signs from the Lord?

XIX

ST BERNARD AND THE ANGLICAN DIVINES

REFLECTIONS ON MARK FRANK'S SERMON FOR THE CIRCUMCISION

> *The text is plain enough, that "at the Name of Jesus every knee should bow" . . . and was there ever more need to do it than in an age where it is doubted whether he be our God or Saviour,—where it is questioned so often whether there were ever such a name to be saved by, and we not rather saved every one in his own?*[1]

THESE WORDS FORM PART OF A SERMON for the Feast of the Circumcision, "On the Name of Jesus," preached by Mark Frank, one of the less well-known Anglican divines, in the chapel of Pembroke College, Cambridge, at the beginning of the seventeenth century. He was speaking to a university assembly, consisting mainly of candidates for holy orders in the newly reformed Church of England, in Cambridge, one of the centers of Puritanism. And yet he speaks within the tradition of the Fathers of the Church, and here specifically in the tradition of medieval preaching typified by St Bernard. This sermon is in fact based on the fifteenth of St Bernard's *Sermons on the Song of Songs: Qualiter nomen Jesus est medicina salubris fidelibus Christianis in omnibus adversis,* with some reference also to St Bernard's first sermon on the Circumcision, *In Circumcisione Domine,* and to the Cistercian sequence, *Dulcis Jesu Memoria.* Mark Frank's

1. Frank, Mark, *Collected Sermons,* Library of Anglo-Catholic Theology (Oxford, 1849), 1:258-272: *Second Sermon on the Circumcision.*

use of St Bernard seems to illustrate some important aspects of Anglican theology and devotion, both in the seventeenth century and today.

Mark Frank was born in 1613, and became a fellow of Pembroke College in 1634; during the Puritan commonwealth, he remained loyal to the king and the established church and therefore left his post; he was restored by Charles II as Master of Pembroke, where he died in 1664. By his time, the Church of England had been in existence for more than a century and had in many ways defined its theology and ethos. Hooker and Jewel had laid the foundations of a specifically Anglican tradition, and at the turn of the century Lancelot Andrewes, in particular, further defined Anglican theology. The idea of being part of the undivided church which looks to the first four Councils and the teaching of the Fathers led these men to make a zealous study of the writings of the Patristic age, especially Chrysostom and Basil, Augustine and Gregory. Andrewes, that "oracle to grave divines," wrote with ease in both Latin and Greek, and turned to the Fathers as readily as to Scripture. This sober patristic and biblical scholarship was combined with a deep concern for the right ordering of liturgy and sacrament; a care for sober and right conduct of life, whether in the family or at court; and a reliance upon Scripture as "the very pure word of God." The seventeenth century divines never explicitly reject the medieval tradition, and in fact some, like Donne, were influenced by Ignatian methods of meditation, but political circumstances in the "new" church tended to turn their attention rather to the Scriptures and the earlier Fathers. Thus there was an unrecognized parallel between their situation and that of a twelfth-century monk like St Bernard—a similar care for right conduct, for simplicity in devotion, and especially a love of the Scriptures and a warm devotion toward them. In Donne and Andrewes there is a constant return to the letter of Scripture, a natural use of the text without direct quotation, which is the method of Anselm, Jean of Fécamp and Bernard.

The seventeenth century in England was the age par excellence of the sermon. The Sunday sermon at St Paul's Cross drew the whole citizenry of London. There were sermons by popular preachers at Whitehall. And, a marked feature of the age, there were sermons in the great households; colleges and schools had their own measure of preaching, as did the parish churches. The sermon was a dynamic force, holding an important position in social and religious life; the great preachers had power to influence devotion and shape religion in an unprecedented way.

These preachers were influenced by the sermons of the Fathers of the Church, not by accident but by their deliberate choice. Donne, for instance, refered to Bernard as the "Father of Meditation," and frequently used the term meditation to describe his own preaching. The Augustinian relationship between knowing and loving God is the basis of both Bernard's preaching and Donne's. Their sermons are meditations because their aim is spiritual development and growth. In his fourth Prebend Sermon, Donne uses the same sermon of St Bernard on the Name of Jesus that Mark Frank used later for his Circumcision sermon:

> . . . from the sole name of Christ thousands of thousands of believers are called Christians, . . . Hidden as in a vase, in this Name of Jesus, you my soul, possess a salutary remedy against which no spiritual illness will be proof. Carry it always to your heart, always in your hand and so insure that all your affections, all your actions, are directed to Jesus.[2]

Donne speaks of this "hiding in the name" but it is interesting to see the differences as well as the similarities between the two:

> We consist in the humility of the ancients; we are Christians, Jesus is merely a Savior, a name of mystery, Christ is Anointed, a name of communication, of accommodation, of imitation; and so this name, the name of Christ, is *Oleum effusum* (as

2. Bernard of Clairvaux, *Sermons on the Song of Songs*, 15, 3-7, *Opera*, I, 84-87. Trans. K. Walsh, *The Works of Bernard of Clairvaux*, Vol, 2, Cistercian Fathers Series 4 (Hereafter CF 4) (Spencer, Mass. 1971) p. 108-111.

> the Spouse speaks); an oyntment, a perfume poured out upon us and we are Christians. In the name of Jesus St Paul abounded, but in the name of Christ more. . . . If we will call ourselves or endanger or give occasion to others to call us from the names of men, Papists or Lutherans or Calvinists, we depart from the true glory and serenity, from the lustre and splendour of the Sunne; this is *Tabernaculum Solis:* here in the Christian church God hath set a tabernacle for the sunne; and as in nature man hath light enough to discern the principles of reason; so in the Christian church (considered without subdivisions of names and sects) a Christian hath light enough of all things necessary to salvation.[3]

Here Donne is presenting the ideal of the Anglican Church as the true and undefiled church, the *tabernaculum solis*, which abhors the "errors both of Rome and Geneva." There is also the world view of the renaissance man, his belief in the "right reason" which is ready to receive the light of Christ in the Church. But there is the same concern and understanding that St Bernard evinces for the relationship of men with Christ Jesus.

Not only the use of the Scriptures, the approach to preaching, the theology and the devotion to the Fathers appealed to the Anglican divines; they were also strongly influenced by the Patristic prose style and use of language. Andrewes based his style on the Fathers just as much as his theology. In St Ambrose he saw a "witty" preacher, in St Bernard a master of antithesis and balanced prose whom he was delighted to follow. The early theology of *kenosis*, the concern with the contrast between the greatness of Christ and the mean conditions to which he descended, found expression in the carefully wrought sentences of these metaphysicians, with their understanding of tension and contrast in ideas and words. The great contrasts of Augustine and Bernard awake again when Donne writes:

> God clothed himself in vile man's flesh that so
> He might be weak enough to suffer woe.[4]

3. Donne, John, *Sonnet XI, Poems of John Donne.* Ed. Herbert J. C. Grierson, (Oxford, 1912), 1:XX.
4. Ibid.

Or when Andrewes exclaims that Christ "that thundereth in heaven cry in a cradle; he that so great and so high should become so little as a child"[5]; and in Mark Frank's introduction to his *Second Sermon of the Nativity*:

> Seeing the infinite greatness of this day become so little, Eternity a child, the rays of glory wrapt in rags, heaven crowded into the corner of a stable, and he that is everywhere want a room.[6]

Their meditations on the Passion followed the same pattern, but with a more clearly medieval devotional tone, as in Donne's phrase about the Cross:

> And thou lookst towards me
> O savior as thou hangest on the tree.[7]

The strange medieval use of the image of a book for the crucified Christ, with the wounds seen as red capital letters finds expression several times in these Anglicans, including Mark Frank.[8]

Andrewes and Taylor especially wrote in the tradition of the Fathers, but they were strongly influenced, though perhaps more by unconscious inheritance than by choice, by the medieval tradition. And here they found in Bernard a writer who combined the theology of the undivided Church with the *affectus* of the *devotio moderna*, and wrote in a prose admirably suited to their way of expression. In theory, of course, St Bernard rejected a careful prose style: "Peter and Andrew and the sons of Zebedes, and all the other disciples, were not chosen from a school of rhetoric or philosophy; and yet through them the Savior made his salvation effective throughout the world."[9]

5. Andrewes, Lancelot, *Second Sermon on the Nativity, Ninety-six Sermons.* (Oxford, 1841), 1:29.
6. Frank, Mark, *Second Sermon on the Nativity, op. cit.,* 1:69.
7. Donne, John, *Good Friday 1613 Riding Westward, op. cit.,* p. 336.
8. See Andrewes, *Sermons on the Passion. Ninety-six Sermons,* 2:XX.
9. Bernard of Clairvaux, *On the Song of Songs,* 36, 1, *Opera,* II, 4; CF 7:213.

But in the very words he uses he belies his theory. The seventeenth-century Anglicans looked to style as well as to meaning; this was in accord with their understanding of the role of words in the expression of right reason and order. "The Holy Ghost," wrote Donne, "in penning the Scriptures delights himself, not only with a propriety, but a delicacy and harmony and melody of language . . . and they mistake it much that think that the Holy Ghost hath rather chosen a low and barbarous and homely style, than an eloquent and powerful manner of expressing himself." Of St Bernard he wrote, "*Pax non promissa sed missa*, says St Bernard in his musical and harmonious cadences . . . St Bernard who evermore embraced all occasions of exciting devotion from the melodious fall of words."[10]

In Mark Frank this appreciation of words finds a less complex expression than in Donne or Andrewes; his prose is often as fine, but less strained, less fanciful, simpler. In his Sermon on the *Circumcision*, Frank relies closely on St Bernard and that in much more than the direct borrowings. The first paragraph introducing the theme of "the Name" is a sequence of prose devices, put together with the simplicity of complete mastery: "A Name that has all things in it; that brings all good things with it; that speaks more in five letters than we can do in five thousand words; speaks more in it than we can speak today; and yet today we intend to speak of nothing else, nothing but Jesus, nothing but Jesus."[11] This combination of warm devotion and good prose is found constantly in St Bernard. Apart from one passage from St Ambrose's *De Virginibus (Omnia Christus est nobis. Si vulnis curate desiderans, medicus est . . .)*,[12] the Bible and St Bernard are the sources for Frank's sermon.

Like St Bernard, he uses several adjectives to describe the Name and deals with them in turn, in the orderly manner of a teacher. They are not precisely the same terms as those used by Bernard, but they fall into the same two basic categories of *majestas* and *pietas.* Frank deals first with the titles of majesty:

10. Donne, John, *LXXX Sermons* (Oxford, 1920) 5:556-557.
11. Frank, *op. cit.*, p. 258.
12. Ambrose, *De Virginibus* (Paris, 1549), 3:110.

"truth and fidelity, might and power, majesty and glory," just as St Bernard does with "admirable, the mighty God, and the Father of the age to come." These titles of the Name "cover heaven and earth with the majesty of its glory. And yet," Frank continues, "so it might and we never the better, but that, fourthly, it is a name of grace and mercy as well as majesty and glory." The remaining titles therefore are, like St Bernard's "Counselor and Prince of Peace," names of mercy—"grace and mercy, sweetness and comfort, wonder and admiration, blessing and adoration." "He wants nothing that has Jesus," Frank continues, "and he has nothing that wants him."[13]

Frank then takes from St Bernard the comparison of the Name to oil: "*Est autem, dico, in triplici quadam qualitate olei, quod lucit, pascit et ungit,*"[14] says St Bernard; and Frank begins: "Thy name, says the spouse, is ointment poured forth, now oil has three special uses: for light, for meat and for medicine."[15] He then asks St Bernard's questions, "Dost thou want health? He is the great physician. Art thou fired in the flames of a burning fever? he is the well-spring to cool thy heat. . . ." The next passage, about "the name of sweetness and comfort too," is based on the parallel passage in the *Sermon on the Song of Songs: "Mel in ore, in aure melos, in corde jubilus,"* says St Bernard, "It is honey in the mouth, it is music in the ear, it is melody in the heart." Frank then refers to a passage, "as says the devout Bernard," which I am unable to trace: *Gyra et regyra, versa et reversa, et non inverties pacem vel requiem nisi in solo Jesu. Quapropter si quiescere vis, pone Jesum ut signulum super cor tuum, quia tranquillus ipse tranquillat omnia*: "Turn you and turn you again, which way you will, which way you can, you can never find such peace and quite as there is in Jesus; you will find none anywhere but in him. If you would fain therefore lay you down to rest in peace and comfort, set the seal of Jesus upon your heart and all will be quiet."[16]

13. Frank, *op. cit.*, p. 262.
14. Bernard of Clairvaux, *On the Song of Songs,* 15, 5; *Opera,* I, 85; Cf 4:109.
15. Frank, *op. cit.*, p. 262.
16. Frank, *op. cit.*, p. 262-263.

"I and this point" he continues, "though so sweet I part with it unwillingly, with a stave or two of devout Bernard's jubilee or hymn upon it."[17] He quotes in Latin two sections of the *Dulcis Jesu Memoria*[18]: "*Nil canitur suavius . . . quid sit Jesum diligere.*" Dom Wilmart has established that this hymn on the Holy Name was produced in the twelfth century, probably by an English Cistercian, but it is so imbued with the thought of St Bernard that earlier ages had no doubt in attributing it to him.[19] Frank translates and comments on it thus:

> There is nothing sweeter to be sung of, nothing more pleasant to be thought of, than this Jesus. Jesus, the delight of hearts, the light of minds, above all joy, above all we can desire; the tongue cannot tell, words cannot express, only he that feels it can believe what sweetness is in Jesus. A long song he makes of it; it would not be amiss that we also made some short ones, some ejaculations, and raptures now and then upon it. Give us but a taste and relish of thy blessed name, O Jesus, and we shall sing of it all the day long, and praise thy name for ever and ever and sing with the same Father *Jesu decus angelicum . . . coelicum:* "O Jesu, thou joy and glory of men and angels, thy name is music in our ears, honey in our mouths, heavenly nectar to our hearts," all sweetness, all pleasure to us throughout, wonderful sweet.[20]

The conclusion of the sermon applies the "sweetness" of devotion in a very practical and Anglican way:

> Bless we ourselves in this name, when we lie down and when we rise up, when we go out and when we come in. . . . The text is plain enough, that "at the name of Jesus every knee should bow," when we hear the name of Jesus I suppose there is none so little Christian but that he will confess that I may lift up my heart and praise him for the mercy and the benefits that I remember and am put in mind of by it; and where I bow my soul, may I not bow my body? Say good of it and

17. Ibid.
18. The whole of this beautiful hymn can be found in PL 184:1317-1320.
19. See "Remarques et Conclusions" in A. Wilmart, *Le "Jubilus" dit de St Bernard: Etudes avec textes* (Rome, 1944) pp. 219-222.
20. Frank, *op. cit.*, p. 266.

> make others say good of it . . . carry ourselves we will, I hope, as men that have a portion in Jesus, a share in salvation . . . . Be we not afraid then of the tongues of foolish men, but open we the morning and shut in the evening with it, begin and end our days with it in our mouths.[21]

This plain concern with conduct, with applying *theoria*, vision, devotion, in practical daily life is something basic to monastic life especially as understood by St Bernard. In the *Sermons on the Song of Songs,* he interprets the text constantly in terms of the humanity of Christ and his relationship to himself and to the monks who were listening. The famous passage on the Name of Jesus has this note of evangelistic piety very clearly:

> For when I name Jesus I set before me a man who is meek and humble of heart, kind, prudent, chaste, merciful, flawlessly upright and holy in the eyes of all; and this same man is the all-powerful God whose way of life heals me, whose support is my strength.[22]

This is a recurring theme in Anglicanism; "Let us," says Jeremy Taylor, "press after Jesus, which is truest religion and most solemn adoration."[23] And it is this unity of warm affection with theology and conduct that Frank expresses in his conclusion, together with that essential monastic dimension of the Parousia:

> Jesus runs through all with us. So then remember we to begin and end all in Jesus; the New Testament, the covenant of our salvation, begins and ends so, "The generation of Jesus," so it ends. May we all end so too; and when we are going hence, commend our spirits with Stephen into his hands; and when he comes, may he receive them to sing praises and alleluias to his blessed name, amidst saints and angels in his glorious kingdom for ever. Amen.[24]

21. Frank, *op. cit.,* p. 272.
22. Bernard of Clairvaux, *On the Song of Songs,* 15,6; *Opera,* 1, 87; CF4:111.
23. Taylor, Jeremy, *The Great Exemplar of Sanctity and Holy Life* (Oxford, 1887), p. 34.
24. Frank, *op. cit.,* p. 272.

XX

THE RELATIONSHIP BETWEEN HERMITS AND COMMUNITIES IN THE WEST

WITH SPECIAL REFERENCE TO THE TWELFTH CENTURY

IN THE SECOND HALF of the eleventh century, Peter Damian, the Prior of Fonte Avellana, wrote about a problem recently raised in his community: 'Many of the brethren, followers of the eremitic life, have asked me whether, since they live alone in their cells, it is right for them to say *Dominus vobiscum, Jube, domne, benedicere*, and the like, despite the fact that they are alone.' He goes on to answer the question himself with a long letter on the hermit life which is known as 'The Book of the Lord Be With You'[1] in which he included the following passage as the kernel of his argument:

> He [the hermit] sees as present with the eyes of the spirit all those for whom he prays . . . he knows that all who are praying with him are present in spritual communion . . . Therefore let no brother who lives alone in a cell be afraid to utter words which are common to the whole Church, for although he is separated by space from the congregation of the faithful, yet he is bound together with them all by love in the unity of the faith; although they are absent in the flesh, they are near at hand in the mystical unity of the Church.[2]

In examining the exact ways in which hermits were connected with communities in external matters, it is essential to have in mind that these external links are meant to subserve and express that deep inner unity in which the hermit is 'bound together with them all by love in the unity of the faith'. When a monk goes to live apart from his brothers it is possible to note and mark the ways in which he is separate from them, but what cannot be assessed in terms of legislation is the main part of his life which is concerned with affirming his unity in Christ with them all; in the mysterious words of St Antony, the father of hermits, 'my life is with my neighbour'.

On the level of external contact between hermits and society, however, this fundamental spiritual link has been expressed in different ways in different ages. I would like to examine here the tradition within monasticism in the West in the Middle Ages, with special reference to some developments in the twelfth century. The material is taken mostly from the lives of saints but I have also tried to show how the relationship between hermits and society was viewed in theory as well as in practice.

The Rule of Saint Benedict was the basis of Christian monasticism from the eighth century to the eleventh. It is often supposed that this Rule formally excluded the idea of the hermit life, and a superficial reading of the text in itself supports this claim. However, no Rule can be assessed truly simply by its written words, and there is ample evidence that hermits continued to exist within the Benedictine tradition and to find their justification within the Rule itself. Cassiodorus, like Jerome and Cassian, had seen the hermit life as a stage within the monastic life, and at Vivarium he provided hermitages for this purpose;[3] it appeared to the early Benedictines that this was the teaching also of the Rule of Saint Benedict. In the first chapter of the Rule, four kinds of monks are discussed, and though the Rule provides most of all for the 'strong race of cenobites'[4] the hermits are described as the end-product of the cenobitic life:

> After long probation in the monastery, having learnt in association with many brethren how to fight against the devil, [they] go out well-armed from the ranks of the community to the solitary combat of the desert. They are now able to live without the help of others, and by their own strength and God's assistance to fight against the temptations of mind and body.[5]

The monastery is 'a school of the Lord's service'[6] in which men attain 'some degree of virtue and the rudiments of monastic observance'[7]; but the Rule claims only to be 'a little Rule for beginners'.[8] For those who 'hasten to the perfection of the monastic life', St Benedict recommends 'the teaching of the holy Fathers . . . the Conferences of Cassian, and his Institutes, and the Lives of the Fathers and also the Rule of our holy father, Basil'.[9] St Benedict himself lived as a hermit, and it is probable that at Monte Cassino there were, as at Vivarium, separate cells for hermits. In the following centuries it is clear that there were hermits attached to monastic houses as a matter of course and, though the perils of such a life and its rarity were increasingly recognized, there is constant evidence of its existence. Grimlaicus, in his Rule for solitaries in the ninth century says, 'to enter the solitary life is the highest perfection; to live imperfectly in solitude is to incur the greatest damnation'.[10] Archeological discoveries have given evidence of hermitages around monasteries, and particularly near Cluny, which was as much a centre for hermit life as for liturgical devotion.[11] Many chroniclers describe hermits, and the fact of their existence is apparent from many saints' lives. Conciliar decrees and monastic customaries tried to exercise some control over the entry of monks into such a life and over their subsequent activities. These hermits had been monks and, after living in a monastery for some time they went, with the blessing of their abbot, to live alone or with one or two companions. Their lives are described in terms familiar from the fourth century and the beginnings of monasticism; solitude, prayer, ascetic practices, and simplicity of life were their characteristics. In the reasons for their choice of such a life and in the paths that led them there they differed widely. There was, for instance, Wulsi of Evesham, a layman who was professed at Crowland in the eleventh century, and who found himself unable to participate in the liturgical and administrative life of a large community; he became a hermit in a cave near Evesham. On the other hand, Maurus, a former abbot of Fulda, chose to enter the eremitical life because he would have leisure there for study.[12] There were monks trained in the East who settled as hermits in the midst of the Western cenobitic communities, like Symeon of Trier and Constantine of Malmesbury, and both were accepted and praised. There were hermits who received the blessing of their abbot to embrace a life of solitude permanently; there were also part-time hermits. Notably, there were bishops and abbots, busy administrators, who had cells to which they could retire. Hermedland, first Abbot of Aindre, always spent Lent in solitude and at the end of his life retired permanently to a hermitage.[13]

There was a peaceful relationship of concord between these hermits and their communities. At times a hermit might be recalled because of the needs of his house, most of all if he were needed as abbot for a time. Monks would visit their hermits and consult them on spiritual matters, and some of the hermits found it proper to their vocation to return to the monastery for the liturgy on Sundays and feast days. Hermits were relatively few, and it was because the numbers remained small that this peaceful co-existence was possible. Customaries sometimes legislated for a percentage of hermits only, out of a community at any time, and this was never more than ten per cent. In all this the tradition both of the West and of the East does not seem to diverge: the hermit was a monk who sought solitude for a longer or shorter time, who maintained links with the monastery in certain ways, and who was allowed for the rest to follow out his vocation as an individual however God called him. It is with the twelfth century that there is a change, and this is closely connected with what is often called the 'crisis of coenobitism' in the West.

It is clear that in the twelfth century a new type of hermit emerged. The traditional pattern of a monk who entered on the hermit life after training in the monastery was still recognized on the same terms as before, but there were many also who had either never been monks or who had found the monastic life in some way unacceptable. With these new hermits a distinction was made between monks and hermits along sharper and less amicable lines. The problems involved were complex and to some extent meant that the term hermit and also the term monk were being re-defined. Since the influence of this is still with us, especially in our concepts of contemplative communities, a closer look at this movement is essential.

There were, first, those who began the hermit life without monastic training. Then there were those who had been monks but had undertaken a hermit way of life more or less as a clearing ground until a concept of community again emerged for them. In the first group there were three famous English hermits: Wulfric of Haslebury, Christina of Markyate, and Godric of Finchale. All of them began their hermit lives outside the monastic structures, though all of them developed close relationships with communities later. Wulfric[14] was born of a middle-class English family in the reign of William Rufus at Compton Martin in Somerset. He was ordained below the canonical age and lived as a careless and worldly cleric at Deverill near Warminster where he neglected his duties for hunting. In about 1125 he underwent a conversion, and was also offered the cure of the village where he had been born. There, under the protection of William Fitzwalter, he became an anchorite in a cell in the wall of the church where he lived until his death. The villagers supported him, and turned to him for spiritual advice, and possibly for practical help since it seems at least possible to deduce from his life that his cell was used as a kind of strong room in which villagers could safely leave their money in the troubled times of King Stephen. Wulfric was known to St Bernard by repute and was approved by him. He was consulted by kings and lords as well as local people, and he had some connection with both the local Cluniac priory of Montacute and the Cistercian house at Ford. The monks of Montecute tried to claim his body after his death, but he was in fact buried in his cell. John, a monk of Ford, wrote his life with admiration and affection.

Like Wulfric, Christina of Markyate[15] did not enter a novitiate in a religious house. This may well have been because she had literally no chance to do so. The opposition of her parents, lack of a dowry, and the prohibition of her doing so by the bishop, debarred her from any monastic house whatever. In order to fulfil her desire for a life of consecrated virginity, she ran away from home and lived among a close net-work of hermits who inhabited the district around St Albans. She joined at first a woman recluse, Alfwen, a hermitess at Flamstead; after two years she went to live with the hermit Roger at Markyate. Roger was one of a remarkable group of hermits who lived near the Abbey of St Albans, and from them Christina received her training as a hermit. After Roger's death she continued, after a year elsewhere, at Markyate and soon made contact with Geoffrey, the Abbot of St Albans. Roger had been a monk of St Albans, and Christina's connections with the monastery were close; it seems almost certain that the St Albans' psalter was written at St Albans for her use. Her friendship with Abbot Geoffrey was deep and continuous, and she was regarded by the other monks as a spiritual guide. It is, however, notable that she did not make her profession as a nun until 1131, after living for many years as a hermit and after being offered the abbatial office at St Clements, York. Her profession, moreover, was made in the monastery at St Albans. Women joined her at Markyate, and though the account of her life breaks off before the death of Geoffrey, it is clear that she continued as a recognized and able abbess for the rest of her life.

Godric of Finchale[16] was an English merchant and sailor who was converted to a more serious Christianity in Jerusalem. He visited Rome, Compostella and Jerusalem, and finally returned to his native Northumbria, where he simply went and lived in solitude. Some land at Finchale was leased to him by the Bishop of Durham, and he also made contact on a spiritual level with the Durham monks. After some years he decided to place himself under obedience to the Prior of Durham, and a more definite relationship with the community emerged. The Prior sent a monk to say mass at the hermitage every feast day, and Reginald, Godric's biographer, a monk of Durham, visited him at those times and also was with him when he became ill at the end of his life. A priory of Durham was established eventually at Finchale.

These hermits were part of a new eremitic pattern, and a more famous one of the same kind shows how this solitude could emerge into a new form of community. Stephen of Muret[17] learned about monastic life while visiting the monks of Calabria, but he did not become a monk in any formal sense. Instead, he went alone to a mountain near Muret and there professed himself. His biographer says:

> He had a ring with which he espoused himself to Christ, saying: 'I, Stephen, renounce the devil and all his pomps, and devote myself to God, Father, Son and Holy Spirit, God Three and One, Living and True'. He also wrote out this formula and placed it on his head saying: 'I, Stephen, promise to serve God in this desert in the Catholic faith, and for this cause I place this form upon my head and this ring on my finger that at the day of my death it may be unto me according to my promise. . . . I ask you, Lord, to restore to me the wedding garment and count me among the sons of the Church at the wedding feast of your Son.'[18]

Other solitaries joined Stephen and the Order of Grandmont was formed. The Grandmontines kept the eremitic life as their basic aim; all the administration was in the hands of the *conversi*, and a standard of evangelical poverty was maintained which foreshadowed that of the Franciscans later. They claimed to follow only the Gospel and not even the Fathers. Their solitude, however, was like that which evolved for other hermits, a corporate solitude, in which each member of the group lived in varying degrees of personal solitude; but the characteristic feature of them as a group was that they were apart from society.

These four did not pass through any formal novitiate nor was their link with the older monastic communities that of formal training and profession. The hermit life was not for them the final stage of a monastic vocation in which they were living out their monastic life under different conditions but basically still as an integral part of their community. They are typical of the new understanding of hermit life in the twelfth century. Stephen of Grandmont provides a link between this kind of new hermit and the more famous kind who were hermit-founders. The new monastic Orders of Camaldoli, Chartreuse, Savigny, Fontrevault, and above all, Cîteaux, were the end product of the hermit explosion of the early years of the twelfth century. Besides these, over fifty other communities which adopted a communal rule of life began from hermit foundations. For instance, there was a group of hermits at Llanthony early in the twelfth century, and by 1120 they had become a house of canons following the Rule of

St Augustine with customs from Aldgate, Colchester and Merton.[19] Besides these, many houses of hermits became affiliated to Cîteaux, including Morimond and Pontigny.

The founders of these communities lived at first as hermits. Romuald, the founder, with Ludolph and Julian, of Fonte Avellana, tried first of all to persuade his community at St Appolinaris in Classe to adopt his ideas, then left it to live alone until a new community formed around him.[20] John Gualbert lived as a hermit at Vallombrosa, and the monastery that grew there continued to be known as the Hermitage, both because of its austerity and its remoteness from the world. Stephen of Obazine, Bruno of Cologne, and Vitalis of Savigny all contemplated a form of solitude which was not that of existing communities. Two things distinguished their idea of hermit life from that of the more traditional hermits: first, their concept of corporate solitude; and secondly, their desire for stability and obedience to recognized authority among themselves. The idea of solitude in a group is different from the idea of personal solitude. St Norbert said, like any hermit in any age, 'I do not want to stay in the towns; I prefer places that are deserted and uncultivated'.[21] But he did not expect to stay in the desert alone. Vitalis of Savigny withdrew to the 'desert', but it was in company with other recluses.[22] The desire for obedience was a corporate ideal, and when combined with the new concept of solitude as being simply away from the towns, led to the evolution of hermits into communities.

Of the new communities, Camaldoli, Chartreuse, Fonte Avellana, and Grandmont came closest to the Eastern concept of a lavra, though with more monks than was usual in the East. The brothers lived in separate cells and the degree of communal life was minimal. At Fonte Avellana, for instance, they met only on Sundays for Mass and Office, while at the Grande Chartreuse they only sang the Office of Vigils together. At Grandmont the separation of the group as a whole from the rest of the world included a stress upon absolute individual solitude as well. The monks in these groups were called hermits. It was not envisaged that they would move on to a greater personal solitude; it was a corporate life in which it was held that the hermit ideal was already realised. It is possible to see this kind of group as a restoration, almost certainly an unconscious restoration, of the idea of the skete which had fallen out of use in the West, the difference being that whereas the Eastern skete was a stage towards the complete hermit life, the hermits of Camaldoli and Chartreuse were basically committed to their monastery. The most famous of these new communities was, of course, Cîteaux, and the differences between the old and new forms of monastic life received dramatic publicity as a conflict between the Cluniacs and Cistercians. The Cistercians were, more than any of the new Orders, concerned to integrate solitude into community. They began as a group of hermits, and called their new home a 'desert'; hermits individually and in groups were to join them later. But the Cistercian way of life was basically inimical to the concept of individual solitude. The Order of Cîteaux claimed to have found the 'more perfect way' of St Benedict's Rule and to have embodied it in their corporate life. This idea of integrated solitude could cause difficulty when members joined who discovered a desire in themselves for the traditional hermit withdrawal; it was seen as a reproach, as opting out of what all wanted and had, and in this it is possible to see the problems that later faced contemplative communities whose members sought greater solitude from a context which *de facto* claimed to have it already.

The hermits formed communities, and with this they posed a new question about the meaning of the term 'hermit'. The topic gave ample scope to the twelfth century's attrait for categorization, but in discussions of the matter the hermit escaped too rigid definition in a significant way. The *Libellus de Ordinibus Diversis*, for instance, lays the stress in differentiating between monk and hermit on the life itself: 'I do not argue much about the name when I see the works performed . . . without the life the name alone is empty'.[23] The term hermit is in this treatise extended to include the new hermit communities. The monk, the writer says, is a hermit when he goes into the desert with like-minded men: 'He will penetrate the innermost part of the desert with Antony where he will merit the aid of the angels against the demons and the company of good men following him for God's sake; when you have done well you must go out into the mountain with Jesus and pass the night there in prayer.' It seems that by the end of the twelfth century the hermit was beginning to be defined as 'ascetic' rather than as one who lives alone. The most extreme example I know of this re-definition is in the accounts of the martyrdom of Archbishop Thomas Becket at Canterbury. When the monks stripped the dead body of this man who had not in life been notable for solitude, either corporate or personal, they discovered that he had worn a hair shirt. 'Lo,' they exclaimed, 'here indeed was a true monk *and hermit*.'[24]

The evidence of the hermit movements in the West in the twelfth century points to several conclusions. First, there is the overall tendency to understand the hermit life as no longer exclusively the summit of monastic life in community. Two aspects of this appear and lead in different directions, both of which have their bearing on contemporary approaches to eremitism in the Church. There were, first of all, those who saw the hermit life as a preliminary to life in community, and from these there emerges a new understanding of the relationship between community and solitary in which the stress is placed upon the solitude of the group rather than the individual. It is from these groups who tried to embody the ideals of solitude within communities that the modern 'contemplative' communities derive in at least certain aspects; and the problems posed for these communities with regard to the individual hermit remain. Secondly, however, hermits were known in the twelfth century who had never undergone any religious training in a community and whose relationship with the monks was not necessarily of a formal nature. This underlines the essentially free and unstructured nature of the hermit vocation and serves to emphasise the fact that there will always be in the Church those whom God calls into the wilderness and keeps there for their love of the Crucified to overflow in ways of prayer. That is the service Peter Damian speaks of in the quotation with which this paper began. It is then for the monks and for the Church to enable them to remain hidden within the quiver of his love.

NOTES

1. Peter Damian, 'The Book of the Lord Be With You', trans. Patricia McNulty in *Peter Damian, Selected Writings*, Faber 1959, pp. 53-4.
2. Ibid., pp. 73-4.
3. Cassiodorus, *Institutiones*, ed. R.A.B. Mynors, Oxford 1937, p. 74.
4. *The Rule of St Benedict*, ed. and trans. J. McCann, London 1952, p. 16.
5. Ibid., cap. 1, p. 14.
6. Ibid., Prologue, p. 12.
7. Ibid., cap. 73, p. 160.
8. Ibid., cap. 73, p. 162.
9. Ibid., cap. 73, p. 160.
10. Grimlaicus, *Regula Solitarium*, cap. 23, *PL* CIII, col. 604.

11. I am greatly indebted for information about Cluny and about the hermit movements as a whole to an unpublished thesis by Henrietta Leyser, 'The New Eremitical Movements in Western Europe, 1000–1150' (Oxford, 1966).
12. Rudolph, *Miracula sanctorum in Fuldenses ecclesias translatorum, Monumenta Germaniae Historica, Scriptores*, XV, i, p. 340.
13. *Vita S. Hermelandi abb. Antrens, Acta Sanctorum Ordinis S. Benedicti*, ed. Mabillon, III, i, p. 396.
14. John of Ford, *Life of Wulfric of Haslebury*, ed. Dom Maurice Bell, Somerset Record Society, vol. XLVII, 1933.
15. *Christina of Markyate*, ed. and trans. C. Talbot, Oxford 1959.
16. Reginald of Durham, *Libellus de vita et miraculis S. Godrici*, ed. J. Stevenson, Surtees Society XX (1845).
17. *Vita S. Stephani confessoris (Muretensis) PL* CCIV, cols. 1013 ff.
18. Ibid., col. 1016.
19. J. Dickinson, *The Origins of the Austin Canons*, SPCK 1950, pp. 111-12.
20. Peter Damian, *Vita Romualdi, PL* CXLV, col. 336.
21. Herman, *Liber III de miraculis S. Mariae Laudenensis*, cap. 3, *Monumenta Germaniae Historica, Scriptores*, XII, p. 656.
22. Ordericus Vitalis, *Historia Ecclesiastica*, Bk. VIII, cap. 27, ed. A. le Prévost and L. Delisle, Paris, (1838-1855), p. 449.
23. *Libellus de Ordinibus Diversis*, ed. Constable and Smith, Oxford 1972, p. 26.
24. *Materials for the History of Archbishop Thomas Becket*, ed. J.C. Robertson (Rolls Series, 1875-1833) vol. I, 12.

XXI

THE WOUNDS OF CHRIST

Reflections on this Devotion in the Middle Ages and in the Methodist Revival

In the Introduction to *A Rapture of Praise*, by Hodges and Allchin, the hymns of John and Charles Wesley are discussed in relation to the framework of Christian doctrine which 'they had received in the Church in which they had been baptised and ordained' (p. 32). The authors make it clear that for the Wesleys the Methodist way was a part of the whole tradition of Christian faith and worship in doctrine and in devotion, and especially in their teaching on the two sacraments of the Gospel. The authors make this suggestion, also, that 'many of the favorite themes of Charles Wesley are to be found in the monastic theology of the early Middle Ages' (p. 43).

It would need prolonged study to follow up this idea fully, but there is one aspect of mediaeval devotion which finds clear expression in the hymns of Charles Wesley, that is, the devotion to the wounds of Christ. The post-Reformation way of isolating such devotions, and treating such matters as the Holy Wounds, the Sacred Heart, or the Precious Blood on their own is something foreign to the early Middle Ages and the Wesleys, but the wounds of Christ, as symbols of the love of God, were of central importance to both. In considering and comparing their treatment of them we find a unity in their understanding of the mystery of redemption and expressing it in popular terms.

In the hymns of Charles Wesley there are many references to the pierced hands and side of the Saviour, and John Wesley defined the object of Methodist preaching as 'to set forth Christ as evidently crucified before their eyes, justifying us by his blood and sanctifying us by his spirit'. In preaching and hymns they set before Methodists 'a faire and lively crucifixe' (Thomas Adams, *Works*, p. 817) to replace the external crucifix which they rejected. The 'Protestant crucifix' of Watts in 'When I survey the wondrous Cross' has its counterpart in many of Charles Wesley's hymns, such as the Eucharistic hymn, 'Lamb of God whose dying love':—

By Thine agonizing pain
And sweat of blood we pray,
By Thy dying love to man
Take all our sins away.

. . . .

Let Thy blood, by faith applied,
The sinners' pardon seal;

. . . .

By Thy passion on the tree,
Let all our grief and troubles cease;
O remember Calvary,
And bid us go in peace!

(Methodist Hymn Book, 181.)

The pictoral expression of these words is to be found in the crucifixes of the early Middle Ages, at that turning point in devotion when the *Christus Victor* image was beginning to be replaced by a more personal attention to the sufferings of the Lord, but the understanding of these sufferings as part of the whole economy of redemption had not been lost. In the hymns of Wesley there is also none of the attention to the sufferings for their own sake, the sort of emotional pity for the Lord of Glory which marred both later Mediaeval piety and later Protestant hymns. When, in 'Arise, my soul, arise', Wesley speaks of 'his precious blood' and the 'five bleeding wounds he bears', it is not to express pity or to dwell on the sufferings but to plead their redeeming power before God:–

The Father hears him pray,
His dear anointed one;

. . . .

His Spirit answers to the blood,
And tells me I am born of God.

(Methodist Hymn Book, 368.)

In Anglican devotion this aspect of the saving Blood of Christ is more frequently associated with the Eucharist, and it is interesting that both the hymns already quoted were written for use at the Eucharist but are now printed in other sections of the *Methodist Hymn Book.*

The hymn which Dr. Newton Flew sees as the finest of Charles Wesley's meditations on the Passion, 'Thou Shepherd of Israel and Mine', is one which John Wesley refused to print, as being too 'mystical'—a strong term of disapproval in the first years after his conversion. Based on the Shepherd passage in Isaiah 40:11ff., and with echoes also of the Song of Songs, it has the same approach to the Passion that one finds in St. Bernard and the Cistercians. The wounds of Christ are seen as clefts in the rock where the lambs find refuge; they are also seen as the bliss of the saints in the 'now' of the eternal Passion:—

Ah! show me that happiest place,
The place of thy people's abode,
Where saints in an ecstasy gaze,
And hang on a crucified God;
Thy love for a sinner declare,
Thy passion and death on the tree;
My spirit to Calvary bear,
To suffer and triumph with thee.

The object of this mystical devotion is Christ eternally crucified and is inspired by a mediaeval type of exegesis. Israel is to Wesley, as it was to St. Bernard, the new people of God, and their Shepherd is Christ. The 'heat of the day' is the noon of the crucifixion and the 'clefts of the rock' are the wounds of Christ. There is a richness of understanding the Scriptures in a Christological sense that is common to the Middle Ages and the Wesleys. It comes from a whole life lived in the conviction that Christ has died and risen and his glory fills the world; that everything that is or that happens in the world has no other meaning than to be a revelation of Christ; and that this truth applies to the interpretation of the words of the Old Testament as much as those of the New Testament.

In the third verse of this hymn there is a still closer parallel with St. Bernard, in text as well as in approach:—

There only, I covet to rest
. . . .
Concealed in the cleft of Thy side,
Eternally held in Thy heart.

(Methodist Hymn Book, 457)

St. Bernard, commenting on, 'O my dove, thou art in the cleft of the rock', writes, 'The literal meaning yields us not much; but . . . the clefts of the rock are the wounds of Christ . . . the rock is the refuge of the conies and where indeed is there complete security and rest for us frail men save in the Saviour's wounds?' As for Wesley, the wounds are not a personal, individual hiding place. He sees them as 'that happiest palce, the place of thy people's abode'. St. Bernard, in the next passage in his sermon on the Song of Songs, calls the rock the Communion of the Saints. For both men the wounds of Christ are the symbol of redemption both now and in heaven, for one and for all.

There is another aspect of the wounds of Christ common to the Middle Ages and the Wesleys, that they are the insignia of the Risen Christ. 'Blessed are the clefts', writes St. Bernard, 'which proved to Thomas that Christ was risen and that he was God'. In the well-known hymn, 'Lo! He Comes', Charles Wesley writes:—

The dear tokens of His passion
Still His dazzling body bears;
Cause of endless exaltation
To His ransomed worshippers:
With what rapture
Gaze we on those glorious scars!

(Methodist Hymn Book, 264.)

This 'rapture' indicates yet another point of similarity between the devotion of the Middle Ages and the Wesleys. The mediaeval writers saw the wounds as symbols of the redemption of the whole man, and in their literal way they paralleled the five wounds with the five senses and worked out the details of their scheme with almost mathematical precision. The *Ancren Riwel* provides one example of this, reflecting a whole school of simple and popular piety, which, if the details were of their age, had a basis which is timeless Lady Julian of Norwich in her detailed and vivid shewings of the Passion also made this link between the five wounds and the five senses, and the whole rejoicing of mankind in redemption:—'a holy marvelling delight in God which is love . . . him verily seeing and fully feeling; him spiritually hearing and him delectably smelling; and him sweetly drinking; And then shall we see God face to face, homely and fully'. It is a different and more earthly kind of language, but it is the same truth that is expressed in Wesley's 'rapture' at the 'dear tokens', and in his longing, expressed in many hymns, for the fulness of God:–

Hear, and all the graces shower,
All the joy, and peace, and power,
All my Saviour asks above,
All the life and heaven of love.

(Methodist Hymn Book, 568.)

At a time when the wounds in the Body of Christ are for us so clearly a sign of the divisions of Christians, and when this has recently been painfully evidenced by the set-back in Anglican-Methodist reunion, it may be of use to look through the wounds of division into their meaning, which is redeeming Love. With the insight of both the Middle Ages and the Wesleys we see, for our encouragement, the meaning of these wounds as love, grace, salvation and everlasting bliss–a way into that unity which God wills, in the way he wills.

* * * * * * * * * * *

BIBLIOGRAPHY

R. Newton Flew, *The Hymns of Charles Wesley: a Study in their Structure,* London, 1953.

M. A. Hodges and A. M. Allchin, *A Rapture of Praise,* London, 1966.

XXII

LAUDABILITER VIXIT

THE DEATH OF THE SAINTS IN SOME 12th-CENTURY SOURCES

'and the moment of death is every moment.'

TO TALK ABOUT death or sanctity is to pursue themes not generally popular in ordinary conversation. Our distaste for the details of death and dying was parodied in the late 'forties by Evelyn Waugh in *The Loved One*, and sanctity has long been out of date: 'the lilies and langours of virtue, the roses and raptures of vice', though, as Chesterton comments, 'If you think virtue is languid, just try it and see'. Perhaps one may at least however try and see what some men in the twelfth century made of both topics; without making recommendations about either.

The texts I have chosen are from the monastic world of the twelfth and thirteenth centuries and from Cistercian sources. They are also from the ordinary monks and nuns, not from the 'stars'. There are many accounts of death among the medieval Cistercian miracle stories, as many as there are of sanctity, and to choose between them has been difficult. As Caesarius of Heisterbach says, there are four ways of dying: to live well and to die well; to live badly and to die badly; and the other combinations of the two possibilities. He himself supplies a very large number of illustrations of each. It was clearly a major interest: how did men die? I think that three stories can be taken as fairly representative; and from those three I propose to discover at least a little of what monks thought about dying. The first story was current at Clairvaux in the second generation after St Bernard; the second was told of a monk of Clairvaux and was later retold in the later stages of the Cistercian movement; and the third was told after 1200 in the German house of Heisterbach. I do not wish to suggest that there is a particular Cistercian spirituality of death; these tales could be paralleled from other twelfth century monastic sources, and indeed from non-monastic sources also. But they serve to illustrate a certain point from texts which will always be of interest to students of the Middle Ages: the *De Miraculis* of Herbert of Clairvaux, the

Exordium Magnum Cisterciensis and the *Dialogue* of Caesarius.

First, a text of the Cistercian movement in its most acute stage: it is, perhaps surprisingly, about a girl, Mary, who entered a convent as a child of nine and died ten years later, a Little Flower of the twelfth century.

For many years she served those who were sick with great devotion and care; at last she herself became paralyzed, so that she could not move either hand or foot and had to be fed with slops. She had to suffer much pain in her body. Now it happened that, in the quietest hour of the night, one of the sisters in another part near the infirmary heard the noise of many voices speaking together. Surprised, she got up and went to see what was happening. She went into the infirmary quietly and saw there a great light blazing, and shining over the bed of the sick nun, who was sitting up, though never before had she been able to move. She called the infirmarian to see this wonder and when they came in together they found her lying still in bed. Next morning . . . she admitted to them that two of the departed sisters of the monastery had visited her and talked with her. On the day when she died, she saw the holy Mother of God descend from heaven with the two departed sisters. The dying nun exclaimed in thanks saying, 'This is our Lady, the queen of heaven, who has deigned to attend the great festival which today we are celebrating, for such a feast has not been celebrated here for many years.' (Herbert, 11, col. 1354.)

Secondly, there is Alquirin, who was a monk of Clairvaux during the abbacy of Pons (1165-70).

There lived in the monastery of Clairvaux a monk called Alquirin whose holiness was as great as his calling indicated. He was a religious and spiritual man, restrained in eating, humble in appearance and severe in chastising his body. He was so circumspect and temperate in everything pertaining to the body that he refused all pleasure and vanity and even used necessities very sparingly, although he often had opportunity to go beyond the limits he had set himself. He was skilled in the art of medicine, and so nobles and great men of that region were always asking his help and drawing him, unwilling and resisting, to many places. Yet he was always solicitous about the poor and needy and would go to any lengths to cure them. Not only did he treat their sicknesses and wounds, but he tended with his own hands their putrid flesh and ulcered limbs with such care that it was as if he were caring for the wounds of Christ. And this really was so, he did everything for Christ, and Christ received everything he did as being done for him, so that at the end he could say to him what was said of those who do works of mercy, 'I was sick and you visited me'.

Having lived his life in this praiseworthy manner, the time came when he would receive in eternity the reward of his labours and his works of mercy, and he fell ill and neared his end. The venerable abbot Pons came to visit him, and asked him what he was doing and how he was. He replied, 'My dear Father, all is very well with me, because I am going to my Lord.' Pons asked him, 'But are you not suffering in body, and do you not fear the agony of death?' Alquirin replied, 'I look upon it all with tranquillity and joy, because I have received beforehand from the Lord the blessings of sweetness, and that has taken all sorrow from my heart and nearly all pain from my body.' Then the abbot asked him, 'I beg you, my dear brother, for the love of God and for our edification, tell us anything that God has revealed to you.' To which he replied, 'Before you came in, I saw, miserable and unworthy though I am, the Lord Jesus who looked at me with a kind and serene expression and showed me the marks of his most blessed Passion, saying: "Lo, your sins are taken away from before my face. Come without fear, come and see, and kiss my wounds which you have loved so much and tended so often." I was so strengthened by this promise that I do not now fear to die, because of the hope which remains in my heart. Tomorrow night, which is the vigil of St Martin [Nov. 11th], I will be taken away at such an hour during divine office.' He died on the very night at the hour he had foretold, and I am quite sure he now rests from his labours. Like a dove whiter than snow, he dwells in the cleft of the rock, hidden in the holy wounds of Christ, who is above all blessed forever. Amen.

And thirdly, the monk Siger of Himmerode, who died young and in great pain.

There was in the same house a priest monk, Siger, a young man and a lover of the Order, a severe chastiser of his body, who amongst other acts of goodness, ardently loved the Holy Mother of God, and by all the ways he could urged others to love her. When the hour of his summons was at hand, his sickness and weakness being very great, a lay-brother, forewarned by the favour of God, whom the Lord frequently deigned to comfort by his secret consolations, saw this vision. He thought that the board of the dead was being beaten and he started to aid in the passing of a brother. And it chanced that whilst going through a palace wonderfully built, he found living in it a matron of venerable bearing, whose face shewed angelic grace and her garments snowy whiteness. Therefore he stopped with his eyes fixed on her, certain that in so desirable a person there resided divine power. Finally, the presence of such divinity giving him courage, he came nearer, having no fear of the danger of rebuff, and joined in friendly talk, saying: 'Most lovely mistress, what reason have you for coming in here to us, since matrons are not allowed here?' Said she: 'I have a special right in your house and I come to visit my friends and members of my household.' Said he, having a pious care for his brothers: 'Behold our brothers depart one by one, young and old and middle-aged, and there is no respect of persons. What then must we do?' She said: 'You must sing the Te Deum.' She made a further reply, but he being a plain illiterate man remembered only these words. Meantime the board was actually beaten and the symbolic vision came to an end. We believe that the good Mother of God, as the mother of pity, did not fail her faithful servant in death and gave him that sign of her coming.

There seem to me to be themes here which recur in stories of Christian death with remarkable persistence and which are not to be dismissed as mere folk tales or pious exaggerations. First of all: in each story there is no pretence that death is easy or simple. It is preceded by great pain and genuine distress: the nun Mary suffered a great deal; Alquirin groaned and suffered agony; the monk Siger was also in agony and remained so. It is not Siger who sees the vision of St Mary, but a lay-brother. That is frequently the case in these tales; it is not the sick man who sees the vision of angels (sometimes it is but not always) but a brother who has a vision of angels or saints helping the dying. For the one who is dying, physical agony remains unabated. And death, the last enemy, has a more subtle and terrifying threat: the agony of damnation, of combat with the devils, the terror of final extinction, lies over the dying; it is the last frontier, the limit of existence and the place of ultimate agony.

Secondly, the dying monks find it possible to link themselves to those who have passed through the grave and gate of death, who have survived that last terrible conflict. The Passion of Christ on the cross therefore colours the thoughts of Alquirin. 'Before you came in', he says, 'the Lord Jesus looked at me and showed me the marks of his Passion.' One is reminded of that greatest of all passages about death in English literature in which Mr Standfast says: 'I am going to see that Head that was crowned with thorns and that Face that was spit upon for me . . .' But Christ is not the only one to befriend the dying. For both Mary and Siger, St Mary the first of saints is their companion. The point of this imagery is that the Christian is never solitary but compassed about with a great cloud of witnesses. In deathbed scenes the dead welcome the living into life and guard them through the greatest of all dangers. This is expressed liturgically in the offertory sentence of the requiem mass: 'O Lord Jesus Christ, deliver the souls of all the faithful departed from the pains of hell and from the depths of the pit: deliver them from the lion's mouth, that hell devour them not, that they fall not into darkness: but let the standard-bearer, St Michael, bring them into that holy light which of old thou didst promise to Abraham and to his seed.' St Michael or St Mary, or the King of Glory himself—or even two recently departed nuns of the same house—the dying immediately enter into the reality of relationship in Christ.

So each story affirms the third fact: for the monk death itself is the gateway of life, because of the death and resurrection of Christ. These stories are after all not photographs but icons; they show not the bare fact of what happened, they are an interpretation, a theology of event, and as with icons, the images are not invented but inherited. The white robes, the angels, the sweet smell all go back to that first icon of resurrection, the Gospel account of Easter morning where the early Church expressed its understanding of the resurrection of Jesus in these terms. Paradise, the garden of Eden, creation restored through the redemption wrought by Christ—these themes shine through the twelfth-century stories as clearly as in the first century. And of course beyond them: the same images are used for the Carthusian martyrs in the sixteenth century, and they are found in accounts of Christian death in our own times. Of Maximilian Kolbe, who died in Auschwitz at the hands of the SS, it was said that 'when the guards entered the bunker they found him still alive, with a scent of sweetness and a light around him, in great peace'.

This imagery of the resurrection of Christ in the accounts of the death of the saints is no facile promise of future bliss. It is rather an affirmation that the Christian dead are alive, more alive in fact than the living. The living are visible; the dead are invisible; that is all. And since it is Christ who gives reality to his own, the saints at the moment of death pass into a closer relationship with Christ and therefore with their fellow-men. It is this which has caused the Church to celebrate the anniversaries of the deaths of the saints, not of their births. It is always the delicate literary inversion of St Ignatius of Antioch that best expresses this truth: 'The pains of birth are upon me. Suffer me, my brethren, hinder me not from living, do not wish me to die . . . suffer me to follow the example of the Passion of my God. (*Epistle to the Romans*, VI.) This is given particular emphasis in the case of monks who have already made their whole existence into the death that is life by living always as those who die.

Finally, there is one more point I want to make about these stories, and it is one linked with sanctity and death in the title of this article: *laudabiliter vixit*. What about the life that preceded death? How did a monk live in order to make this passage into heaven? For the Cistercians at least were clear that those who lived and died in the Order need not fear a long journey or a long delay in purgatory; the monastery itself was the antechamber of heaven and the monk could pass straight in, if—and of course there was an 'if'—*laudabiliter vixit*. It is said of Alquirin in this story, it is carved on monastic tombstones of the Carthusians. Not a life full of wonders, for the monks have always had a certain restraint about marvels among themselves, not even a life of astonishing revelations, insight and understanding. Nor is it virtue, in the sense of doing good. It is rather life lived as a repentance, and therefore a service towards all, that counts. In these stories a life of mundane service prepares for death: Mary served her sisters in the convent infirmary; Alquirin served both rich and poor as a doctor; Siger was known as a servant of the brothers. The moments of vision, the great insights, the clear exposition of principles were not what prepared a man to die. Perhaps the very close connection between how a man lived and how he died is brought home for scholars by the story of Master Serlo. He dreamed one night that a pupil of his who had died appeared to him in agony, wearing a heavy cloak made up of scraps of paper covered with syllogisms of the schools that Serlo had taught him; it was so heavy that his sweat ran down and burned Serlo's hand. Next morning Serlo fled in terror from the life of the university and became a monk; and which of us would not do the same, confronted with a departed fellow-scholar eternally obsessed by unchecked footnotes? The monk must live well in order to die well, live in that antechamber of heaven not in wonders but in plain and unobserved repentance. *Laudabiliter vixit*: as Thomas Merton once laconically translated it, 'He did all right.'

The above article was originally read as a paper at the Conference of the Ecclesiastical Society held at Durham in 1979.

XXIII

Saints and Sybils:
Hildegard of Bingen to Teresa of Avila

> How could I presume to teach or advise you who are favoured with hidden knowledge and in whom the influence of Christ's anointing still lives so that you have no need of teaching, for you are said to be able to search the secrets of heaven and to discern by the light of the Holy Spirit things that are beyond the knowledge of man. It is rather for me to beg that you may not forget me before God or those who are united to me in spiritual fellowship.[1]

That is a remarkably humble letter from the greatest theologian of the twelfth century, Bernard of Clairvaux. It is his reply to a letter he had received from the Abbess of Mount St Rupert, Hildegard, who describes herself as '*paupercula femina forma*' ['a poor little womanly figure']. Bernard, the theologian of prayer, is filled with admiration for one who prays but does not analyse; there are two spheres, separate and distinct, and it is the woman who prays who is admired by the man who analyses and not vice versa. Four hundred years later in the relationship between John of the Cross and Teresa of Avila there has been a change in which both mystics also apply their minds to the analysis of experience. The change is in the women visionaries rather than in the men theologians and it seems worth comparing Hildegard of Bingen and Teresa of Avila in some detail in order to see where the differences lie. Much of the contrast they present may be attributed to differences of literary genre, of culture or simply of temperament but it may be of deeper significance to explore the exalted position of women in the medieval Church as true 'theologians', that is, as seers and sybils, visionaries and intercessors, and to see why they were so respected and if this position was changed then they turned their minds also to the analysis of the life of prayer. With Hildegard and Teresa who wrote so much and in such variety it is only possible to indicate here where some of the differences lie and to offer a tentative suggestion about the reasons behind them.

Bernard of Clairvaux wrote about the journey of the soul to God with such insight that he influenced deeply and permanently the way in which prayer was both experienced and discussed in his own day as well as later. It is at first sight remarkable that he should have been so impressed by the prophetic and mystical experiences of a woman, but he makes it clear that Hildegard was everything he admired and, he thought, failed himself to become. Above all she was taught by God, the clear structures of learning which Bernard deplored had never closed her mind to divine truth; she saw by what she called the divine light and she saw truly. Like the unlettered lay brothers at Clairvaux, she heard and saw the world of the spirit directly. The parallel Bernard saw between them was in part, of course, a fantasy; Hildegard constantly claims to be 'simple' and 'unlearned' but this modest phrase is deceptive. Unlike the lay brothers of the Cistercian Order, many of whom really were unable to read and write, Hildegard knew Latin and dictated books of considerable complexity. She was a woman of renown in her times, and her writings comprise almost the greatest range of literature of any medieval author. What Bernard meant and what Hildegard claimed, was, rather, a lack of formal academic training. What they agreed upon in a positive sense was that just because of this 'ignorance' she could receive direct inspiration from God which could not be argued with. Moreover, it was an authority that even the most rational minds of the twelfth century accepted as final: what Hildegard wanted done, was done, not on account of her undoubted ability either as a writer or as a monastic superior, but because she was held to enjoy a knowledge far superior to any merely rational method of inquiry.

Hildegard was admired by many besides Bernard. He recommended her to Eugenius, the Cistercian Pope, and arranged for him to meet Hildegard at Trier on his way to Rheims for the trial of Gilbert de la Porée since Bingen is on the Rhine only thirty miles from Trier. Eugenius became one of Hildegard's fervent admirers and they wrote letters to one another; she corresponded with successive popes, Anastasius IV, Adrian IV and Alexander III; she wrote to churchmen, to religious, and also to secular rulers such as Conrad III and his son Frederick Barbarossa, Henry II of England and his wife Eleanor of Aquitaine, the Empress Irene and Philip, Count of Flanders. She undertook journeys, preached to monks in their monasteries and clergy in their synods, and laymen in towns; she gave spiritual counsel, she exorcised, she argued and she prophesied. She was clearly a woman of very great force of character, but all she did was in the name of the light which was not her own, a claim that was recognised and accepted.

Hildegard was respected not in spite of her tendency to strange and emotional ecstasies but because of them: they marked her out as a prophetess. It seems that she was not suddenly visited by heavenly inspiration as a nun and abbess but had been accustomed to such visions from early childhood. In 1141 when she was forty-two she felt herself commissioned to reveal the visions, which she did by dictating them to two close friends, the monk Volmar and the nun Richarda:

> A fiery light of the greatest brilliancy coming from the opened heavens poured into all my brain and kindled in my heart and breast, a flame that warms but does not consume as the sun heats everything over which he casts his rays . . . I said and wrote . . . not according to the curious invention of my heart but as I saw, heard and perceived them in a heavenly way through the secret mysteries of God. And again I heard a voice from heaven saying unto me, 'Cry aloud therefore and write thus.'[2]

This description, couched in the personal and emotional language of the twelfth century, is nevertheless replete with traditional imagery. The 'prayer of fire' associated with the descent of the Holy Spirit is a main theme of Eastern theology and the final quotation links her ecstasy with the Book of Revelation and the vision of St John (cf. Rev. 1.19). Moreover, her revelations belong to the tradition of compunction, that piercing of the heart by fear and love for a further inner knowledge of the divine which Gregory the Great articulated for the West and which formed the basis of such popular meditations as those of Anselm of Canterbury.[3] At times it is the theme of wonder and glory that seizes her:

> I saw as it were the mystery of God in the southern sky, a wonderful and beautiful image in the form of a man whose face was so beautiful and brilliant that I could more easily have looked into the sun . . . 'I am the high and the fiery power that kindled all living sparks . . . I burn in the fiery life of the substance of divinity above the beauty of the fields, and I shine in the waters and I burn in the stars . . .'[4]

At other times, it is the terror of distance from God and the burden of sinful mortality that oppresses her:

> Whither am I, a pilgrim, going? Into the valley of death. In what way do I go? The way of error. What consolation do I have? That of a pilgrim. Others deride me, saying, 'Where is your honour now?' Oh, where am I? Whence did I come? What consolation do I seek in this captivity? How can I break my chains? What eye can see my wounds? What hands will anoint them with oil? Who will show pity on my grief? Therefore He will hear my cry.[5]

Such deeply emotional and self-revealing experiences by no means removed Hildegard into a realm of mysterious ineptitude. What she wrote about was not only or even especially religious. She was interested in botany, in medicine, in minerals, she composed music and her visions inspired pictures of a wild and impressive kind. Her advice was very practical, and her administration of her abbey so effective that the small and rather undistinguished little group which she met at Disiboden (when she arrived there as a child of eight to be educated by the hermitess Jutta) had, when she died as abbess in 1179 at the age of eighty-two, become a large and flourishing abbey on excellent land at Bingen. This move was an example of the force of a visionary woman upon very practical men. The monks closest to her convent as confessors viewed her proposal to move from Disiboden with alarm and hostility. They were unwilling to lose both nuns, who were without exception and by a deliberate policy of the abbess, high-born ladies, and their endowments. Hildegard wrote to the monks in these terms when she heard of their opposition to the move:

> In accordance with what I had seen in my true vision I said to the father abbot, 'The serene light says, you shall be father to our provost (the monk Volmar) and father of the salvation of the souls of the daughters of my mystic garden. But their alms do not belong to you or to your brothers – your cloister should be a refuge for these women and if you are determined to go on with your perverse proposals, raging against us, you will be like the Amalekites . . . justice will destroy you. And when I, poor little creature, had with these words petitioned the abbot and his confrères for the freehold of the site and domains of my daughters they all granted it to me, entering the transfer in a codex.[6]

Hildegard was listened to and respected as a sybil, as a prophet, one through whom the Spirit of God spoke most clearly but at the same time her influence and practical activity were undoubted. In this she was a highly significant figure for her times. There is no doubt that the twelfth century saw a change in the kind of activities open to women. The political and economic power they wielded with ease and confidence earlier was drastically limited. They were excluded from Latin education by the rise of the universities as never before. The disaster of the cult of courtly love isolated them by glorifying them. But in certain spheres the women prospered. One was the emergence of vernacular literature and another was the prophetic and mystical role which opened increasingly to them.

From Hildegard of Bingen in the twelfth century to Teresa of Avila in the sixteenth there was an increasing number of prophetesses, many of them women of discernment and influence. The thirteenth and fourteenth centuries in particular saw an explosion of women visionaries: the great ladies of Helfta, Gertrude and Mechtild, and particularly their younger contemporary Mechtild of Hackborn; Elizabeth of Schonau; Hadewijch, Beatrice of Nazareth, Margeret of Oignt, Catherine of Sienna, Catherine of Genoa, Bridget of Sweden, Margery Kempe, Julian of Norwich, to name only the most obvious. Like Hildegard, these were women visionaries, highly respected and attended to: dreams, visions, prophecies, trances, locutions, suspension of the faculties, all were there. With the more able and controlled visionaries, they committed their revelations to writings which exercised influence and commanded respect. Of course, men were also equally open to the influence of mystical experience but it seems that this mostly took the form of analysis of the life of prayer in writing, exhortation to it in preaching, or counsel about it. Many of the revelations of the women mystics were written about by men by whom they were highly, even hysterically respected, as having a specially direct and mysterious contact with divinity which was its own justification. Though deeply immersed in the central activity of prayer with all its demands for solitude, silence and detachment, the women visionaries were also active, busy women, aware of the world and its needs, and prepared to involve themselves and their experiences of prayer in the affairs of their day. Catherine of Sienna, for instance, was at the centre of ecclesiastical politics for most of her adult life yet was pre-eminently renowned for her visions and ecstatic experiences. One can only conclude that unlike ourselves, the Middle Ages regarded the exterior phenomena of the mystic as a passport to credibility, not the reverse. This link between paranormal phenomena, sound theology and practical common sense presents certain problems for those in a very different psychological and theological atmosphere. There are perhaps at least two preliminary differences in the understanding of reality to bear in mind when approaching this question, which were true for the sixteenth as well as the twelfth century.

The first major difference to notice is the extent to which medieval theology was linked to ancient concepts of anthropology. The human biology of the ancient world depended on the theory of the elements and the humours. Man was the microcosm of the universe, and both were made up of the elements of earth, air, fire and water. Man and woman together formed the perfect human being and the elements were divided between them: men were predominantly air and fire, women earth and water. Air and fire made for the critical intellect, earth signified fruitfulness and water was a spiritual principal which opened women to visions and dreams. The twelfth century pushed many things to logical conclusions, it was a great age for categorising and making lists and they did it with this world view also. Man issued from the hand of God, male/female. The airy and fiery elements opened him to reason, the earthy, watery elements to divinity unalloyed. Hildegard put it like this:

> 'Oh humans, look at the human being! for it contains heaven and earth and all other creatures within itself and is one form and all other creatures hide in it.'[7]

The part of this whole which was directly open to heaven was, therefore, feminine; woman was man's love, his heart, and his direct route to the powers of the air. She was therefore seen as being by her very nature the dreamer, the prophet, the visionary.

Secondly, there was a different understanding throughout the Middle Ages of the significance of the flesh. On the one hand, extreme illness was not regarded as merely unfortunate; it could be a gift, opening the mind to heaven: Hildegard, Teresa and many, perhaps all, other women mystics began their inner, mystical life through this liberating breaking of the external senses in severe illnesses. On the other hand, interior vision was naturally accompanied by external phenomena: the visionaries saw, heard, smelled, touched, even tasted the celestial visions, reacting visibly to inner experience with their senses. These physical phenomena were recorded vividly and with reverence, a fact which is often forgotten by those who concentrate on the very strong and theologically sensible content of the visions. For the Middle Ages, the reactions of the body were not seen as improper but as authenticating. Where people were peculiarly open to God it was expected that the effect would show in their bodies. This is not perhaps completely alien to our experience. After all, human beings only have five senses to register whatever happens to them; the spirit does not invent new and spiritual matter for itself. Even now, it is a common experience that serious illness can become the gateway to deeper apprehensions of reality. On the other hand, great personal grief or complete desolation does not make one pale and romantic but is so disorientating that it will be as likely as not to cause vomiting and a blinding headache. So the coming of the Spirit of God on a human being was thought to use the normal make-up of that person. Thus, the eyes closed, the breathing changed, those so visited seemed to speak automatically, to rise from the ground, become rigid and immovable or even impassible for hours on end; they heard sounds inaudible and saw sights invisible to others – all these things earlier ages took for granted and even required in their mystics.

Such physical reactions might alert people to the presence of something unusual but in spite of this it would still seem to us that such personal revelation was in itself uncheckable. If I say I have a vision, you cannot say I have not. The problem of authentication of visionaries has always exercised serious-minded people, but in earlier ages the external symptoms had greater weight. There were women visionaries whose ecstasies seem to us pointless, neither significant nor helpful to others. Perhaps Christina the Astonishing falls into this category as someone we regard as simply neurotic. She is said to have been frequently in trances so deep that they were mistaken for death; on one occasion her body had been carried into church for burial when she revived. At once, her corpse flew up to the roof where she perched like a bird until the people were cleared out, for it was known that Christina could not stand the smell of human flesh. Among her more pointless escapades was her habit of getting into ovens where she sat down, presumably under the impression that she was a bun. She would climb on to the mill wheel and go round with it, and once she sat down in the font when it was full of water.[8] This tomboy athletic style of sainthood seems to us unedifying since totally devoid of theological or moral content but her contemporaries were prepared to accept what they did not understand; there was sufficient respect for her trances for her to be included in the calendar of the saints. The reactions of the body were regarded as the work of the Spirit upon flesh and that was sufficient for wonder and awe; they were signs of the hidden approval of God, beyond human judgments and opinions.

While these two ideas about the human person and about the significance of the flesh are unfamiliar to the twentieth century, they continued long past the sixteenth century to shape European notions of reality. It is not, therefore, that a change occurred in the sixteenth century. Rather, a new caution began to be felt about the significance of bodily phenomena in prayer. There was a new stress on what was intellectually orthodox, accompanied by more caution about the possibility of demonic deception especially for the untutored mind. In a united Europe, where Christian teaching was mostly clearly articulated and heretics were few, visionaries had been easily accepted and indeed cherished, their orthodoxy unquestioned. In the sixteenth century under the pressure of heresy, the evidence of the experiences of the ecstatic visionaries was received with a new caution. Those faced with a visionary who might well be a heretic and perhaps, like Elizabeth Barton, the Fair Maid of Kent, used in secular political matters, could no longer be impressed solely by her states of trance; they might suspect quite other spirits of speaking through her. A vision itself was no longer authenticating. Visionaries had to be examined for uprightness of life and their visions had to be checked by their content; was what they said in ecstasy worth saying? Was it in accordance with Scripture? With church doctrine as agreed by the consensus of Christian people? Did it lead to the virtues of charity, faith, hope, peace? Was it edifying to others?

Such analysis did increasingly take place and one of the foremost in offering such criteria for authenticity was a woman who was herself subject to extreme and alarming mystical states. Teresa of Avila was within this tradition of women visionaries. Like them, she was a woman of great influence and continual activity; like her predecessors, she claimed ignorance of both Latin and scholastic methods, the traditional *deprecatio* which nevertheless was intended to show that the writer's mind was not confined along particular and defined ways. She writes, she says, about what she understands from within, not from exterior information. Like most of the women mystics after Hildegard, Teresa wrote in the vernacular. Subject to trances, visions, ecstasies, she, like the rest, was widely consulted and was most highly regarded for her prayer; so highly regarded that people would act upon what she said. But there was a change; for one thing, the Inquisition was demanding examination of those who experienced paranormal states; and for another, Teresa herself offered detailed analysis of such experiences as part of a whole structure of the life of prayer.

In the last books of the *Life* and in the *Interior Castle*, Teresa set down a great deal about the different kinds of visions experienced by those who pray.[9] They were, perhaps, merely sensory, perhaps imaginary, perhaps intellectual; if accompanied by physical phenomena, that was a sign of a weak integration of body and spirit and should be disregarded. And always the central check for the one praying was perseverance in the way of charity which is the following of Christ. Teresa did not refuse to give attention to the subject of visions and saw them as a valid part of the life of prayer, but it is clear that her approach was more subtle than that of Hildegard.

Teresa herself was seized by ecstasy of one kind or another for most of her life, and in order to communicate anything about these moments of vision, she used new images rather than old arguments or descriptions. Like all the mystics, she used language of a poetic, mysterious nature, but here joined to an analytic intellect, which combined both the experiential and the expository sides of mystical writing in a new way. Her use of images in describing the way of prayer is very like the explicitly visionary language of Hildegard. For instance, the central image of the *Interior Castle* is a crystal ball shaped like a castle; it is described with intense imaginative beauty, matching anything in the visions of Hildegard or Mechtild, and it was revealed to her first of all, it seems, in a vision:

> On the eve of the festival of the Most Holy Trinity, she (Teresa) was thinking what subject she should choose for this treatise, when God who disposes all things in due form and order granted this desire of hers and gave her a subject. He showed her a most beautiful crystal globe, made in the shape of a castle, and containing seven mansions, in the seventh and innermost of which was the King of Glory, illuminating and beautifying them all.[10]

It sounds very like a vision of Hildegard, but there is a distinct difference. Teresa did not simply experience a vision, but saw the way in which she was to analyse prayer in the form of a vision. Like the men who wrote about prayer, she provided an interpretation. Given this vision, she asked herself questions about its precise significance for others. She saw the crystal ball as the soul, the castle is within, and every visionary detail was clearly interpreted according to her understanding of prayer. The image in the vision was linked to the Scriptures and she had good precedent for seeing the 'many mansions' of the Father's house (John 14.2) as the person, the temple of God which is within. Other writers had used the image, though not in quite the same way; the *Proslogion* of Anselm, for instance, begins with an invitation into the 'inner chamber' where one seeks God who is within, the ground of being, while Hugh of St Victor used a particular house, Noah's ark, for his discussion of the life of the soul in prayer.[11] The difference is that Teresa presented the image as a result of a direct vision from God, and with this she combined a strict analysis of the life of prayer. The interior castle was not with Teresa simply an amazing celestial building whose every piece might be replete with changing, shifting images of wonder; it provided, rather, a structure for articulating rational thoughts about prayer.

For Teresa such images were not an end in themselves. She considered prayer, and particularly any visionary experience, to be linked indissolubly with asceticism; not as a way into prayer but a result of it. From the other end, so to speak, the body had its place in prayer also for Teresa, not as the vehicle of divinity so much as the place where love planted in the heart would then overflow into all the senses and all of life. In this sense it is interesting to note that for herself, 'betrothal to the Lord' meant acute desolation and the inner rooms of the crystal castle were full of darkness.

It is necessary to distinguish between Teresa's deliberate and conscious use of imagery and her accounts of experiences of a paranormal nature, but in a way they come from the same apprehension of life. Through both she says prayer is not either emotional or intellectual; mind and emotion are linked to the flesh for her as much as for Hildegard, and she was well aware that the impact of the divine upon the human body could take extraordinary forms. There are what Teresa calls 'lesions', that is, gaps between vision and experience. For example, absorption in prayer can so dislocate the normal unity of the self that the one who prays may begin to drop things, forget things, not react on a natural level very quickly, become clumsy, not quite functioning, something that was reverenced in earlier mystics but with Teresa is treated with a brisk compassion. Though Teresa never denied her own experiences of trance and vision, such manifestations were to be hidden and disregarded. She saw them as 'the least of the gifts' – not things to be afraid of, but not to be regarded or sought. They might be of God or they might not; if they were, then there would be an increase of charity in daily life: charity towards men, love towards God, a humility which thinks itself unworthy of notice. For herself, she used to test such revelations by asking others whose opinion she respected about them. There had been enough false mystics and some of them close at hand for her to have learned not to trust the externals even for herself with the simplicity of the earlier mystics.

No doubt Teresa would have classed most of Hildegard's visions as 'corporal', a kind of vision with which Teresa says she was not personally acquainted. Her own visions she called either 'imaginary' or 'intellectual', and she discussed them for their content and meaning alone. What was external in visionary states was for her at best peripheral, at worst a temptation to pride; they were to be examined with care and related to the whole of Christian life. The most famous of her own experiences, when she felt that her heart was being pierced by the fiery spear of a seraph, is an example both of the similarity of language about mystical experience and the difference between its apprehension in the early Middle Ages and the sixteenth century.[12] Hildegard described a vision of seraphs in terms remarkably similar to those of Teresa:

> These signify the Seraphim because they are burning with the love of God, having a very great desire for the vision of Him . . . the secrets of God appear in them wonderfully as they do also in those loving souls who seek eternal life in the sincerity of a pure heart. These love God ardently and embrace him with a pure desire.[13]

In her *Life* Teresa also speaks of a seraph and of love, and this is one of the very rare passages where she describes a 'corporal' vision of her own:

> It pleased the Lord that I should sometimes see the following vision. I would see beside me, on my left hand, an angel in bodily form – a type of vision which I am not in the habit of seeing

> except very rarely . . . He was not tall but short, and very beautiful, his face so aflame that he appeared to be one of the highest types of angels who seem to be all afire . . . In his hand I saw a long golden spear and at the end of the iron tip I seemed to see a point of fire. With this he seemed to pierce my heart . . . he left me completely afire with a great love for God. The pain was so sharp that it made me utter several moans . . .[14]

It is clear that Hildegard and Teresa write within the same tradition of angelic visions but there are significant differences. Both connect the seraphim with light and with the inner mysteries of the vision of God and with desire for him. The metaphor of fire has been used for centuries about prayer connected both with the heart, the most central part of the person and with the Holy Spirit. While Hildegard records what she 'sees' with amazement and delight and regards her vision as something to be communicated to all, Teresa writes about the 'fire' as a personal and inner experience of immense pain, and of something so intimate that she was distressed when others connected such things with her. It is significant that the transverberation happened at the end of her quiet life as a simple Carmelite nun; it overflowed into the next years of active service of others until her death. The famous statue by Bernini of Teresa with her heart being pierced by a seraph says nothing else – love in the centre of the soul, so that it affects every action and thought. To refer that baroque expression of devotion to Teresa is perhaps hardly to our taste or in line with our view of her; nor is the equally well-known poem upon the book and the picture of the 'Seraphical Teresa':

> O thou undaunted daughter of desires
> by all thy dower of lights and fires
> by all the eagle in thee, all the dove
> by all thy lives and deaths of love
> by thy large draughts of intellectual day
> and by thy thirsts of love more large than they
> by all thy brim-filled bowls of fierce desire
> by thy last morning draught of liquid fire
> by the full kingdom of that final kiss

that seized thy parting soul and sealed thee His
by all the heaven thou hadst in Him
fair sister of the seraphim
by all of him we have in thee
leave nothing of myself in me;
let me so read thy life that I
unto all life of mine may die.[15]

It sounds much more like Hildegard than Teresa, and the reality which completed that 'final kiss' did not seem to Teresa like anything of the kind. A few days before her death, Teresa was carried reluctantly in extreme sickness to the house of a friend who wanted her there while she, Donna Anna, bore a child, a sentimental desire to treat Teresa as a saint which she disliked and mocked. There on 9th October, 1571, she died; she was repeating over and over again Psalm 51: 'the sacrifice of God is a troubled spirit, a broken and a contrite heart, O God, thou wilt not despise.'

The writings of or about the medieval mystics reveal some shifts in the way revelation was understood and received from the twelfth century to the sixteenth. With Hildegard, the fact of her ecstatic states was authenticating for her other activities; their place in the whole tradition of Christian life was taken for granted; both she and others were simply impressed by the actual experiences themselves which were seen as authentication given by God himself. The visionary states themselves created awe and were left open for interpretation; the activity and actual influence of the visionaries were simply the results of the impact of mysterious divinity and it was rare to find any of the early visionaries exploring and analysing their visions as a scheme of prayer or of life in detail. Teresa was as much a visionary as any of them, and exceeded even Hildegard in the activities of her work for the Carmelite Reform and in the force of her influence on others. But there is a most significant difference between them, for where Hildegard merely saw, Teresa analysed and classified. She applied her mind to the analysis of any visionary experiences, her own or others, and made them a part of a whole structure for understanding and pursuing the life of prayer and charity. In the case of all the visionary women, there is a unifying theme of direct and intimate receptivity in prayer towards divinity which was seen as their 'theology', even when it was eventually combined with the analytic presentation of prayer. At least with Teresa, the analysis of visions did not diminish their value as a direct participation in divine life, however this may have been later. With her, the rational intellect was seen as balancing and not negating – though at times as subsidiary to – intuitive understanding, a balance which seems to have swung in the opposite direction for far too long a period.

NOTES

1. *Letters of St Bernard of Clairvaux*, trans. Bruno Scott James (London, 1953), Letter 390, p. 460.
2. *Hildegardis Scivias*, ed. A. Fuhrkotter, A. Carlevaris, *Corpus Christianorum Continuatio Mediaevalis*, xlii–xliii A (Turnhout, 1978), Preface, pp. 3–4 (hereinafter referred to as *Scivias*). Hildegard's other works are found in PL 197. Of the recent English versions of Hildegard's works, I have either used the translations provided in Peter Dronke's excellent chapter, 'Hildegard of Bingen' in *Women Writers in the Middle Ages* (Cambridge, 1984) (hereinafter referred to as Dronke) or attempted my own translation of Hildegard's unusual Latin.
3. Cf. *Prayers and Meditations of St Anselm of Canterbury with the Proslogion*, trans. with introduction, Benedicta Ward (Penguin Books, 1979/87).
4. Hildegard, *Liber Divinorum Operum Simplicis Hominis*, Vision 1, PL 197, col. 74.
5. Hildegard, *Scivias*, 4th Vision, p. 62.
6. Hildegard, *Letters*, PL 197, col. 1065 (Dronke, p. 153).
7. Hildegard, *Causae et Curae*, Dronke p. 172; Latin Text, Dronke p. 241.
8. Thomas de Cantimpre, *Vita Baetae Christinae Mirabilis Trundonopoli in Hasbania*, Acta Sanctorum Jul.1,5 (Paris, 1868) pp. 637–60; English translation by M. King in *Medieval Women's Visionary Literature*, ed. E.A. Petroff (Oxford, 1986) pp. 184–9.
9. (The Works of St Teresa will be referred to in the translations of E. Allison Peers (London, 1946) by their English titles with references to chapters only.) Teresa, *The Interior Castle*, VI.ix,4ff. Cf. *Revelation* IV,14. Teresa's discussion of visions is analysed and compared with the teaching of St John of the Cross by E.W. Trueman Dicken,

The Crucible of Love: a Study in the Mysticism of St Teresa and St John of the Cross (London, 1936), pp. 374–406.
10. Teresa, *Interior Castle*, Introduction, p. 10.
11. Hugh of St Victor, *De Arce Noe Morali*, PL 176.
12. Teresa, *Interior Castle*, cap. v; *Life*, xviii. Teresa's teaching on union is discussed by E. Truman Dicken (op. cit. note 9), pp. 407–30.
13. Hildegard, *Scivias*, vi, pp. 106–7.
14. Teresa, *Life*, xxix.
15. Richard Crashaw, 'The Flaming Heart: Upon the Book and Picture of the Seraphical Teresa'.

XXIV

'FAITH SEEKING UNDERSTANDING'

Anselm of Canterbury and Julian of Norwich

At first sight Anselm of Canterbury and Julian of Norwich seem to have little in common. The one, a monk from Normandy who became Archbishop of Canterbury under William Rufus, was one of the greatest of medieval scholars, writing his prayers and meditations in beautiful, highly-wrought Latin in the eleventh century. The other, an unlettered lay-woman, a recluse in the town of Norwich, who wrote (or perhaps dictated) her revelations and meditations on them in English in the fourteenth century. Both wrote a short devotional work, however, Julian's *Revelations of Divine Love* and Anselm's *Prayers and Meditations*, and it seems clear that they both belong to the same tradition of Christian prayer.

In comparing them it is not suggested that there is any actual dependence, for two reasons: first that Julian would not have been able to read the Latin prayers if they had been available to her; and secondly that they were not, as a clearly defined body, available to anyone before the present century. This is because within a few years of Anselm's death the original prayers were surrounded by a host of prayers by other writers in the same vein all of which were attributed to him. It is only in the past fifty years that the genuine prayers and meditations have again been distinguished, in the form in which Anselm meant them to be used, and it is only now that Anselm's teaching as an ascetical theologian can really be appreciated. The body of genuine prayers was not available to Julian, but there can be no doubt that she was influenced by the ethos that Anselm had been so largely responsible for creating, and that there are very significant similarities between them. It is of more interest for us to see the same methods, the same approaches, the same understanding in two such dissimilar people, than to attempt any more academic discussion of them. It may be, who knows, that the tradition they both used can be of real significance for us in the same desire for God.

In the first place Anselm and Julian are both people who can truly be called 'theologians', in the sense of the theologian as 'one whose prayer is true'. Anselm was pre-eminently a theologian, formed by the undivided tradition of Christian doctrine, and bending all the powers of his mind to understanding that faith. This total acceptance of Christian dogma was equally present in Julian, as she says: 'I shall always believe what is held, preached and taught by Holy Church . . . it was with this well in mind that I looked at the revelation so diligently.' (Ch.9.) In his greatest philosophical work, which is also the greatest of his Meditations, Anselm approaches his search for God in the same way: 'I desire to understand a little of your love, which my heart already believes and loves . . . unless I believe I shall not understand.' *(Proslogion* Ch.1.) The original title Anselm gave to the *Proslogion* was in fact 'Faith Seeking Understanding'. a phrase which sums up his whole approach to theology and prayer, and is as true of Julian as of him.

In both of them there is this complete unity of belief and understanding, the mind at the service of the heart, that makes them truly Christian scholars. To accept the truths of the faith was for them a liberation not a restriction. No one could accuse either of them of being simply echoes of other men's ideas: in both there is originality and personal insight to an astonishing degree. It is to be expected, perhaps, that Julian, whose book-learning was limited, should not have quoted other writers very often; but that Anselm, one of the most learned men of his—or any—age, quoted equally infrequently is more surprising. The Bible, of course, permeated their thought and writings, but even there they rarely quote. They have, it seems, so absorbed and made their own the revelation of God in Christ that they were free to speak for that revelation in terms of their own personality and understanding.

The idea of 'faith *seeking* understanding' is another concept that they have in common—the mobile, flexible, developing nature of faith lies behind their works. Julian reflected for thirty years on the meaning of her revelations, making an interior journey ever deeper into 'the Lord's meaning', and Anselm taught a reaching forward to the knowledge of God, a continuing inner journey: 'Come now, little man, stir up your torpid mind . . . flee a while from your occupations . . . enter into the inner chamber of your mind . . . close the door and seek Him.' (*Proslogion* Ch.1.) This inner world of movement and discovery demands for its proper realisation, however, a measure of withdrawal, of solitude, of stillness. It is essentially an interior adventure, made by Anselm in the 'inner chamber', and by Julian in her anchoress's cell.

Firmly based in theological truth both Anselm and Julian prepared to 'seek understanding' in solitude, and they sought it by paths that are very similar. In both of them there are stages of spiritual progress, stages which were to be most clearly described by St. Bernard. At the beginning of the *Revelations* Julian says: 'Through the grace of God and the teaching of Holy Church, I developed a strong desire to receive three wounds, namely, the wound of contrition, the wound of genuine compassion, and the wound of sincere longing for God.' (Ch.2.) This threefold pattern of prayer is the same in the teaching of Anselm. It has, of course, a long history in the spirituality of both

East and West but at the end of the eleventh century Anselm articulated it for the West in a new way. Against the background of a liturgically-centred tradition of prayer he set out a way of personal, interior prayer in the pattern of three wounds or piercings of the soul by God. The first wound was that of contrition, true sorrow for sin and self-abasement; the second wound was that of compassion, known through the sufferings of Christ; and the third wound was that of longing desire for God. These three wounds were to pierce and break the hard heart so that God's work of prayer could really begin. In each of the Prayers this pattern is followed. It is not a once-for-all way, in which one stage is finally left behind and then another undertaken; rather it is a continual pattern of prayer, into which one enters more deeply all the time.

The first wound that Anselm sets at the beginning of all his Prayers is that of sorrow for sin and he uses every verbal means to bring this home to himself: 'I am afraid of my life; for when I examine myself closely, it seems to me that my whole life is either sinful or sterile.' (Med.1.) 'Alas for my wretched state, how my sins cry out against me . . . immoderate offence, offence against my God.' (Prayer to St. John the Evangelist,1.) 'The Judge Himself is my stern accuser and I am clearly a sinner against Him.' (Prayer to St. Paul.) In Julian there is the same awareness of sin: 'Sin is the sharpest scourge'; 'holy Church shall be shaken at the world's sorrow, anguish and tribulation' (Ch.28); 'the shame that our foul deeds caused'. (Ch.77.)

This awareness of sin and self-abasement is not, in either Anselm or Julian, a matter of psychological or personal guilt; it is rather a deep theological awareness of the infinite glory of God, and of the contrast of the horror of any sin which offends against it. 'How can you call any sin small' Anselm asks, 'when it is committed against God?' In Julian it is not reflection upon her own misdeeds but the sense of 'our foul, black, shameful deeds which hid the fair. splendid and blessed Lord God' (Ch.10) that provokes contrition.

It is in the second wound, however, that the similarity between Anselm and Julian is most marked: this is their 'compassion' with the sufferings of Christ. The whole of Julian's writing is based on her immediate and vivid experience of the passion of Christ: 'I had' she says, 'some experience of the passion of Christ, but by his grace I wanted still more. I wanted actually to be there with Mary Magdalene and the others who loved him . . . I would be one of them and suffer with him.' (Ch.2.) This is Anselm's approach in his Prayer to Christ, an imaginative consideration of the details of the sufferings of Christ which found its ultimate term many years later in the emotions of the 'Stabat Mater'. In the Prayer to Christ he asks: 'Why, O my soul, were you not there to be pierced by the sword of bitter sorrow . . . Why did you not see the nails violate the hands and feet of your Creator?' 'Would that I with happy Joseph might have taken down my Lord from the cross, wrapped him in spiced grave-clothes, and laid him in the tomb.' This desire to experience personally the human side of the sufferings of Christ and of his mother received new impetus from Anselm and coloured the prayers and the art of the later middle ages as, incidentally, did his understanding of the tenderness of the child of Bethlehem and his mother. The 'homely', as Julian would say, was seen as an integral part of the 'holy'.

The third 'piercing' for both Anselm and Julian is that of longing desire for the joys of the vision of God. In both writers this theme counter-balances their emphasis on sin, pain and estrangement. In Anselm each prayer ends with a passage full of longing for God and the bliss of heaven: 'He fell asleep in the Lord', he says of St. Stephen, 'happy man, to rest in joy and joy in rest; safe home, you are filled with glory, your joy does not change, your light does not fail . . . O rich and blessed peace, how far I am from you; alas for my unhappiness, where I am not, where I am, and, alas, I know not where I shall be.' This theme of the longing of the exiled soul for God lies at the heart of Anselm's understanding of prayer; it is the restoration of man to the image of God, a fundamental monastic theme in any age which goes with a great longing and a great and positive joy. In Julian there is always this longing for God, and there is also a great deal about joy. It is the joy of God which she sees most of all, his joy in his work of redemption and our joyful response to that work in delight and thankfulness: 'When we are done with grief, our eyes will suddenly be enlightened . . .' (Ch.83) 'we shall partake of God's blessedness forever, praising him and thanking him . . .' (Ch.85.)

One further similarity of these writers in this connection is that 'this holy marvelling delight in God which is love' is expressed in terms of the physical senses. Julian writes, for instance: 'We shall see him truly and feel him fully, hear him spiritually, smell him delightfully and taste him sweetly.' (Ch.43.) Anselm frequently uses this sensual imagery, especially about eating or tasting the sweetness of the word of God, and in the last chapter of the *Proslogion* he describes the joys of the saints in terms of the perfect fulfilment of all the senses.

For both Anselm and Julian the centre and pivot of their approach to God by the three 'piercings' resolves itself into one word–Jesus. In Anselm's first Meditation, when he has thought with anguish of the terror of the Last Judgement, he exclaims: 'But it is he, it is Jesus; the same is my judge between whose hands I tremble . . . Jesus, Jesus, be to me for thy name's sake, Jesus.' Julian says simply: 'I wanted no other heaven but Jesus, who shall be my bliss when I come there.' (Ch.19.) The essence of this approach is perhaps found in the Cistercian *Jesu dulcis memoria*—'Jesus, the very thought is sweet'—but in none of these writers is this concentration on Jesus sentimental or naive. Julian chooses Jesus for her heaven 'whom I saw only in pain at that time'; 'the strength of your salvation, the cause of your freedom, the price of your redemption . . . through this, and not otherwise than through this, will you remain in Christ and Christ in you, and your joy will be full.' (Med.3.)

This combination of pain and joy, sorrow and bliss, points to the last and perhaps deepest point of similarity between Anselm and Julian. Their ability to see in the details of suffering the truth of glory is brought out in an unusual and striking way in the concept they share of Christ as our mother. This idea of the maternity of God is found in the Old Testament, and in St. Paul, and had found echoes in several medieval writers of the eleventh century, but Anselm gave it a profound and disturbing meaning in his great Prayer to St. Paul. He sees St. Paul as his mother in the faith, and then turns to apply the same terms to Christ: 'And you, Jesus, are you not also a mother? It is by your death that we have been born; longing to bear sons into life, you tasted death and by dying you begot them.' Christ is seen here as bearing sons by his passion on the cross, a deeper understanding of the meaning of suffering than a simple analogy about the love of Christ being like that of a mother for her children. Anselm sees love as essentially life-giving, not as sentimental or easy. Later in the same prayer he pictures the sinner hiding under the wings of Jesus: 'You, my soul, dead in yourself, run under the wings of Jesus your mother, and lament your griefs under his feathers. Ask that your wounds may be healed and that, strengthened, you may live again.' This is not the gentleness of a mother with a child, but a fundamental concern with our relationship to Christ and the integral meaning of atonement.

Julian expands this theme in several chapters. 'In our mother Christ we grow and develop; in his mercy he reforms and restores us; through his passion, death, and resurrection he has united us to our being.' (Ch.58.) And: 'Jesus is the true mother of our nature for he made us. He is our mother too by grace, because he took our created nature upon himself.' (Ch.59.) Both are saying that Christ bore us as his children by his death on the cross. The pain he suffered was the pain of labour, so that we are his very flesh and blood, and his joy over us is also the cause of all our joy. They are also making a startlingly modern statement about the nature of God: 'Fatherhood, motherhood and lordship, all in one God', says Julian. 'God is both father and mother' according to Anselm. Not that our images of God are 'fatherhood' or 'motherhood', but that God himself contains and completes the whole man. Salvation is a new birth of the whole of humanity by the whole God—all mankind is made whole by the whole of God.

Anselm and Julian were three centuries apart in time, and we are six hundred years further on again. The gap of general concepts and culture which lies between them and us is wider than in any other century. Yet they represent an unchanging dimension in the relationship between God and the human being who seeks him from which we can perhaps learn still. They both accepted the objectivity of God as something other than themselves and, in order to seek him, they withdrew into solitude and really set themselves to an *ascesis*, a hard labour, to prepare for finding him. They experienced the sense of their own sin before the glory of God; they found mercy through the new life brought to them by Christ on the cross; they learned to rejoice with all their being in Christ and to long for the bliss of his abiding presence in heaven. For both the final word is the same: love. Julian, in the last chapter of her book, says that after more than fifteen years meditation on the revelations it was shown to her that 'love was his meaning'. Anselm, writing in exile forty years after the rest of the Prayers came, in his last Meditation, to the same conclusion: 'Thus have you loved me! Draw me to you, Lord, in the fullness of love. I am wholly yours by creation; make me all yours, too, in love.'

NOTE:

Quotations from St. Anselm are taken from *The Prayers and Meditations of St. Anselm*, translated by Sister Benedicta Ward SLG. Penguin Classics 1973.

XXV

JULIAN THE SOLITARY

AT THE END of her marvellous novel, *The Man on a Donkey*, H.F.M. Prescott describes the sweet fool of the book, Malle, returning to the recently dissolved nunnery of Marrick and wandering down to the banks of the Swale carrying with her various leaves torn from manuscripts which she gathered up in the cloister. She laid a stone upon the painted pages lying in a bright litter at her feet, and began folding them one by one into little boats. On one of these pages were the words

> It is true, that sin is the cause of all this pain; but all shall be well, and all manner of thing shall be well.

And the poignant conclusion of the scene continues:

> When Malle had made all the little ships ready to sail, she set them on the water, where it lapped, trembling and bright, close to her feet. They bobbed and curtseyed there, loitering a minute till the strength of the river caught them. Then they went dipping and dancing away towards the sea. [1]

It is a fiction, and its main point is in its subtle underlining of the loss of the old ways of religion at the dissolution of the monasteries, but perhaps it is permissible to give it a shade of meaning more closely connected with the text written on those paper boats, for when making any comments on the *Revelations of Divine Love* it is useful to remember that the original text of the *Revelations of Divine Love* is lost.

The Texts

Julian, in the late fourteenth century, wrote two books: the 'Short Text', the record of the revelation, written shortly after 1373, and the 'Long Text', her meditation on the revelation over the next twenty years which was finished about 1393. Both books were copied; her own manuscripts have not so far been found. The oldest surviving copy is that of the Short Text preserved in a collection of devotional works, British Museum Additional MS 37790, where it occupies nineteen pages of a beautifully written fifteenth century manuscript, which was in the possession of a Yorkshire Catholic family and then in the library of Lord Amherst until it was presented to the British Museum in 1909. There are no known copies of the complete Long Text earlier than the mid-seventeenth century; it is known exclusively through three manuscripts now in Paris and London, with some selections in a manuscript at Upholland and one in the Westminster Cathedral Archives. All are in difficult seventeenth century hands, and differ significantly from one another. One of the London manuscripts was perhaps copied out in the mid seventeenth century by Dame Clementina Cary, foundress of the English Benedictine nunnery in Paris. The selections of the Westminster manuscript are associated with the English Benedictine nuns at Cambrai. The first printed edition was made by Dom Serenus Cressy in 1670 for members of this community. Older copies may have survived among the English nuns on the Continent, giving them an interest in Julian, but if so they have disappeared. Cressy's edition was reprinted in 1843 but commentaries on and translations of the Long Text did not appear until thirty years later. It was only at the end of the last century with the burst of enthusiasm for the Middle Ages characterized by the Pre-Raphaelites in literature and devotion as well as in art that the *Revelations* began to be read, studied and translated into a more modern English. The first attempts at the very difficult job of making a critical edition of the Long Text were begun fairly recently, and the process is by no means complete.

The Short Text, unknown until the beginning of this century, was printed two years after its discovery and other modernizations and commentaries have now appeared. Between the writing of the texts and the twentieth century, however, almost no references to the *Revelations* have been discovered in contemporary literature and perhaps none were made. Knowledge of this important work is very rare indeed before this century. Since the autograph by Julian herself is lost and there are so few and such late copies, the fact is, we do not know exactly what she wrote; the text is a difficult one to establish let alone interpret.

The image of bright scraps of parchment on the river is correct.

Monastic Commentators

It will be clear from what I have just said that any attention that was paid to the *Revelations of Divine Love* after the Reformation seems to have come initially from the organized religious orders, whether Benedicine, Dominican or Jesuit. It seems to me also that the fact that Julian was 'discovered' by religious who were interested in her primarily as theologians themselves accounts for a special emphasis on the Long Text which has coloured thinking about the author ever since. It is often asserted as known fact that 'when young she entered a religious house . . . and was still there . . . in her fiftieth year'.[2] It has been tentatively suggested several times that she might not have spent her life in a convent but usually that has only been proposed in order to be rejected. Every effort has been made to place her in the tradition of theologians, educated writers, and monastic orders. It is now generally assumed that she was a nun, probably at Carrow, before she became a solitary. Her latest editors, the Jesuit Walsh and the Augustinian Colledge go so far as to assert that when she says 'This work was begun by God's grace but it is not yet performed' she 'is obliquely stating her intention to retire from monastic life to the yet more severe rule of solitary enclosure';[3] one could hardly get a more blinkered reading of the text. It is concentration on the Long Text by those dedicated to the religious life that has produced this monastic Julian.

For myself, I am interested in the *Revelations* first of all as a historian, and not as a theologian, and it is therefore not the Long Text with all its extraordinary flights of sublime theology that most interests me but the older manuscript of the Short Text. It seems to me that who Julian was can affect the reading of the text, perhaps not in any major way but in some details, and I therefore propose to look again at Julian herself and especially to challenge the assertion that she was at any time in a convent and to suggest a very different background for the author of this priceless text. I do this not only out of historical curiosity, but because a close attention to this work and a study of the tradition of the solitary life has suggested this to me;[4]

also, I find that my reading of the *Revelations* is enhanced by having this idea in mind; she speaks more truly and consistently, and many of the minor difficulties of the text disappear. I do not give this as any more than my opinion; at each stage the evidence I produce can be interpreted differently; but the cumulative effect seems to me convincing. I do this of course in direct opposition to Julian's own preference that no attention should be given to herself but only to her message;[5] however my excuse is that attention has already been given to her and the picture which is being presented is already proving a block to her message by making it appear to be difficult and complex rather than profound and simple.

The Solitary Tradition

There has always been a tradition in Christian ascetic practice of men and women who become hermits without any previous training in a monastic house. Almost always they have later had contact with a community, and very often this is why details of their lives have been preserved; but it has by no means been the rule at any time that a hermit or anchorite must belong to a community of religious first. In England especially the idea of the individual solitary, this do-it-yourself approach to solitude, seems to have been more than usually popular and never so closely linked with the monasteries as elsewhere.

In the first years of the conversion of the Anglo-Saxons, for instance, there were many solitaries, particularly under the influence of Ireland, who had no training in religious communities at all. The variety of relationship between the different Christian vocations was re-established from the first: there were married men, like Drythhelm, who left his wife and children and went to live as a recluse near the monastery of Melrose,[6] or Columba, a princely solitary and exile, fleeing from the results of his own arrogance to the island of Iona, around whom a group formed.[7] Aidan combined a life of mission in Northumbria with frequent withdrawals into solitude,[8] while Cuthbert was a monk of Melrose and Lindisfarne before he went as a solitary to Farne, returning as a bishop for a few years before going back to die in his island hermitage. He seems to have puzzled the monks of Lindisfarne greatly by this, and it took a man of marvellous and quiet insight, Bede, even to glimpse the meaning of his life.[9] Guthlac, a kind of Robin Hood in his early life, became a hermit in the fens at Crowland with only fourteen months spent in a monastery in order to learn, it appears, not the monastic but the clerical life, before he went into life-long solitude.[10]

The tradition of solitary life seems to have survived the Conquest and both in chronicles of the times and in romances hermits are a familiar part of the landscape, for consultation by kings, knights and travellers.[11] The tradition of non-monastic solitaries in England seems to have continued and they became still more popular as a class recognized and valued in themselves. There still continued to be monks and nuns, also, who after monastic training chose the solitary life, but the three best-known solitaries in England between the eleventh and fourteenth centuries had only had a tenuous connection with monasteries and were none of them trained there: Godric of Finchale, that unique individualist, began life as a poor boy, a scavenger, and became a self-made merchant trader who may have married and who left his eminently successful career in middle life to become a self-made solitary at Finchale; it was only after he had lived there for some years that he formed links of friendship with the monastery at Durham.[12] Wulfric of Haselbury, after a dissolute youth, though in priest's orders, was at once enclosed as an anchorite in a cell built against the church in his village of Haselbury when he underwent conversion, and only after his death was he of interest to the monks of Ford and Montacute.[13] Christina of Markyate, the only English woman to be the subject of hagiography in this period, was a young woman betrothed against her wishes, who fled from her home not into a nunnery, since they would not receive her, but into the woods around St Albans where she lived at first with the anchoress Ailwen and then in a cell adjoining that of Roger, a solitary attached to St Albans; her biography in its present state breaks off when her solitary life ended and she went to a nunnery as abbess.[14] A most revealing account of solitary life, called *The Ancren Wisse*, was written in England in the twelfth century for three lay women who lived as anchoresses, advising them about both the spiritual and practical aspects of their life, which was specifically to be outside any of the existing monastic rules.[15]

In the fourteenth century as in the fourth, Christian life in either monastery or family could equally be a preface to a vocation to solitude. Moreover, the solitary life seems to have been regarded officially as special and different from both lay and monastic life though linked to both; when the *Liber Vitae* of Lindisfarne listed the glorious dead, solitaries were placed in a class alone after the first class of the kings and before the class of bishops and abbots. In the liturgy for All Saints, 'holy hermits' are a separate rank of sanctity. The author of the *Libellus de Diversis Ordinibus* says that he has 'decided to deal with the orders and callings in such a way that the hermits . . . are placed first', and he describes several kinds of solitary life before turning to the monastic orders.[16]

The Fourteenth Century

But it seems that in fourteenth century England at least, the gap between the spirituality of the cloister and the hermitage was growing. The desire for intense prayer rarely led people into the cloistered life; the 'stars' were all outside it or tenuously associated with the newer orders of friars or canons. There were solitaries who had begun as members of religious orders, like John de Lacy, a professed Dominican friar who became a hermit at Newcastle-under-Lyme,[17] or Bartholomew, who was a monk, albeit a marginal one, at Durham before he became a solitary on Farne.[18] But real spiritual vigour was beginning to be manifested in movements of lay piety rather than in the religious orders: the *Imitation of Christ* after all, came from Thomas à Kempis and belonged more to the *devotio moderna* than to the religious orders.[19] In England the individual independent strain that was always present, deepened, and the works of the English mystics of the fourteenth century were associated not with the religious orders but with solitaries.

The first in time and the best known in his own time, Richard Rolle, simply sent himself down from Oxford and made himself into a solitary, wearing a dress belonging to his sister; far from being a monk he was critical of monasticism and even insisted that it was impossible for monks in monasteries to undertake contemplation at all.[20] It was not monks but laymen following the solitary life who were the recipients of advice about prayer, whether from Richard Methley, the Carthusian,[21] Walter Hilton, the Augustinian, or the unknown author of *The Cloud of Unknowing*; it was not to the cloister but to the hermitage that their counsel was offered.

Moreover, the tradition of non-monastic solitaries was not confined to the 'stars'. Of its nature, the life of a solitary is hidden and unknown, but there are glimpses of other women who became independent solitaries, some of whom had been married. In the fourteenth century Loretta of Hackington, who had been the the wife of the Earl of Leicester became at his death an anchoress at St Stephen's Church, Hackington; Joan, the widow of Sir William Clapton, was enclosed in the church of Lower Quinton in Gloucestershire; Katherine of Ledbury who had been the wife of Robert Fitz Parnell, Baron Dudley, became a recluse in 1323, having reared two sons and a daughter after the death of their father in 1299. The mother of the wife of Sir John de Beauchamp was also enclosed as an anchoress.[22] The fourteenth and fifteenth centuries in England have been called the golden age of the solitary life; these solitaries, I suggest, were as often from ordinary lay life as from the religious orders.

It is in this tradition of the lay solitary following a special vocation, called from the world rather than from the cloister that I would place the author of the *Revelations of Divine Love*. In the light of this I suggest that Julian was not a nun at any time; I go further and say that she may well have been a young widow and also have been a mother before she became an anchoress. I present my reasons for these conclusions under three headings: external evidence; absence of evidence; and internal evidence in the Short Text itself.

The External Evidence

First, what evidence external to the *Revelations* is there about its author? Very little indeed and none which connects Julian with a nunnery. There is the sentence with which the scribe who copied the Short Text introduced the *Revelations*; there is some evidence to be found in certain Norwich wills; and there is the account of a visit paid to Julian by Margery Kempe of Lynn. The scribe who copied the Short Text in the fifteenth century describes the author as 'a devout woman and her name is Julian that is a recluse at Norwich and she is still living in this year of our Lord 1413'.[23] The Short Text, then, was written during Julian's lifetime, by someone who had either met her or known someone who had. Julian is described as a recluse and a devout woman, but not a nun, which is suggestive. She is referred to as a recluse'of Norwich', of a town, not of a nunnery; and she is called Julian.

Can anything be made of her name and the dedication of the church to St Julian? 'Julian anchorite at St Julian's in Norwich' is the name given her in one of the wills. It is possibly a co-incidence that her name was 'Julian' also, but there are instances of religious people changing their names in accordance with a change in life-style and perhaps she called herself after the patron of the church where she lived. It may be that the dedication to St Julian meant more to her than simply the name of a saint. Seventeen Julian's are listed in the *Acta Sanctorum* and of the seven churches in England known to have been dedicated to St Julian, it is usually Julian the Hospitaller that is meant, a married man said to have been a kind of latter-day Oedipus, who accidentally killed his parents and then as a penitent lived a life of solitude and service to the poor and sick, with his wife alongside him.[24] Such a dedication would perhaps attract a lay anchoress in her choice of church, or rather, seem an additional confirmation of a choice made for more practical reasons. There was a tradition of anchoresses there after Julian and often with the same name. The information that she was living beside the church of St Julian is supported by two things: the discovery of the remains of an anchorhold there, and by evidence from wills.

There are many wills of the fourteenth and early fifteenth centuries leaving money or goods to solitaries as well as to religious, to monks presumably for them to offer masses, to the solitaries for their prayers. A number of wills made in Norfolk in the fourteenth century contain references which seem to be to Julian.[25] In 1394 when Julian was fifty-one there was a bequest of two shillings by Roger Reed of Norwich to 'Julian the anchorite', and Thomas Edmund of Aylesham in 1404 left one shilling to 'The anchorite Julian at St Julian's in Norwich' and some pence to her servant Sara. In 1415 John Plumpton of Norwich left forty pence to 'the anchoress in the church of St Julian at Conisford in Norwich', and twelve pence each to her maid Alice and her previous maid, additions which suggest that John Plumpton had at various times consulted the anchoress and had been received with kindness by her servants. In 1416 Isabel Ufford died and left forty pence to 'Julian a recluse in Norwich',[26] but this may have been another Julian by that date. It seems though that the Julian of the first three wills may well have been the 'devout woman' of the Short Text.

What connection is there between Julian, a recluse at Conisford, and the nunnery at Carrow? The convent of St Mary at Carrow was built by two women, Seyna and Lescalina in 1146, on land granted them by King Stephen. It prospered and in 1273 a papal injunction ordered them only to accept the number of nuns that their income could maintain. Thereafter the number of sisters was never above twenty, with adults, not children, as recruits. At the Dissolution, Carrow had eight nuns 'of very good name by repute in the county', with an income under 100 pounds a year; the only complaints the sisters had made to the Commissioners were trivial grumblings about certain sisters who made themselves girdles of silk, about the thinness of the beer provided at table, that some thought the Office was chanted too quickly. In the early fifteenth century, during Julian's lifetime, matters had not run so smoothly at Carrow: in 1396 the prioress, Edith de Wylton, was prosecuted for giving sanctuary to the murderess of William Koe of Trows, and in 1443, the mismanagement of another prioress, Alice Waryn, caused the bishop to intervene and place the affairs of the priory in the hands of a local gentlemen for two years. Carrow seems to have been deeply embedded in the life of the local countryside, a house of no great pretentions to spirituality and certainly with no school, library or concern with education.

As a small house, Carrow priory needed an income and part of this came by holding the advowson and income of certain churches despite the fact that such practices were contrary to canon law. One of these was the church of St Julian at Conisford. The connection was a formal one, the prioress and her administrators appointed the priest who had charge of the church and would be aware of any anchorite who lived there. Such a link cannot be stretched to mean that the sisters could be hermits there; an anchoress in a parish would be under the authority of the bishop, and not that of a prioress, and there by his blessing. A nun who wanted to be a solitary would be given a place near the convent and would continue to be protected by her community.

Some nuns became solitaries and another 'Julian', Juliana Lampit, may have been one at Carrow. The Norwich wills mention frequent bequests to Dame Julian Lampit, a recluse who lived with her household in the grounds of Carrow priory; earlier writers suspected that she was the Julian who was the author of the *Revelations*, but it seems to be only the coincidence of names that connects her with this text. In the wills Juliana Lampit is consistantly referred to as either 'Dame Julian, anchoress at Carrow' or 'the anchoress of Carrow'. In 1466 a payment was made 'to the anchoress at Carrow' on occasion of the funeral of John Paston, which the prioress of Carrow attended with her maid. Juliana Lampit may have been a nun of Carrow before she became an anchoress in the grounds of the priory. Anchoresses were supported either by a religious community or by gifts, while sometimes part of their lands would supply their income. In the case of Juliana Lampit it may have been a mixture of all three. One more inference can be drawn from these wills: bequests to Juliana Lampit are listed along with bequests to the prioress and each of the nuns of the priory; in other words, a nun-recluse was considered legally to remain a member of the community. The wills leaving money to Julian, the anchoress at Conisford, however, are direct bequests, with no mention of the priory at all.

There is one other direct reference to Julian as a respected anchoress living in Norwich and that is in Margery Kempe's account of her visit to Norwich specifically to consult Julian, which is well-attested and of great interest. The married visionary of Lynn consulted William Southfield, a friar of Norwich and afterwards was 'commanded by our Lord' to go and see 'an anchoress in the same city who was called Julian'. This was in 1413 when Julian was in her seventieth year, having completed both versions of her revelations and already become known for her wise advice in matters concerning the inner life. Perhaps it is significant that it seemed appropriate for Margery to go to consult Julian about her inner experiences at a time when she had borne a child and decided it should be her last; Julian commended her choice of chastity, 'for all chaste livers are temples of the Holy Ghost' and urged her to have confidence in her own experience of God and not to be swayed by criticism. They seem to have had more than one conversation, in which Julian took seriously Margery's account of her revelations, so different in style from those of Julian herself: 'great was the holy conversation that the anchoress and this creature had through talking of the love of our Lord Jesus Christ for the many days that they were together'.[27]

Absence of Evidence

Secondly, if Julian had been a nun, what is there that is missing? She is never mentioned in any existing records of Carrow Priory or any other nunnery. She never refers to her sisters or addresses any remarks to or about nuns or monks; all her concern is for 'mine even Christians', the lay folk, the holy people of God. She makes no mention of any monastic practices or formation whatsoever, and her writings bear no marks of the cloister at all. Moreover, is it at all likely that a nunnery with such a member, known in her own time as an outstanding counsellor and visionary, would not have done two things: made a fuss to ensure her burial in their grounds and boasted of it; and made sure of having copies made of her *Revelations* and both keeping them securely, and making them available? The virtual disappearance of her work and the almost total silence about it suggests few copies were ever made; and it follows perhaps that this was because she did not belong inside any settled monastic community with a scriptorium. Her name and where she came from are both entirely unknown; but had she been a nun at Carrow there is one external event which makes it highly unlikely that she would have been able to leave the cloister for the anchorage: in 1369 when Julian was twenty-seven, the plague called the Black Death recurred; of the sixteen nuns then at Carrow four died; hardly a moment for the community to agree to the enclosing of another young nun as an anchoress.

Internal Evidence

Thirdly, what can be learnt from the *Revelations* themselves, especially the Short Text, the surest source for information about the author? Some of the meagre hints can perhaps be fleshed out by reference to the context of her times. First, from her own words it is possible to establish that she was born in 1342 by her reference to her age of thirty and a half in 1373; most probably from her use of English she was born in England though not necessarily in Norwich; Yorkshire has been plausibly suggested from the evidence of the dialect she uses. Thirty and a half is a long time to account for in the life of a medieval woman; what was she doing then? She could have been a nun but I think it most unlikely, not only because of her silence about religious life but because of one very simple fact: she would have been six when there occurred the first onslaught of the plague known as the Black Death (to distinguish it from other plagues and now thought to have been a kind of anthrax affecting people) which eventually destroyed one third of the population of England. The instinctive reaction after great disasters is towards marriage and childbearing. It was in just such a situation that Julian grew up and no one was to know if the plague would return. At marriageable age it is most unlikely that Julian would have remained unmarried and there is no reason to suppose that she herself wished for anything else.

The passages in the *Revelations* which have been alleged to contradict this are, first, her early desire for the three gifts of God, 'mind of His Passion, bodily sickness in youth and to have the three wounds in her life of very contrition, kind compassion and steadfast longing towards God';[28] and secondly, by the phrase addressed to her by God, 'I thank thee for thy travail and especially in thy youth'.[29] For the first point, the three wishes are exactly in line with devout aspirations of lay people of her times and were not confined to novices. The fact that she then forgot about them suggests that they were certainly not for her a determining factor leading to monastic life; had this been the case, she would have built upon them; had they prefaced a life in the cloister, they are just the kind of thing a devout little novice might remember and live from. But any pious girl might have thought of just those desires; the piety of her times taught her to do so; but whereas a nunnery would have been a place where they were remembered, marriage, especially a happy marriage, with the responsibility of a household, might well cause anyone to forget such ideas until the coincidence of illness at a significant age (that mysterious thirty that marked the beginning of the public ministry of Christ) reminded her of them. For the second point, 'young' could well refer to Julian at the age she was when the revelations began, since in the fourteenth century up to thirty was counted, in theory at least, as 'youth'. This comment of the Lord could therefore be seen not as saying she had consecrated her childhood (the modern sense of 'youth') to God but as meaning her consecration to him at that moment through suffering. In the next chapter she supports this idea of 'youth' as a theological concept when she says 'every man's age will be known in heaven'.[30]

Thirty may have been 'youth' to the theologians through a calculation based on biblical numerology; for the realities of life, with fifty as the usual but not invariable limit of life, thirty was middle age, by which time a woman should have been married for at least fifteen years. At thirty Julian fell seriously ill and all she says about her situation fits more easily with the idea of a household than with a nunnery. In her illness her bedside was crowded with friends, not sisters; her mother was also there and they were all prepared to laugh heartily. She sent for 'the parson, my curate', a phrase suggesting either a chaplain to a private household or the parish priest, and he came with a boy and a cross.[31] Later she mentions a conversation with a cleric at her bedside, again involving laughter. No abbess or infirmarian seems to have come near her. In place of some mention of prayers at her bedside for a dying nun, Julian says she wanted to warn those around her to love God more and leave earthly vanity. At the end of the Short Text it is Julian's even-Christians that still occupy her mind: 'God wants us always to be strong in our love and peaceful and restful as He is towards us, and He wants us to be for ourselves and for our fellow-Christians, what He is for us. Amen.'[32] I suggest that Julian wrote those words as a young widow living in her own household with her mother and her servants.

The Long Text is a most carefully wrought piece of theology, and one which retains very little of the personal links of the Short Text with Julian's actual experience of the revelations in her sickness. But it seems to me that there is something to be detected in one of the most striking sections in the Long Text where Julian gives a detailed image comparing the work of Christ to that of a mother. Clearly, this flows naturally from her meditations and is an integral part of her thought. There is no need to suppose she had ever heard of the rare uses of this image by any predecessors; it is there in the Scriptures, if you want a literary source. The beauty of the imagery is clearly her own and belongs naturally to her thinking. But it is one with other intimate images that occur to her about the body and it is an extended image of great detail and tenderness. It always worried me to think that a woman of Julian's maturity still held such memories of her own mother but showed no warmth at all in her solitary mention of her; in fact, her own mother totally misunderstood her, and attempted to close her eyes when all Julian wanted was to have them wide open: 'I did not want to be hindered from seeing because of my love for Him.'[33]

If it could be permissible to suppose her to have borne at least one child, as married women should, all the language of motherhood takes on a new and more natural meaning:

> the mother's service is nearest, readiest and surest, readiest because it is most loving and surest because it is truest . . . Our bodily bringing to birth is only little, humble and simple . . . still it is He who does it in the creatures by whom it is done . . . A kind, loving mother who knows and sees the need of her child guards it very tenderly as the nature and condition of motherhood will have it. And always as the child grows in stature, she acts differently but she does not change her love; and when it grows older she allows it to be chastised to destroy its faults so as to make the child receive virtues and grace.[34]

Can one go further and suggest that a child, loved and watched and guarded in this way had died, perhaps in the recurrent onslaughts of plague? In 1361 when Julian would be nineteen a form of plague occurred which was especially fatal to children. The imagery of one passage which occurrs soon after her use of the image of motherhood at least suggests a memory of such a thing:

> I saw a body lying on the earth which appeared heavy and horrible, and without shape and form, as it were a swollen pit of stinking mud, and suddenly out of this body there sprang a most beautiful creature, a little child, fully shaped and formed swift and lively and whiter than a lily, which quickly glided up to heaven . . . It is more blissful that man be taken from from pain than that pain be taken from man, for if pain be taken from us it may come again.[35]

Had her young husband died either of plague or in war? So many died of the attacks of plague and many others in the wars of the times; and then perhaps a child died also? No wonder she was most deeply concerned with the problem of pain; no wonder Margery Kempe found a ready listener in Julian when she consulted her as a married woman and a mother.

Literary Sources

The question of Julian's education and what she had read has been one of the chief industries for writers on Julian recently, and is one of the main arguments put forward for her connection with a nunnery. One writer goes so far as to say,

> What is . . . beyond any doubt is that when [*sic*] the young Julian had received an exceptionally good grounding in Latin, in Scripture and the liberal arts, and that thereafter she was able and permitted to read widely in Latin and vernacular spiritual classics.[36]

This would be an exceptional education for anyone, especially all of the liberal arts which as far as I know were unknown in their entirety in medieval Europe. Julian's extensive book-learning is asserted in spite of the fact that there is no evidence in her writing of such extraordinary learning and that what she says herself is that she 'could no letter', meaning of course that she was no scholar in Latin.

I have three points to make in disagreeing with this view of Julian, and the first is this: Why should she have had to have literary sources for her work? There are, in fact, few direct quotations and the ones there are come from either the Bible or popular works easily accessible by eye or ear; beyond that, only parallels can be drawn with other authors. If there is truth, whether in mathematics or in theology, surely it is only sensible to recognize that good thinking can arrive at the same answers independently? There is a kind of presumption in supposing that she could not possibly have thought for herself, that the little lady would need male instruction and had to have books to read. Why not suppose the simple truth that she thought for years and came up with a startlingly new and immensely cohesive work? There are original thinkers; Anselm of Canterbury was one, Julian was another, and neither gives footnotes.

Secondly, of course Julian could read; 'could no letter' means, as with Teresa of Avila, that she was not a professional scholar. It is clear from the text that she knew the Scriptures well; a good deal she would learn from the liturgy and from preaching, but as a married woman in her own home she would also need to read and write for the management of her household, and it would be no great matter then for her also to read her Bible for herself; there were Bibles already in English and not all of them known as heretical. It was after all a time of lay education, especially among the tradesmen, of whom there were a great many in Norwich, with close contacts through trade with the burgeoning life of the spirit in the Low Countries. Given even an averagely devout husband, there could be far more contact with the world of thought through discussion and table-talk than for any novice in a great abbey with its restricted possibilities for both reading and talk.

Thirdly, the suggestion that she went to school with the nuns at Carrow I think can be discounted entirely; there is no evidence whatever that the sisters ever had a school. For financial reasons they had several people, families or individuals, who lived near the priory as 'borderers' at various times, a few of whom had children with them, but like the other nunneries in England, they had no schools open to outsiders and were constantly being discouraged from taking children into their households like other nobles.[37] Since the twelfth century when the Carrow priory was founded, nuns had not accepted children into the cloister as novices, so the need for a school for such had passed; all that was needed was instruction for the novices in singing the Office and other conventual duties. Carrow in particular was always a very small priory, and as I have shown, it was known for other things than education. Like other convents of England after the glorious days of the Anglo-Saxons, the nuns were noted not for their scholarship but for their embroidery.[38]

The Anchorhold

For all these reasons, then, I suggest that when Julian received the Revelations and wrote her short account of them, she was a young widow living in her own house with her servants and her mother. Were the next years which produced the Long Version of the Revelations passed in her own house so that she became an anchoress only when the second book was finished? Or did she go to her anchorhold at once and produce the Long Text out of the next years of silence and solitude?

I do not think it at all likely that Julian rose from her sick bed and went into her anchorhold. It seems to me probable that the Short Text at least was written in her own household. After all, it would be difficult to dispose of her responsibilities in a flash, with her mother living there, perhaps other children as well, she would hardly be free the moment she recovered from her illness. It may be that after she had completed her Short Text and arranged her responsibilities she went to the anchorhold and by prolonged meditation there wrote the Long Text; indeed the Long version feels like the work of someone with time to concentrate totally on it. That is not, of course, conclusive, and perhaps Julian was not like us; perhaps she did not need a sabbatical in order to think. It is perfectly possible that she wrote the Long Text also in her own home before becoming a solitary; perhaps that is another reason why it took her so long.

In either case, the Long Text of the *Revelations of Divine Love* is remarkable and almost unique among writings that have been produced from within the solitary life. Solitaries have not often been renowned for their literary productions, especially the ones who had no monastic background. Often enough they chose the solitary life partly because they were not interested in reading, writing and arithmetic. With some notable exceptions, like Thomas Merton, what have even the monastic hermits produced in the way of theology or literature of the soul? The works of the hermitage are not often sustained works of such superb theology. In the desert, Evagrius and Cassian were both writing aside from the regular pattern of prayer in the cell; most of the hermits wove mats. Bilfrith, a hermit of Farne, made a jewelled binding for a Gospel book; Cuthbert simply prayed; it was a solitary who made the first Latin and English grammar; in his hermitage in Newcastle-under-Lyme John de Lacy produced second-rate illuminated manuscripts on request.

There is plenty of writing about solitaries and to solitaries: descriptions of their way of life fill the accounts of visitors to early Egypt; in England the lives of Godric, Wulfric and Christina were written by others. The author of *The Cloud of Unknowing* was advising a solitary; so were Aelred of Rievaulx, Walter Hilton, and the author of *The Ancren Wisse*. But what about the solitaries' own inner life, their continuing and deepening knowledge of God? Arsenius turned to pray towards the setting sun and was there to see it rising, but what did he see in the darkness?[39] There are hints from some: there are Richard Rolle's lyrics, the meditations of the hermit of Farne, Godric's English songs. Nearly always it is poetry that comes from the hermitage, 'The hint half guessed, the gift half understood'. The solitary has something other to do than the analysis of experience.

A fourteenth century writer described the real work of the solitary like this: 'Nailed and spread fast on the rood in my holy order as Thou wast nailed for me on Thy hard rood.'[40] In the Eastern Church there is a familiar icon which shows a hermit, wearing the great schema, nailed to a cross, with the words 'I am crucified with Christ' written under it. It seems to me that this is all the hermit life has to say to the world; it is not specifically to do with monastic life or clerical life or analysing or teaching. Is is a kind of enlarged version, stripped down to its barest essentials, of what baptismal life is about for every Christian. The hermit is not looking towards the Crucified; there is no other figure on the Cross; he is crucified with Christ. So perhaps Julian, who saw so clearly and wrote so truly about the Crucified, lived for many years afterwards; and in the silence of that anchorhold in Norwich, who knows what prayer and compassion followed on from the *Revelations of Divine Love* that she gave to her even-Christians? If, in fact, Julian wrote about the Revelations of the love of God when she lived in her anchorhold, then they are a rare text which comes directly out of the silence of the cell and has to do with the essence of the solitary life.

With all the saints, it is the day of their death, their entry into heaven that is celebrated each year. With Julian, no one knows when she died but we know exactly when she received the Revelations of love, and it is that date which is celebrated for her, whether it was the VIII or the XIII of May, either the Third Sunday after Easter or a Friday.[41] The truly remarkable thing about Julian is not herself; there are no miracles or cult of Julian, and no Life. It is her message that matters and that is, that the Cross of pain is also the Cross of glory, that the Cross reveals the love of God.

The *Revelations* are not, like every other devotional piece of the time,[42] a description of the Crucified written to invoke pity and repentance; they are not in the tradition of the *Stabat Mater*; they are serious theology of the love that is God. To Julian the Crucified says not 'Are you sorry your sins crucified me?', but 'Art thou well pleased that I suffered for thee?', and she says simply, 'Yes'.[43] For her the Cross is the revelation of the love that is God; and having faced steadily all the implications of this, in the end she can write, 'Love was our Lord's meaning':

> He beholds his heavenly treasure with so great love on earth that He will give us more light and solace in heavenly joy, drawing us from the sorrow and darkness we are in. Thanks be to God. Here ends the book of the revelations of Julian the anchorite of Norwich on whose soul may God have mercy. Amen.[44]

XXV

DATES PROPOSED FOR JULIAN OF NORWICH

1342	Born, probably in England.
	(1348–9 Black Death)
	(1361 Children affected by Black Death)
	(1374 Four out of sixteen nuns at Carrow die of Black Death)
	In this period Julian perhaps married, bore a child/children, one or more of whom died, and was widowed.
1373	Illness and Shewings in her own home at 'thirty and a half years old'.
	Dates for Shewings:
	P reads: 'the xiii daie of May'
	SS both read 'viii daie of May'
	May 8th 1373 was after the Feast of St John of Beverley (cf. Ch. 38), also the Third Sunday after Easter, May 13th was a Friday. Time is given as four in the morning; there was a clock that struck the hours on Norwich Cathedral by 1325.
	Julian enclosed as an anchoress at St Julian's in Norwich in this period.
1393	Long Text completed.
1393	Bequest by Roger Reed of Norwich to the anchoress at Norwich.
1404	Bequest of Thomas Edmund: 'Juliane anchorite apud St Juliane in Norwico' with money also to her servant Sarah.
1413/6	Visit of Margery Kempe. See *The Book of Margery Kempe*, Ch. 18. Margery lived in Bishop's Lynn (now King's Lynn) 40 miles from Norwich. The *Book* was written in 1436, 'twenty years or more' after Margery's conversion which must therefore be placed about 1416. She visited Norwich soon after the birth of her last child.
1413	Short Text reference: 'Here is a vision shewn by the goodness of God to a devout woman whose name is Julyan. She is a recluse at Norwich and is yet alive in this year of Our Lord 1413.'
1415	Bequest by John Plumpton of Norwich to the anchoress Julian at Norwich and also to her maid Alice and to her former maid.
1416	Bequest by Isabel Ufford of 20s. to 'Julian recluz of Norwich'.
1429	Bequest to 'an anchoress in the churchyard of St Julian's.' Therefore perhaps still alive at 87.
Death	date unknown.

Dates for manuscripts and printed texts of her works:

1413	Short Text MS British Library Additional MS 37790
1500c	Selections from Long Text (Westminster Cathedral Archives MS)
1640c	Selections from Long Text (St Joseph's College, Upholland MS)
1650c	Long Text (Paris MS Bibliothèque Nationale Fonds anglais 40)
1650c	Long Text (British Library, Sloane 2499)
1700c	Long Text (British Library, Sloane 3705)
1670	Long Text printed in London from text by Dom Serenus Cressy.
1843	Cressy Long Text reprinted.
1877	Modernization of Cressy Long Text printed by H. Collins.
1901	Grace Warrack's version.
1911	Short Text recognized two years after acquired by British Library and printed in a modernized edition by Dundas Hartford.

NOTES TO *JULIAN THE SOLITARY*

1. H.F.M.Prescott, *The Man on a Donkey*, London, Eyre and Spottiswoode, 1952, pp. 698–9.
2. Julian of Norwich, *A Book of Shewings to the Anchoress Julian of Norwich,* ed. E. Colledge and J. Walsh, Toronto, Pontifical Institute of Medieval Studies, 1978 (hereafter referred to as Colledge and Walsh), Introduction, Vol. I, p. 43.
3. Ibid. p. 21.
4. I have chosen to use the word 'solitary' throughout rather than either 'hermit' or 'anchorite'; this is because although 'anchor' is in Middle English neuter and therefore appropriate for either man or woman, 'anchor' sounds too much like 'anchor' and at once gives a nautical turn to the subject which I do not intend, although there is precedent for such a fantastic etymology as early as the twelfth century *Ancren Wisse*. 'Hermit' would be another option, or 'ascetic', but both have come to have rather limited meanings, and 'hermit' is used to mean one living alone in a solitary location as distinct from an 'anchorite' whose cell is attached to a building. The term 'anchorite' was much more loosely used in the Middle Ages and the only English word which keeps this wide range of meaning is 'solitary', which I have used to mean one who lives alone for a religious purpose.
5. Short Text of the *Revelations of Divine Love*, Ch. 6. (I will refer to the works of Julian hereafter as 'Short Text' and 'Long Text' giving only the number of the chapters.)
6. Bede, *Ecclesiastical History of the English People*, ed. and trans. Colgrave and Mynors, Oxford University Press, 1968, Bk. V, Ch. 12.
7. Adomnan, *Life of St Columba*, ed. and trans. A.O. and M.O. Anderson, London, Thomas Nelson and Sons, 1961.
8. Bede, op. cit., Bk III, Ch. 16.
9. Bede, *Life of St Cuthbert* in *Two Lives of St Cuthbert*, ed. and trans. B. Colgrave, Cambridge University Press, 1940.
10. *Felix's Life of St Guthlac*, ed. and trans. B. Colgrave, Cambridge University Press, 1956.
11. E.g. *The Quest of the Holy Grail*, trans. P. Matarasso, Penguin Classics. 1969.
12. Reginald of Durham, *Life of St Godric of Finchale*, ed. J. Stevenson, London, Surtees Society, 1838.

13. John of Ford, *Wulfric of Haslebury*, ed. M. Bell, *Somerset Record Society* XLVII, 1933.
14. *Life of Christina of Markyate*, ed. and trans. C. Talbot, Oxford University Press, 1987.
15. *The Ancren Wisse*, ed. J.R.R.Tolkein, Oxford, Early English Text Society, 1962.
16. *Libellus de Diversis Ordinibus*, ed. and trans. G. Constable, Oxford University Press, 1978.
17. MS 71, St John's College Library, Oxford.
18. *The Monk of Farne*, trans. The Nuns at Stanbrook Abbey, with Introduction by D.H. Farmer, London, Darton, Longman and Todd, 1961.
19. Cf. Thomas à Kempis, *The Imitation of Christ*, trans. Leo Sherley-Price, Penguin Classics, 1972.
20. Cf. Richard Rolle, *The Fire of Love*, trans. Clifton Wolters, Penguin Classics, 1972, Ch. 13, pp. 82–83.
21. Richard Methley, 'Letter to Hugh Hermit', ed. James Hogg, Salzburg, Austria, *Analaecta Carthusiana,* 1978.
22. For further information about English solitaries in the Middle Ages see R.M, Clay, *The Hermits and Anchorites of England, London,* Methuen and Co., 1914, especially Appendix C, pp. 203–283.
23. Preface to the Short Text.
24. For Julian the Hospitaller, cf. B. de Gaiffier, *Analaecta Bollandiana*, XLIII (1945) pp. 144–219.
25. Cf. N.P. Tanner, *Popular Religion in Norfolk with Special Reference to the Evidence of Wills, 1370–1532,* unpublished D. Phil. Thesis, Oxford, 1973.
26. Cf. Introduction to Colledge and Walsh, op. cit., Vol I, p. 34.
27. *The Book of Margery Kempe*, trans. B.A. Windeatt, Penguin Classics, 1985, pp. 76–79.
28. Short Text, Ch. 1.
29. Short Text, Ch. 6.
30. Short Text, Ch. 2.
31. Ibid.
32. Short Text, Ch. 24.
33. Short Text, Ch. 10.
34. Long Text, Ch. 60.
35. Long Text, Ch. 64.
36. Colledge and Walsh, op. cit., Introduction, Vol. 1, p. 44.
37. Walter Rye,

37. Walter Rye, *Carrow Abbey*, Norwich 1889, pp. 48–52.
38. Cf. Eileen Power, *Medieval English Nunneries*, Cambridge University Press, 1922, Ch. VI, pp. 237–281.
39. *Sayings of the Desert Fathers, The Alphabetical Collection*, trans. Benedicta Ward, London, A.R. Mowbray and Co. Ltd., 1975/83, Arsenius 30, p. 12.
40. *A Talkyng of the Love of God*, ed. M.S. Westra, The Hague, Martinus Nijhoff, 1950, p. 58.
41. I prefer the date XIII to VIII since it is easier for the copiest's eye to have mistaken an X for a V than vice versa.
42. For further discussion of this point see S. Bhattacharji's article on Julian of Norwich in *Word and Spirit*, 1989.
43. Short Text, Ch. 12.
44. Long Text, Ch. 86.

INDEX